The Ambivalent State

The Ambivalent State

*Police-Criminal Collusion at
the Urban Margins*

JAVIER AUYERO
KATHERINE SOBERING

OXFORD
UNIVERSITY PRESS

OXFORD
UNIVERSITY PRESS

Oxford University Press is a department of the University of Oxford. It furthers the University's objective of excellence in research, scholarship, and education by publishing worldwide. Oxford is a registered trade mark of Oxford University Press in the UK and certain other countries.

Published in the United States of America by Oxford University Press 198 Madison Avenue, New York, NY 10016, United States of America.

CIP data is on file at the Library of Congress
ISBN 978-0-19-091554-4 (pbk.)
ISBN 978-0-19-091553-7 (hbk.)

1 3 5 7 9 8 6 4 2

Paperback printed by Marquis, Canada
Hardback printed by Bridgeport National Bindery, Inc., United States of America

The Ambivalent State: Police-Criminal Collusion at the Urban Margins. Javier Auyero,
Oxford University Press (2019). © Oxford University Press.
DOI: 10.1093/oso/9780190915537.001.0001

Contents

The Ambivalent State: Police-Criminal Collusion at the Urban Margins. Javier Auyero, Oxford University Press (2019). © Oxford University Press.
DOI: 10.1093/oso/9780190915537.001.0001

Preface and Acknowledgments

A series of fortunate events brought us together to work on this book. Before this joint work, we were working on quite different (but, we would come to learn, theoretically related) projects.

Katie had been conducting an ethnography of "equality projects" in Hotel Bauen, a worker-run, worker-recuperated business in central Buenos Aires. For years, Katie was immersed in the organizational life of this hotel that had been closed by its private owners, occupied by its workers, and restarted as a worker cooperative. While much of her fieldwork focused on reorganization of service under worker control, she also observed the cooperative's long-term political campaign to legalize its use of the downtown hotel. Summer after summer, she documented the actions of myriad state actors—from building inspectors and ministry staffers to judges, city council members, and national senators—who promised very different futures. While some advocated for the hotel to be expropriated by the state (which would secure its tenancy), others threatened closure, eviction, and the almost certain dissolution of the cooperative. As state agents simultaneously proffered hope and fear, members of the cooperative were left in a legal limbo that is still unresolved at the time of this writing.

While marginal in its organizational form (an occupied hotel, a worker cooperative), Hotel Bauen enjoyed a very central geographic location just blocks from the national Congress and steps off of one of the busiest intersections in Buenos Aires. Most members of the cooperative, however, made long commutes from poor and working-class neighborhoods in the province. If you board a bus near Hotel Bauen, it takes nearly an hour and a half and two transfers to arrive in Arquitecto Tucci where Javier has studied

The Ambivalent State: Police-Criminal Collusion at the Urban Margins. Javier Auyero, Oxford University Press (2019). © Oxford University Press.
DOI: 10.1093/oso/9780190915537.001.0001

daily violence since 2009 (Auyero and Berti 2015). In a very different context, he also documented the intermittent, contradictory, and highly selective state presence among the urban poor. That examination of the state action was mostly a reconstruction of the ways in which one actor (the state police) *appeared* and was experienced in the lives of the most dispossessed: sometimes in the form of a visible police operation (a raid on a drug selling point, a full day of stop-and-frisk operations) and other times in the form of a secret deal between a street policeman and a local drug dealer. The original study remained mostly at the phenomenological level. Because the analytical focus of that research project lay in what he called "concatenations of violence," he did not go behind the scenes to examine that modality of state intervention. But Javier remained curious about that backstage of state action—whose illicit aspects are an open secret among residents of many a marginalized neighborhood and among students of poor people's daily lives.

During the course of our separate research projects, we now realize, both of us were grappling with analogous issues: how to make sense of conflicting and inconsistent state interventions (the police, in Javier's case; the city council, national legislature, and the courts, in Katie's case) among vulnerable and precarious groups.

In addition to our related lines of inquiry, we also share a vision of how to approach our research. We both believe that "the contemporary state can best be captured . . . in the way that it deals with its poor and its delinquents, its immigrants and its detainees, in the manner that it administers sensitive urban neighborhoods and waiting zones at the border, correctional facilities and detention centers, in its use of practices at once opaque and spectacular, deviant, or illegal" (Fassin 2015:3).[1] With concepts and images such as assemblage, field, and pieces, plenty of recent scholarship has disaggregated and de-reified the state, ultimately questioning its unity and integrity.[2] In this book, we sought to take a step further into the direction signaled by this exciting body of work. We make an argument about the character of the state in a specific time and place (Argentina during the first two decades of the 21st century) by dissecting the resources, practices, and processes at the center of the clandestine relationships that link state actors to groups engaged in actions that the state itself defines as criminal.

Now to the series of fortunate events (and the people behind them) that made this book possible. Event One: While we were engaged in our other projects, Karen Cerulo, the editor of *Sociological Forum*, invited Javier to write an essay on the relationships between the state and the urban poor in the global South. That invitation prompted our initial dialogue about what we thought was missing in current scholarly conversations in urban ethnography and ways of conducting systematic research on the unseen and potentially illicit activities of state actors. A careful reading of newspaper accounts and investigative journalists' "crónicas" alerted us to sources of much-needed information (court cases and wiretappings) that we had not seen carefully analyzed. We would soon learn that there was a handful of exemplars in the use of wiretapped conversations[3] and even more in the use of legal archives.[4]

Event Two: Renowned Argentine journalist Cristian Alarcón put us in touch with two intrepid and extraordinary journalists and *cronistas*, María Florencia Alcaraz and Silvina Tamous. "They might be able to help," he told Javier when he asked if the court cases cited in news reports might be accessible. And helped they did. Florencia and Silvina located the court cases for us and provided extremely valuable background information to help us understand them. We are immensely thankful to both. The thrill of opening a file and having access to unedited wiretapped conversations is hard to describe. The energy we gleaned from the initial success of that search in turn prompted us to revisit previous ethnographic material and undertake a new round of interviews conducted by María Fernanda Berti, Javier's co-author of *In Harm's Way*.

Event Three: Fernanda was willing, able, and eager to go back to the field. *Gracias, Fernanda*, for the research that was integral to developing our arguments in Chapters 2 and 3. In addition to

Fernanda's invaluable fieldwork, we owe a special thanks to the residents of Arquitecto Tucci who have participated in this study since its inception. This project would not be possible without your trust and collaboration, and we are indebted to your generosity and willingness to share your experiences.

Thanks also to our colleague, Mary Ellen Stitt, who helped us sharpen the argument about pathways of violence that we present in Chapter 3. A version of that chapter was published as a paper in the journal *Social Forces*—we thank the anonymous reviewers of the piece for their helpful comments. Parts of Chapter 3 were also published as an article in the *Latin American Research Review*. Thank you also to Aníbal Pérez-Liñán, Guillermo Trejo, and the anonymous reviewers for helping us refine our argument about legal cynicism.

As we developed a shared reading list in political sociology, criminology, and adjacent fields, we began to dig deeper into a transactional world made visible in the wiretapped conversations. During this period, many scholars helped us make sense of our findings, pointing to research to aid in our intellectual expedition, listening to us present at conferences, and reading early versions of parts of this manuscript. We want to thank Pablo Alabarces, Desmond Arias, Nino Bariola, Sarah Brayne, Abby Cordova, Matías Dewey, Scott Decker, Gabriel Ferreyra, Sandra Ley Gutiérrez, Tina Hilgers, Alisha Holland, David Kirk, Pablo Lapegna, Benjamin Lessing, Aníbal Pérez-Liñán, Jenny Pearce, Shannan Mattiace, Marcelo Saín, Gemma Santamaría, Sharon K. Schierling, Svetlana Stephenson, Guillermo Trejo, Federico Varese, Loïc Wacquant, Vesla Weaver, and Melissa Wright. Thanks to you all!

Dennis Rodgers read many, many, many versions of this manuscript and provided incredibly helpful and detailed comments. *Muchas, muchas, muchas gracias, Dennis!* Next time we see each other, dinner is on us—but we choose the place.

Karen Cerulo, editor of *Sociological Forum*, first heard our general argument when she invited us to submit a paper for a special issue of the journal she so deftly edits. Thanks, Karen, for that initial invitation. As we said above, this book is the product of that initial endeavor.

We presented parts of this book, either preliminary arguments or earlier versions of various chapters, at the Humanities Center at Wesleyan University, the Universidad Diego Portales in Santiago de Chile, the Institut Barcelona d'Estudis Internacionals, and in the sociology departments at Boston College, Harvard University, Johns Hopkins University, UNC–Chapel Hill, Tulane University, the University of Buenos Aires, UC–San Diego, the University of Georgia–Athens, and the University of New Mexico. We wish to thank the organizers and all those in attendance for their questions, comments, and criticisms.

We also participated in workshops at Concordia University, the University of Chicago, the University of Notre Dame, and the Universidad de Los Andes in Colombia. Participants in the workshop "Argentina en Perspectiva Sociológica" at UT–Austin heard our first full argument and provided invaluable feedback. *Gracias,* María Akchurin, Claudio Benzecry, Daniel Fridman, Mariana Heredia, Amalia Leguizamón, Luisina Perelmiter, Ariel Wilkis, and (again) Matías Dewey and Pablo Lapegna.

We conceived this book while we were both at the Urban Ethnography Lab, a collaborative institutional space at the University of Texas at Austin that supports qualitative research. We presented an earlier version of this work in the 2017 brownbag series. Thank you to all who attended for your feedback, and for being a part of an intellectual community that encourages creativity and collaboration.

Finally, we would like to thank our families near and far. To Gabriela, Camilo, and Luis, the loves of Javier's life, *gracias* "foreveranever." To Cindi, who offered extraordinary help copyediting the final proofs, thank you! And to Melissa, thank you for being a steadfast partner and the shining light in Katie's life. This collaboration was made possible through the depth of their love and support.

Introduction

Carolina's Plight

For all her life, Carolina has lived in Arquitecto Tucci, a poor district on the outskirts of the city of Buenos Aires with record high rates of homicide.[1] At 37 years old, she shared a two-story house with her husband, Raúl, and their three sons close to a local elementary school. As is typical in Arquitecto Tucci, Carolina's modest home was made mostly of exposed bricks with a shingled roof and unfinished concrete floors. At night, two street lights provided very little visibility on the unpaved street that flooded when it rained. In addition to keeping house and raising her sons, three times a week she took two buses into the city of Buenos Aires, where she worked as a maid. Her commute required nearly two hours each way.

When we first approached Carolina to learn about her *barrio*'s most pressing problems, she seized the opportunity to talk about what mattered most to her: the jarring journey of her eldest son in and out of addiction. "My son Damián started smoking weed a few years ago and then he began doing *paco*,"[2] she explained. "I have seen him all drugged up many times, and I know it's not good for him. It is as if he is on high alert, as if he is somewhere else, his eyes are somewhere else. He doesn't understand you, he doesn't listen to you."

Carolina's description of her son on paco is characteristic of the drug's effects. Cheap, accessible, and highly addictive, paco is a mixture of cocaine byproducts and a medley of other toxic fillers, which produces an intense but short-lived high. After its effects

The Ambivalent State: Police-Criminal Collusion at the Urban Margins. Javier Auyero, Oxford University Press (2019). © Oxford University Press.
DOI: 10.1093/oso/9780190915537.001.0001

rapidly wear off, users are left depressed, paranoid, and in search of the next hit.

In addition to the dramatic changes Carolina witnessed in Damián's personality, her family had also been affected by his erratic schedule and health problems. She told us, "[H]e would come back [to the house] at 4 a.m. I couldn't sleep." She described her anguish over seeing his mouth full of sores: "Because when he smokes, he burns his mouth. . . . It's so sad." Even worse, Carolina's two younger sons were exposed to the uncertainty and strife created by Damián's addiction. She explained, "[M]y son Brian, who is five years old, used to cry a lot because his brother was not around. Brian is the one who has suffered the most."

Carolina spoke passionately about her difficulties trying to manage Damián's addiction: "I used to lock him up so that he couldn't go out to smoke." But her attempts to restrain him to the house backfired: "[O]nce he jumped out of our balcony and broke his leg. The drugs were really hurting him."

When he wasn't at home, Carolina often didn't know where Damián was or when he would be back. "[W]e spent the whole year chasing after him, rainy day after rainy day, always looking for him," she remembered. "It was hard. We all suffered. . . . It's horrible, you can't even imagine. You feel your legs and your hands shaking, you have no idea what you are going to find when you are searching for him." Perhaps worst of all, Carolina worried about the violence that Damián may have encountered as he bought, used, and rebounded from drugs: "I feared he was going to be killed, or raped. . . . My biggest fear was to find him stabbed or shot because of the drugs."

Her powerlessness to curb Damián's addiction manifested in deep-set frustration. When her son was high, she explained, "I wanted to kill him." She recollected, "[O]ne night, I went out to look for him. And he was super high. . . . I beat the shit out of him, but he doesn't remember anything. He looks at you as if in shock, with that stupid face, as if he doesn't know what you're talking about."

Carolina was quick to identify the streets—where Damián spent most of his time—as the source of his addiction. She explained, "When I ask him why it is so difficult to stop, he says the drugs are in his face, everywhere he goes, drugs are all over. They sell them on the corner, they sell them across the street. He says that he cannot leave the house, because drugs are right there and they tempt him. Anywhere he goes in Arquitecto Tucci, there are drugs."

For some like Damián, dependence on highly addictive drugs like paco was a fact of life. But many others were caught in the crosshairs of the production, distribution, and consumption of illicit drugs and the violence these processes engender. "You cannot go to work without thinking you are going to get mugged," Carolina explained as she told us about her long commute. "There are kids who steal so that they can get money to buy drugs. I'm always watching my back. You cannot walk on the streets. Anywhere you go, you have to take a car service. We can't live like that." What is more, Carolina did not feel protected by law enforcement: "The cops don't do anything. The cops are all dealers [*La policía es toda transa*]. They catch a dealer on this street and they let him out on the next corner."

In describing her son's addiction and the fear and violence in her neighborhood, Carolina gives voice and texture to the shared experience of many residents of Arquitecto Tucci. She also articulates what constitutes the empirical object of this book: the collaboration between police and drug dealers.

The Priest's Remorse

Father Mariano Oberlín was an outspoken critic of paco.[3] The drug was having, he repeatedly asserted, devastating effects on the lives of poor youth in the shantytown where he lived and worked, a hot spot of drug dealing on the outskirts of Córdoba, Argentina's second largest city.

The son of a union and church activist who was kidnapped and disappeared in the mid-1970s by paramilitary forces, he also publicly supported the activism of Mothers against Paco. This organization, which was also very active in Arquitecto Tucci where Carolina lived is composed of mothers whose children are addicted to what is called "the poor man's drug."[4] As a result of his visibility, Father Oberlín received death threats from local drug dealers. "Five thousand pesos for whoever kills the priest," he once overheard as he was clearing the grounds of an abandoned plot in front of a local school.

Given the recurring intimidations, the local government assigned him a bodyguard. On December 22, 2016, according to the police report, the priest was mowing a lawn near his church when two teenagers approached him and demanded his cell phone, necklace, and the weed wacker he was using. His bodyguard came running toward him and fired several shots. A bullet killed one of the assailants, a boy named Lucas.[5] Oberlín was devastated by the murder. In a public Facebook post the next day, he wrote:

> I could never have imagined that the bullet I had thought for a few weeks was going to hit my head could end up in the head of a fourteen-year-old boy. If I could trade my life for this boy's, I swear I would trade it. But even if I die, he will not be brought back to life. Today, I feel nothing makes sense. Neither the struggles of so many years, nor the convictions, nor the words so often said, nor the tireless work trying to change at least one tip of a system that is rotten to the core. I do not know how life will go on. I just know that I do not want to continue to feed this machine of violence, exclusion, and death.

This story vividly encapsulates the transformations of violence at the urban margins in Argentina and elsewhere in Latin America. Hector Oberlín, the priest's father, confronted the threats of state and paramilitary forces until he was abducted and then killed in a state-run concentration camp during Argentina's last military dictatorship (1976–83). His son, Father Mariano, confronted a different form of danger: one posed by local drug dealers.[6]

Drug-related violence affects not only its users and dealers but also other residents. Men, women, and children living in poor communities are oftentimes caught in the middle of disputes between drug dealers. As Carolina knew well, drug addiction and consumption generate other types of interpersonal physical aggression: a violent mugging on the street, a brutal beating perpetrated by a mother on a son. As this book will closely inspect, what scholars and journalists call "drug-related" violence is not confined to participants in this illicit market but travels beyond its confines, affecting relations both on the streets and inside homes.

Violence in Latin America

During the first decades of the 21st century, most Latin American countries have witnessed an increase in urban violence, making Latin America the only region in the world where lethal violence (measured in homicide rates) is still growing without being at war.[7] Political scientist José Miguel Cruz (2016:376) eloquently describes this process:

Year after year, statistics reveal signs of worsening, hitting new highs boosted by drug wars and street gangs. The latest consolidated reports on homicide rates based on data from 2012 suggest that the region's average surpassed 20 murders per 100,000 inhabitants long ago. By 2015, Latin America and the Caribbean were home to eight of the top ten most violent countries in the world. In some of the countries of the so-called Northern Triangle of Central America (El Salvador and Honduras), Venezuela, and the Caribbean (Jamaica and Trinidad and Tobago), homicidal violence appears to have gone out of bounds, with rates ranging from 50 to 103 homicides per 100,000 inhabitants. In Venezuela, for instance, approximately 128,580 people have been killed between 2001 and 2011, averaging 11,689 murders per year. Guatemala, Colombia, and Belize register rates greater than 25 homicides per 100,000 inhabitants. And Brazil, with the largest population in Latin America, is just above the regional average, although in absolute terms, violence there far exceeds any of the others.

This violence, analysts agree, is not evenly distributed socially or geographically, but instead concentrates in the territories where the urban poor dwell—known as *favelas, colonias, barrios, comunas,* or *villas* in different countries of the sub-continent.[8] Argentina has levels of violence that are comparatively lower than the rest of Latin America but demonstrates a similar clustering of violence in poor areas and among certain people (predominantly poor young men).[9]

Social scientific studies point to a number of factors associated with this increasingly ubiquitous character of violence in low-income neighborhoods: poverty, unemployment, inequality, the accumulation of structural disadvantages, the lack of social cohesion and informal social control ("collective efficacy"), and the twin influence of the illicit drug trade and the fragile legitimacy of the state's monopoly of violence.[10] This book focuses on the relationship between these last two factors, dissecting the secret and illicit connections between drug dealers and members of the state security forces.

We zoom in on these connections aware of the fact that they are part of a larger universe of state-criminal links—relations that are central to comprehend the maelstrom of violence in the region. Again, Cruz (2016:376) puts it well: When citing the cases of top government officials (in Mexico, Honduras, and Guatemala) who were involved in criminal activities, he argues that to truly understand the high levels of violent crime in Latin America it is imperative to "study the participation of the state and its operators as *perpetrators* of criminal violence" (*our emphasis*).[11]

In his persuasive call for a re-invigoration of a comparative sociology of urban marginality, sociologist Loïc Wacquant (2008:11) contends that social science research needs to:

> specify the degree and form of state penetration in neighborhoods of relegation as well as the changing—and often contradictory— relations their inhabitants maintain with different public officials and agencies, schools and hospitals, housing and social welfare, firefighting and transportation, the courts and the police. These relationships cannot be assumed to be static, uniform, univocal.

Wacquant continues, "Among the institutions that stamp their imprint on the daily life of the populations and on the climate of 'problem' neighborhoods, special attention must be accorded to the police" (p. 12).[12] Our book heeds this call for a close inspection of the "causal dynamics, social modalities, and experiential forms that fashion relegation" (pp. 7–8). In the chapters that follow we focus on one particular form of state penetration in territories of urban perdition—that of the police—and we zoom in on one specific set of relations: *the clandestine links between police agents and drug dealers.*

Pulling Back the Curtain

This book draws on a unique combination of data. These include ethnographic evidence collected over 30 months of fieldwork in Arquitecto Tucci and documentary evidence from several court cases involving drug market groups in Argentina—evidence that includes hundreds of pages of highly revealing wiretapped conversations between drug dealers and members of the state security forces, including agents of the State Police, Federal Police, Naval

Prefecture, and National Guard. With these sources, we dissect the actual content of what is known as "police-criminal collusion" and examine its connection to poor people's perception of law enforcement and the depacification of their daily lives.

We are the first to admit that the material on which we rely in this book is indeed "messy" and does not lend itself to construct the stylized facts and neat descriptions upon which much theory-testing and modeling in the social sciences are done these days. We understand that terms such as "cohesive state apparatus" or "fragmented sovereignty" serve analytic purposes and have been useful in advancing knowledge on the origins and forms of violence.[13] But we prefer to focus on fine-grained, micro-interactive processes involving members of drug market organizations and police forces. We do this not simply because we think there are fascinating—and highly consequential— dynamics at work, but also because we think that we can contribute to the construction of a more solid foundation for sociological research on the relationship between police-criminal collusion and interpersonal violence. The following short vignettes anticipate the kinds of data we draw upon to unpack collusion.

In Argentina's third largest city, Rosario, a member of the powerful trafficking group called Los Monos had a phone conversation with Murray, the group's leader.[14] Unbeknownst to either speaker, their phones had been wiretapped by state detectives.

"The guy from Vehicles Division [of the State Police] called [me]," the member warned Murray. "He says there's going to be a raid on Fifth Street. They say there are high quality cars there and motorcycles.... I think that place belongs to you." Later on, Murray spoke on the phone with an officer from the State Police. He asked, "Are you guys working tomorrow?" "Yes," the policeman replied, "we are starting at 6 p.m. We have 12 search warrants." Murray wanted to know where raids would take place: "Not towards our side, correct?" The officer then provided details about their whereabouts: "We are going to the Chacarilla area where there's a tire shop, but that'll be on Saturday."

In another wiretapped conversation, all of which are included in a 408-page indictment against members of Los Monos, another police officer told Murray: "This afternoon, the *bunker* [drug-selling point] at [address] will be raided."

Far from the city of Rosario, in the district of San Martín in the west of the Conurbano Bonaerense,[15] Nélida—one of the leaders of a different drug-dealing group—asked the local police chief when he was going to raid her main competitor's stash house. According to transcriptions nested in another set of court proceedings, Nélida said, "I was wondering if something was going to be done about my little problem." The police chief responded, "Yes, the thing is that I still don't have the arrest warrant. I'm waiting for the prosecutor, do you understand?"

The Ambivalent State

The ethnographic material and judicial proceedings that we examined throughout this book portray the views of ordinary citizens on the law and police (mis)behavior, the widespread fear of interpersonal violence they experience, and a variety of interactions between members of groups engaged in criminal activity (specifically drug trafficking and street sales) and members of the state's repressive apparatus. The data we analyzed fill in our understandings of police-criminal "collusion"—a term that is repeatedly heard in the news but whose actual substance remains vague and unspecified both in public discourse and in the scholarship on the topic.[16]

Taken together, the material we inspect gives concrete shape "to what would otherwise be an abstraction ('the state')" (Gupta 1995:378). "[T]he state as an institution," write Aradhana Sharma and Akhil Gupta (2006:11), "is substantiated in people's lives through the apparently *banal* practices of bureaucracies" (*original emphasis*). People learn about the state in the sphere of everyday practices, such as waiting in line for a subsidy,[17] paying a traffic ticket, attending a court hearing, or, as we will see in this book, suspecting or witnessing police break the law.

Research on the state in the 21st century has criticized the still widespread dichotomy between "weak" states and "strong" states.[18] Cruz (2016:378), for example, points out that "the excessive focus on the debate of strong states versus weak states has hampered exploration of the complexities surrounding the role of the state in common violence." Political scientist Enrique Desmond Arias (2006a; 2017), in turn, argues that we need to inspect the specific kinds of *engagements* between state and criminal actors. His research in the favelas of Rio de Janeiro dissects such engagements between criminal organizations, community associations, police, and politicians. As he describes:

> Relations between police and traffickers are both violent and disorganized. Residents report that while one shift of police takes direct payments from the traffickers, other shifts maintain more distant relations. Most police do not directly take bribes from the gang. Rather, they arrest traffickers, confiscate contraband, and then ransom the jailed traffickers' freedom and sell the drugs and weapons to other gangs.[19]

As readers will note, our description of the clandestine connections between drug dealers and police agents share many similarities with those described in Brazil. By examining drug market organizations that are relatively younger and levels of violence that are relatively lower compared to well-studied cases such as in Brazil, Mexico, and Colombia, our book contributes to a better comprehension of the dynamics of collusion by examining data at a granular, interpersonal level.

The overarching argument of our book is that, when closely inspecting the interactions between law enforcement and criminal actors, the state that emerges is neither "weak" (as in descriptions of poor neighborhoods as abandoned by the state or "governance voids") nor "strong" (as in descriptions of poor neighborhoods as highly militarized spaces firmly controlled by the state's iron fist).[20] The set of clandestine interactions between drug market participants and state actors unearthed and analyzed in the pages that follow point to a state that is a *deeply ambivalent organization*, a state that enforces the rule of law while at the same time (and in the same place) functions as a partner to what it defines as criminal behavior.

When highlighting the ambivalent character of the state, we are not referring to "sociological ambivalence," a concept elaborated by Robert K. Merton and Elinor Barber (1976:5) to denote the ambivalence that comes to be "built into the structure of social statuses and roles." Rather, we use the term "ambivalent" in the literal sense, defined by the *Oxford English Dictionary* as "having either or both of two contrary or parallel values, qualities or meanings; entertaining contradictory emotions (as love and hatred) towards the same person or thing; acting on or arguing for sometimes one and sometimes the other of two opposites; equivocal."[21]

We embarked on the project of unearthing clandestine connections between state security actors and drug dealers with the dual aim of understanding not only violence but also the type of state with which the poor interact on a daily basis and the meanings conveyed through these interactions. In the pages that follow, we do not provide a comprehensive review of what the state is and what it does (or should do).[22] Rather, our approach to the state emerges from a general consensus around its definition as the set of organizations that hold a monopoly on the use of legitimate force. The state is "defined as a complex of interdependent institutions, differentiated from other institutions in society and legitimate, autonomous, based upon a defined territory and recognized as a state by other states," and "characterized by its administrative capacity to steer, to govern a society, to establish constraining rules, property rights, to guarantee exchanges, to tax and concentrate resources, to organize economic development and to protect citizens" (King and Le Gales 2012:108). The state also has a symbolic dimension in which the production of belief in the state and its authority (i.e., legitimation and its recognition) takes center stage. Attention to this dimension will prove key to making sense of poor people's understandings of law enforcement and their feelings of betrayal by members of the security apparatus.[23]

Most students of the modern state would not list *coherence* as its defining characteristic.[24] According to Bob Jessop (2016), for example, the state is a "polyvalent, polymorphous assemblage" in which various "state projects" compete with one another (p. 26). Ambivalence with respect to the law is a feature, in Jessop's view, of every modern state: "[M]any states routinely infringe their own legality—whether openly or beneath the cloak of official secrecy, whether at home or abroad—by relying on a mix of terror, force, fraud, and corruption to exercise power" (p. 28). For Pierre Bourdieu (2015), to cite another example, the state is a field, an arena where a plurality of agents, groups, and institutions are in constant struggle. Tensions and contradictions are, in other words, germane to the state. Although contending actors endowed with different resources and "unusual strengths" pursue various and sometimes conflicting agendas, they all share a general orientation (p. 32). In this field, action is "oriented largely toward imposing the state's will on society at large" (Steinmetz 2014:5).

Most scholars of the state would thus probably find our claim about the state's ambivalence tautological. States, they would almost certainly argue, are *always* ambivalent. We concur. What we will show is that state agents *simultaneously* enforce and break the law in the *same* marginalized space and among the *same* relegated people. In this book, we provide empirical evidence of a more specific, grounded instantiation of ambivalence in the lower regions of the social and geographical space. The state might always be ambivalent, but the specific ambivalence we will uncover, based on detailed attention to the *resources, practices,* and *processes* that link state agents and drug dealers, shape interpersonal violence and produce a widespread mistrust of law enforcement agents.

What is more, state action and intervention are not isolated from other institutions. As Jessop (2016:57) explains well, "How and how far state powers (and any associated liabilities, vulnerabilities, and incapacities) are actualized depends on the action, reaction, and interaction of specific social forces located in and beyond the state." Although he did not have illicit links in mind, Jessop's point still applies: Clandestine connections pull state actors away from "imposing the state's will" (as Steinmetz [2014:5] argues) and into a different and illicit direction. As we will demonstrate, state security agents involved in collusive relations abdicate the orientation to impose the state's will on others and instead attempt to enforce their own will for their own benefit. They do so by using the power that comes from their belonging to the state apparatus.

The empirical evidence we will present points to a state whose presence at the urban margins displays, as we said above, two coexisting and seemingly contradictory qualities: acting simultaneously as an *enforcer* of the rule of law and an *accomplice* to criminal acts.[25] Security forces patrol the streets, conduct sudden raids, and set up checkpoints. Police agents use violent stop-and-frisk tactics and excessive force to fill jails and prisons. These are not, to reiterate, signs of an absent or a weak state.[26] Rather, we will show that the same state concurrently partakes in criminal activities in a variety of concealed ways. This participation has important consequences. As Cruz (2016:377) perceptively notes, it "increases the repercussions of crime, reproduces impunity, makes state institutions partners in crime, and transforms the parameters of legitimacy of the regime."

We set forth to make an argument about the state's ambivalence by meticulously *showing* (as different from simply telling and theorizing) the inner workings of collusive relations. In order to unpack collusion, *The Ambivalent State* presents, in as close empirical detail as possible, the exchanges of material and symbolic resources between drug dealers and state agents, as well as the practices and relational processes that constitute collusion. We argue that illicit relationships help drug market organizations in their efforts to establish an economic monopoly over a certain territory that is central to their illegal trade. We also demonstrate that this set of clandestine relationships between police officers and dealers (a) shape the systemic violence that often accompanies the market for illegal drugs and contributes to the constitution of what Janice Perlman (2010) calls the "violence stew" in poor urban areas,[27] and (b) give form to what criminologists call "legal cynicism"—the shared belief that law enforcement agents are "illegitimate, unresponsive, and ill equipped to ensure public safety" (Kirk and Papachristos 2011:1191).[28] Poor people share the belief that, when it comes to the drug trade and controlling the related violence, the state is inept and biased and that it engages in what we will call *disorganized organized crime*.

Joining the "relational turn" in the social sciences, sociologist Matthew Desmond (2014) makes a case for "relational ethnography."[29] He argues that ethnographers should shift the substantive and analytic focus of inquiry from groups and places to relations, conflicts, boundaries, and processes.[30] *The Ambivalent State* further develops a two-decade long research agenda that has scrutinized the relationships between the state and the urban poor.[31] Although we spend a lot of time and effort trying to figure out how residents, police officers, and drug dealers—alone or in groups—think, feel, and act, our analytic object lies in the *relationships* between them. To make clear our focus: Think of clapping. We are not examining the hands that strike each other but the percussive sound that is produced by—and *figuratively* lies between—those striking hands. This is a study not of a neighborhood (Arquitecto Tucci), a group of people (its residents), or an organization (the police force or drug gang) but of the relations (sometimes overt, sometimes covert) of conflict or cooperation between them—and the experiences and actions that result.[32]

These relations, it is important to note, do not exist in a vacuum but are shaped by particular economic and political contexts. Economic and political forces and structures determine—in the sense of setting limits and exerting pressures, as Raymond Williams (1978) would say—the resources exchanged, the practices in which actors engage, and the processes that link them. Of particular importance in understanding what "constrain[s], impel[s], and impress[es]" (Salzinger and Gowan 2018:62) upon the dynamics of collusion are the transformations in the policing and drug trafficking, which we review in Chapter 1.

A Note on Methods: Ethnography and Court Case Analysis

This project is a continuation of the examination of violence and urban poverty initiated in the book *In Harm's Way* (Auyero and Berti 2015). That book touched on collusion between drug dealers and police agents but did not fully examine the preliminary data found on the topic. For this book, we re-analyzed the extensive fieldwork conducted for that project, collected several more interviews in Arquitecto Tucci focused specifically on the links between drug consumption, trafficking, violence, and police (in)action, and scrutinized court cases involving members of drug market organizations and state security forces.

Ethnography, Revisits, and Re-analysis

Between April 2009 and August 2012—with the interruptions of the winter and summer academic recesses—María Fernanda Berti, one of the co-authors of *In Harm's Way*, registered her activities as a primary school teacher in a field diary. These included her experiences in the neighborhood where she worked combined with the stories recounted by her students, those told by other teachers and school personnel, and information shared by parents. She always used pseudonyms to identify the people she discussed. Agustín Burbano de Lara joined the project as a research assistant in 2010 and 2011. He visited Arquitecto Tucci two or three times a week for six months and established a trusting relationship with the coordinators of a local soup kitchen. Through them, he got to know many other residents: first, neighbors who visited the soup kitchen and then others through those connections. The interviews he conducted had a more informal character than the unidirectional exchange typical of research protocols and were conducted after weeks, and sometimes months, of mutual acquaintanceship.[33]

For this project, we re-examined the data produced during that fieldwork. Our analysis involved a re-coding of field notes and previously transcribed interviews. But this time, we focused on interactions between police, drug dealers, and neighbors. Specifically, we concentrated our attention on residents' descriptions and evaluations of what they called the "arreglo"—the illicit relationships between police agents and drug dealers. In this text, we use the pronoun "we" when describing this ethnographic fieldwork to refer to the team-based nature of its collection, not our own exclusive presence.

At the time of writing, María Fernanda Berti still works as a teacher in Arquitecto Tucci. In 2018, she conducted 14 additional interviews with five political brokers, the local priest, and eight additional residents. These new interviews focused on their personal experiences with collusion, violence, addiction, and the ways these individuals navigated nearby drug-selling operations and rumors about corrupt police. This rich qualitative fieldwork and interview material constitute the data used to not only inspire the rest of this study but also to orient our discussion of collusion and legal cynicism that we develop in Chapter 3.

Legal Documents and Newspaper Articles

The bulk of our archival research was based on a close reading of court cases (judicial indictments and transcribed wiretappings) involving members of drug market groups operating in different areas in Argentina, including groups we call Los Vagones (Arquitecto Tucci, Buenos Aires), Los Monos (Rosario, Santa Fe), Los Pescadores (Yapurá, Corrientes), and La Banda de Raúl (San Martín, Buenos Aires). In addition to these legal documents, we collected news articles related to these court cases to better understand the context of the indictments. These cases document collusion between drug dealers and members of various state security forces. These include federal agencies like the Federal Police (Policía Federal), National Guard (Gendarmería), and Naval Police (Prefectura),[34] as well as state police forces. Each state in Argentina has its own police force made up of state-level agencies and local precincts. When we refer to local police, we mean the state police agents operating in a particular neighborhood.

The cases we analyzed are not the only legal cases involving illicit relationships between police and drug dealers. We focused on these four in particular because, with the help of two journalists (Silvina Tamous and María Florencia Alcaraz), we were able to access the complete court cases without redactions. These cases represent well the existing variation in terms of size, territorial extension, and, most importantly, diversity of relations with security forces among drug market organizations.

For obvious reasons, evidence of the "actual links between state agencies and illegal actors or activities" is not easy to come by (Dewey 2017a:15). Typically squeezed out of newspaper accounts, information about the internal operations of criminal organizations and their connections to state agencies overflows in documents that social researchers do not readily have access to: judicial proceedings and their accompanying investigations. In the study of clandestine connections between criminal groups and state agents, court records are a significant source of information. Several hundred pages of transcribed phone conversations that were wiretapped by the police are nested within the court documents we reviewed, offering a rich source of data. According to criminologists Paolo Campana and Federico Varese (2012:15), "Data drawn from wiretap records have the advantage of capturing conversations as they occur in their 'natural' setting and may yield a fuller picture of the group, including conversations involving lower-level and upper-level actors." And, we would add, between these actors and members of the police forces. Despite these strengths, they still constitute a "relatively neglected source of data" (p. 27).[35]

We are certainly not the first to use court records to uncover knowledge hidden from public view. "Microhistory" also relied on trial records—notable among them, and our main sources of inspiration, were Carlo Ginzburg's *The Cheese and the Worms*, David Kertzer's *Amalia's Tale*, and Natalie Zemon Davis's *The Return of Martin Guerre*. Rather than "recovering buried history" (Kertzer 2008:190), our effort was to retrieve state records and put them in dialogue with ethnographic and qualitative material in order to describe and theorize the micro-dynamics of collusion.

There are three prerequisites for minimizing bias and potential sources of error with wiretapped conversations: coverage, duration, and self-censorship.[36] The wiretapped conversations we analyze meet all but one of these requisites. Our data include a reasonably wide coverage of actors and activities (approximately three months for each case). But in two of the four primary cases, the wiretappings did not fulfill the requisite of "no self-censorship." Although some individuals seemed aware of surveillance—and censored their conversations accordingly—we interpret this as evidence to better understand the workings of collusion. Moreover, while recording conversations without consent is inconsistent with our ethical standards for qualitative data collection, we use these transcripts not as data produced through in-depth interviews but as a legal archive produced by the state.

We coded and analyzed these judicial documents and wiretappings using open and focused coding.[37] We concentrated both on the activities of these groups and on their relationships with security forces. We paid particular attention to the types of material and informational resources exchanged between various actors. When violent episodes were mentioned (for example, an attack on a drug-selling point or a murder), we triangulated these references with news articles to see if there was any further evidence in journalistic reports. We also relied on news reports, particularly those produced by investigative journalists, to better understand local drug market activities and the trajectory of each group.[38] To analyze the court cases, we applied the evidentiary criteria normally used for ethnographic research: Higher evidentiary value was assigned to individual acts or patterns of conduct that were described repeatedly in the court proceedings and/or referred to in wiretappings.[39]

Court cases do not afford an unobstructed view into the *arcana imperii*, the secrets of state power. Many critical data are still inaccessible. We are also deeply aware of the fact that some of these court cases, or parts of their evidence, might be the very outcome of a jockeying for power among rival security agencies, politicians, and actors in the judiciary.[40] Although shadowy turf wars within the state are beyond our purview, it would be naïve for us not to consider the obvious fact that many a case could be the result of a dispute between what Schneider and Schneider (2003:34) call "pieces of the state." This does not make our evidence irredeemably fabricated. Rather, it points to its inevitably partial character. Having reviewed several cases in different parts of Argentina involving different state actors as well as the extensive media coverage of the topic, we are confident in the validity of our evidence of the patterned ways in which clandestine connections operate.

Case studies constrained by accessibility prompt us to consider how well the findings travel beyond the specific sites. For us, the question—posed ad nauseam to ethnographers in particular, and qualitative researchers in general—is not whether security forces are behaving in the way we describe here in other states or countries. Further empirical research should determine that. The important question for us is whether the analytic and methodological approach we put forth in this book—combining ethnographic and archival research to unpack collusion and dissect its effects on poor people's daily lives—can be deployed to analyze other contexts. By the end of this book, we hope readers answer this question in the affirmative.

What we cannot achieve with the kind of data we have at our disposal is to explain why some drug dealers and police officers engage in this type of illicit activity or when and why they get caught. Collusion has its limits. The indictments and trials we present below are evidence of that. An analysis of when, where, and why some collusive relationships begin and when and why they end up in court would require data that, as far as we know, are not available (for example, about the universe of active dealers with and without close ties with police officers). Because of these limitations, this book focuses on how collusion works rather than when and why it develops, succeeds, or fails. The same can be said about the relationship between collusion and violence. Given the nature of our data, we cannot speak to absolute changes in levels of drug-related violence; rather, we will argue that collusion shapes and channels interpersonal violence.

On Studying Poverty and Violence

Areas like Arquitecto Tucci—and many other poor neighborhoods throughout the Americas—are persistently stigmatized and criminalized by states, the media, and other fearful citizens. These places and the people who live there are often homogenized to evoke a "threatening criminal imaginary" (Schneider and Schneider 2003:352). The last thing we intend to do by studying and then publishing the stories of life in Arquitecto Tucci is to reproduce dominant stereotypes about the poor. Rather, we focus on these experiences because they are critical to understanding the depacification of marginalized spaces and the difficult predicament their residents face on a daily basis. People like Carolina, it bears repeating, are the ones who are suffering the most from the inner workings of collusion and escalation of violence. We embarked on this project because we wanted to better understand how state actors produced and perpetuated her (and many others') afflictions.

Our focus on poor, structurally disadvantaged areas and on the clandestine links between drug dealers and members of the security forces (who more often than not come from the same neighborhoods and are similarly disadvantaged) is not meant to suggest that illicit liaisons are inherent or exclusive to urban marginality. They are not. To emphasize this point, we paraphrase the 1993 report of the Italian Parliamentary Anti-Mafia Committee, which stated: "Consideration of Mafia connections should not focus only on the 'lower branches' of politics. It is unthinkable that the vast phenomenon of collusion with Mafia in communities of the South could have developed as it has without some sort of *participation of political actors at higher levels*" (quoted in della Porta and Vannucci 1999:220, *our emphasis*).

Although we are not studying the Mafia, the same general point applies. Illicit relations are not exclusive to low-level police officers or isolated to poor urban areas. Research on money laundering and electoral campaigns, for example, shows that clandestine connections also exist between higher-level actors and pose a serious risk to the integrity of democracy.[41] Other studies have uncovered and analyzed the relations between politicians, members of the judiciary, police, and criminal actors in a variety of illegal enterprises.[42] For example, the Center for Socio-Legal Studies, the foremost human rights organization in Argentina, notes that both police agents and actors within the judiciary "use" the law and legal and administrative procedures in a "discretionary and instrumental" way to "protect allies, punish competitors and cover up their own crimes" (CELS 2016:109).[43] In other words, what sociologist Matías Dewey (2015) aptly calls the "clandestine order" extends well beyond the specific empirical focus of our study and includes actors other than police officers and drug dealers.[44] One of us has shown, for example, that clandestine relations between police agents and political brokers have been central in the making of episodes of collective violence.[45]

Our focus on the inner workings of collusion at the local level was to a great extent informed by what we observed on the ground in Arquitecto Tucci. It was the many tales of collusion and rumors of extortion that circulated among residents that sent us on our quest. Our focus was also prompted by the availability of data at the time of writing—availability that is very much a function of the power of certain actors to avoid being detected. Nevertheless, the court cases we analyze offer an unprecedented window into social interactions, including private conversations, that often remain obscure, even to the most astute and embedded ethnographer.

To our knowledge, this book is the first to combine ethnographic data with evidence culled from judicial proceedings and transcribed wiretappings. In principle, the combination of ethnographic and legal evidence could certainly be *scaled up* to examine police-criminal connections at the state and federal levels. It could also be *expanded* to study other sorts of connections, hinted at in the case of Los Pescadores (Chapter 6) but not fully developed in the cases we present below. Despite these exciting possibilities, the availability of reliable evidence remains the prime obstacle to such an empirical and theoretical endeavor.

Uncovering the Covert

Describing the predicament of "the American writer" in the mid-20th-century United States, Philip Roth (2017:27) notes that the writer's hands are full "in trying to understand, describe, and then make *credible* much of American reality. It stupefies, it sickens, it infuriates, and finally it is a kind of embarrassment to one's own meager imagination." The hidden reality we reconstruct in the pages that follow produced a similar type of challenge to our *sociological* imagination. By digging into different sources of data (qualitative fieldwork and legal documents), we sought to make connections between "things" (social facts) that are not usually related; for example, the suffering of a mother due to her son's addiction, a domestic dispute, and a police officer's deal with a drug dealer (what many political sociology textbooks would call "society" and "state").

Why do people who care neither about Argentine politics nor the relationship between its state and the poor read this book? What can it tell readers about some larger issue? These questions recurrently haunt researchers like us who work in the United States but write about other areas of the world. For us, this book is the product of our collective effort to uncover and analyze the covert interactions and resolutions that were never intended to be seen, read, or examined. While popular television shows, movies, and documentaries sometimes go "behind the scenes" to dramatize crime and punishment, scholars of poverty, the state, and violence rarely make such attempts. This book calls for analytic attention not only to the clandestine dimension of state-society interactions but also to the ways in which these shape the daily life of poor residents. Rather than offering a theoretical manifesto, we set out to show *how collusion works*.

In the pages that follow, we engage with different types of scholarship. Some has been produced by sociologists and anthropologists in Argentina about Argentine reality; others are by sociologists, political scientists, and anthropologists working in the United States who examine the conditions, problems, and dynamics in Latin America and other parts of the world; and still others have been produced by sociologists based in the United States about

U.S. issues. Therein lies another broad lesson of our study. We draw on diverse literatures not out of scholasticism but out of the need to make sense of the empirical material we encountered. Scholars, and particularly urban sociologists, should attempt a similar kind of engagement with scholarship that goes beyond disciplinary and national boundaries so as to avoid the parochialism that still characterizes much of the field. We believe that U.S. urban sociologists have much to learn from what is written in other parts of the world. This book offers an empirical demonstration of how scholarship can be produced through transdisciplinary and transnational scholarly engagement.

A third broad lesson of this book is related to our methods. Ethnographic work shows the virtues of capturing the relational nature of a certain phenomenon from various positions: for example, understanding eviction in Milwaukee from the perspectives of the evicted and the landlord (Desmond 2016) or interrogating policing in Los Angeles by studying patrol officers and the homeless (Stuart 2016). Sometimes this can be done by conducing multi-sited ethnographic fieldwork. Other times, given the illicit character of the activity under investigation (and the risks associated with researching it), other methods have to be mobilized. Our study shows how different types of data collection– in this case, ethnographic fieldwork and archival research—can be merged in a productive way.

* * *

Our book proceeds as follows. The first chapter situates this study in scholarship on the illicit networks between state officials and drug market organizations. Here, we utilize the notion of *intreccio* that Italians use to refer to the connections between Mafiosi and state officials to understand the emergence and inner workings of "state-sponsored protection rackets." Both concepts clearly illustrate the existence of clandestine connections between participants in criminal activity and members of the state repressive apparatus, what our respondents referred to as an arrangement, or *arreglo*. Although studies have signaled the importance of such clandestine connections, very few scholarly works have dissected the actual content of these covert relationships. This book not only fills this important gap but also goes beyond description to connect the content of police-criminal collusion with the actual responses of actors involved and the lived experiences of those affected by these relationships. We then provide a brief historical context of drug trafficking and police corruption in Argentina.

With this theoretical and contextual foundation, we begin our empirical analysis of clandestine connections from the ground up. Chapters 2 and 3 draw primarily on our ethnographic and interview data to detail the routine encounters with crime and violence that take place on the streets and in the homes of Arquitecto Tucci. In Chapter 2, we describe neighbors' daily experiences with this violence, documenting the pathways through which drug-related violence enters residents' homes. Like Carolina, whose story opened this introduction, most of the neighbors we talked to had personal experiences with violence, strong opinions about the police in the neighborhood, and suspicions about police extortion and complicity with the drug dealers, all of which deeply informed the generalized distrust of local law enforcement that we describe in Chapter 3.

The next three chapters depart from the fieldsite (Arquitecto Tucci) and move to *where the collusion is*. Through a detailed analysis of court cases indicting both participants in the drug trade and members of security forces, we zoom in on actual relationships of collusion across Argentina. These chapters move from the outskirts of Buenos Aires in Chapter 4, where we analyze the clandestine relations between a group we call Los Vagones (The Train Cars) and members of the local police, to the poor neighborhoods around the city of Rosario in Chapter 5, where members of Los Monos (The Monkeys) relied on close connections with several different security forces. In Chapter 6, we travel to Argentina's northern border to analyze a well-connected drug trafficking organization we call Los Pescadores (The Fishermen) and then return to the Conurbano Bonaerense to delve into the inner workings of La Banda de Raúl (Raúl's Gang). Together, these three chapters present evidence of the actual content of collusion and show the important exchanges of material and informational resources that accompany the well-studied provision of "protection."

In Chapter 7, we take a step back from the cases to theorize collusion through a close examination of the resources, practices, and relational processes at work. The deep and routine entanglement between drug dealers and members of the security forces we dissect in this book is not a perennial characteristic of the polity in Argentina—or in Latin America for that matter. Change can happen. Aware of how pernicious collusion is for democratic institutions, we conclude this book with a re-assertion of the value of public social sciences, and with an empirically grounded speculation about ways that collusion can be stamped out. The ambivalence of the state we uncover here does not make Carolina's plight, frustration, and impotence less painful. But we hope that it makes it at least more understandable.

1

Clandestine Relations Matter

> Clandestine: Secret, private, concealed; usually in a
> bad sense, implying craft or deception; underhand,
> surreptitious.
>
> *Oxford English Dictionary*

Carolina and her neighbors in Arquitecto Tucci are not alone in be-
lieving that members of the state security forces and participants in
criminal organizations have some kind of mutual arrangement or,
as locals call it, an *arreglo*. The clandestine relationships that people
suspect between police and drug dealers have been the object of
much scholarly attention by sociologists, anthropologists, historians, and political scientists. What follows is not a complete review
of all the social science literature on the topic but a summary account of the scholarship that guided our data collection and helped
us to make sense of our empirical material. This chapter begins
by introducing what anthropologists Jane Schneider and Peter
Schneider (2003) call the *intreccio*—the Italian word that refers to
the thick entwining of criminal enterprises and state officials.[1] It
then moves to more specific works that inspect the networks that
develop between drug market organizations and state authorities
in Latin America, and concludes with an examination of police and
drug market activity in Argentina that serves as the general context
for our analysis.

The Ambivalent State: Police-Criminal Collusion at the Urban Margins. Javier Auyero, Oxford
University Press (2019). © Oxford University Press.
DOI: 10.1093/oso/9780190915537.001.0001

What is the relationship between the violence in a given area and what the state does or does not do?[2] When examining unprecedented levels of interpersonal violence in many marginalized spaces, and given that state structures "operate through, and in turn transform, the ordering of surrounding networks of social relationships and practices" (Clemens 2016:94), political sociologists are compelled to ask: How does the state police poor neighborhoods? What is the relationship between that intervention and the violence on the ground?

Answers to these questions have been dominated by two main perspectives: one that identifies the state's neglect of poor areas and another that focuses on the state's harsh and punishing presence. Three decades ago, social scientific research depicted marginalized urban areas as governance voids deserted by the state.[3] Poor barrios, inner cities, and African American ghettoes were described as spaces "abandoned" by the state. The main indicators of this desertion were the striking lack of social services and the notable absence of police. More recent scholarship in the Americas and Europe portrays poor areas as militarized spaces firmly controlled by the state's iron fist.[4] Far from being "neglected", marginalized urban areas are now seen as deeply penetrated and oftentimes brutalized by the state repressive apparatus.

In the United States, and despite this changing state presence, the urban poor face many of the same challenges documented by urban sociologists in the 1980s and 1990s, such as limited job prospects, failing neighborhood social institutions, high levels of segregation, a predatory "poverty industry," and chronic interpersonal violence in the street and, for some, at home.[5] But they must also contend with disturbing trends in state surveillance, policing, containment, and punishment practices spurred by a highly racialized "war on drugs" that has targeted poor communities of color through the institution of practices such as "gang injunctions," "roundups," and "stop-and-frisk" and the increasing militarization of domestic police forces.[6]

In Latin America, answers to questions about the relationship between state intervention and urban marginality have been highly influenced by political scientist Guillermo O'Donnell's (1993) notion of "brown areas": "neofeudalized regions" where legality is obliterated and where residents enjoy, at best, a "low intensity citizenship." Shantytown dwellers (along with peasants, indigenous populations, and women), according to O'Donnell, "often are unable to receive fair treatment in the courts, obtain state services to which they are entitled, or be safe from political violence" (p. 1361). In Latin America, the poor meet a state that routinely breaks the rule of law and frequently violates human rights.[7]

Although both sets of literature illuminate important aspects of the interactions between the state and its poor citizens, neither in the United States nor in Latin America has much attention been given to a mode of state intervention that *engages* with illegal actors and conducts illicit actions as part of its daily operation.[8] It is still true that those living in marginalized areas are sometimes neglected by the state and other times are over-policed (and abused) by it. But they are also subjected to what Enrique Desmond Arias (2006a:324) calls "police-criminal collusion": an "active political constellation" of state and illicit actors that not only erodes the rule of law but also institutes "a separate, localized order" that can reproduce high levels of interpersonal violence.[9] In addition to their state-sanctioned routines, members of security forces actively and secretly make illicit deals with members of criminal organizations. Borrowing the language of one of the court cases we will review in chapters that follow, people refer to these deals as "arrangements" (*arreglos*). Many of these deals have a "fluid and permanent" character, constituting a patterned set of relations that organize the actions of both state actors and criminal organizations.[10] Before turning to describe this form of state clandestine action, let us briefly review the scholarship that inspired us to unpack the illicit connections between state authorities and participants in illicit drug markets.

The Intreccio

Political scientists, organizational theorists, and economists have studied collusion in a variety of contexts.[11] We define collusion as one sub-type of corruption, referring to the "abuse of public resources for private gain, through a hidden transaction that involves the violation of some standard of behavior" (della Porta and Vannucci 1999:16).[12] A common term deployed to discuss the misuse of the power associated with public duties, corruption involves "an informal/illegal and secret exchange of formally allocated resources . . . in which at least one corrupt party has to have formal membership/affiliation or at least a contractual relation with the organization from which the resources are extracted" (Jancsics 2014:359). Corruption takes place "between two or more corrupt parties" and always consists of a "deviation from social rules or expectations of some kind" (p. 359).[13] Collusion, in turn, refers to situations in which state actors *actively collaborate over an extended period of time* with non-state actors who engage in criminal activity. Although the term is increasingly common in popular culture and the media,[14] the micro-dynamics of collusion are not well understood.

As will become clear, we do not seek to *prove* in legal terms that corruption exists (which is the ultimate goal of the court cases we analyze). Given the nuanced and multifaceted character of the clandestine arrangements documented in court records, we are more interested in providing a thorough description of the resources exchanged, the practices involved, and the processes at play in order to theorize the kind of state with which the poor interact at the urban margins.[15]

Over the past two decades, social science research has documented a variety of clandestine links between state officials and criminal enterprises.[16] The presence of these illicit relationships has challenged approaches to what the state is and does. While some continue to classify states as weak or strong based on their capacity to monopolize the use of legitimate force, others have moved beyond this binary to examine plural forms of domination.[17]

For our purposes, the Italian notion of *intreccio* best captures these illicit liaisons. The term refers to the "dense interweaving" between Mafiosi and the state officials who take measures to protect them. In their study of the Sicilian Mafia, Jane Schneider and Peter Schneider (2003) call for analytic attention to the interconnections between organized collective violence and state and party politics Mafiosi, they assert, share with some state and political elites a moral and political space that Palermitans (residents of the Sicilian town of Palermo) call the *intreccio*.[18] "More than a simple reciprocity between the Mafia and the state," the term points to "a vast gray area where it is impossible to determine where one leaves off and the other begins" (p. 34).

In an insight that will become crucial as we move into our empirical material, the Schneiders assert that to truly understand the workings of this foggy moral and political nexus,

> it helps to recognize that the state is not unitary. In Italy, indeed, it is common to use the expression "pieces of the state," which immediately conveys a generally high level of internal inconsistency and the possibility that, through a kind of relay system, one state element might engage with fractious local groups to gain advantage over another. (Schneider and Schneider 2003:34)

What Italians call "the wicked deal"—referring to the collusive participation of society's legitimate institutions—is a key ingredient in the development and operation of Mafias: "Political connections, extending into the criminal justice sector, are especially necessary to avert arrests, abort police investigations and trials, and procure licenses to conduct business and carry arms" (p. 363).

Along similar lines, sociologist Pino Arlacchi (1983:117) describes what he calls "the fundamental complementarity" between the authority of the state and the power of the Mafia in this way:

> [A]ll the fundamental activities of the mafia did *not* take place, save at a few moments of official rigidity, *in frontal opposition to the tasks and functions of the organs of the state.* . . . [Rather] mafia and organs of the state, theoretically competitors for the monopoly of the control of violence, in fact *collaborated* often with very similar methods, in the repression of the most serious malfunctions and threats to the established order. In many episodes of banditry or common criminality, as in other cases of organized political dissent or trade-union activity, the intervention of the armed power of the *Mafiosi* on the side of the official forces of order was decisive in the killing, capture or neutralization of the deviants. (*our emphasis*)

Collusion between "bandits and bureaucrats"[19]—understood as a "situation in which the state actively cooperates with non-state armed actors that are geographically intermeshed with its areas of operation" (Staniland 2012:249)—is also one of the ways that authority is distributed between insurgent and state actors during armed conflict. Drawing from examples that include the cooperation between discreet and unitary actors (e.g., Sri Lankan government with "flipped" Tamil insurgent groups) and between parts within the state and insurgents (e.g., Afghan soldiers and police cooperating with the mujahedeen), political scientist Paul Staniland (2012) makes two assertions that will prove relevant to our analysis of clandestine connections between state actors and drug dealers. Collusive relationships, he asserts, are (a) "complex," "fluid," "intricate," and "often-surprising,"[20] and (b) structure the on-the-ground dynamics of violence. We ask readers to keep these two insights in mind as we move into the empirical material in the next chapters.[21]

State-Sponsored Protection Rackets

In countries across Latin America, drug market organizations establish close, almost symbiotic relationships with state authorities. Colombia and Mexico offer two clear examples. In the city of Cali, Colombia, for example, a massive judicial process known as "Proceso 8000" documented the links between drug traffickers and state senators, governors, and mayors.[22] Mexico also has a long history of complicity between criminal organizations and state actors. Luis Astorga (2005), for example, carefully reconstructed the deep intertwining of politics and illicit drug production and trafficking in 20th-century Mexico. Guillermo Valdés Castellanos (2013) also details the many instances of complicity and protection between diverse criminal organizations and Mexican state authorities from local, state, and federal police forces, elected officers, and members of the judiciary.

Although not using the term "intreccio," recent comparative research highlights the existence of the kind of state protection analyzed by the Schneiders in Italy as a key factor in the growth and consolidation of illicit market organizations.[23] The complicity between state officials and illicit actors—such as the drug dealers we will meet in this book—usually takes the form of state-sponsored protection rackets, or "informal institutions through which public officials refrain from enforcing the law or, alternatively, enforce it selectively against the rivals of a criminal organization, in exchange for a share of the profits generated by the organization" (Snyder and Durán-Martínez 2009:254; see also Flom 2018; Dewey 2017b).

Protection rackets are based on a relatively straightforward exchange: Drug market organizations pay state officials to leave them alone. In this arrangement, drug dealers are expected to make regular payments to state agents. They may also be asked for favors as another form of payment, such as information about competing organizations or desistence from using violence when order and peace are in the interest of state officials. State officials, in turn, are expected to provide protection in the form of non-enforcement and information about the operation of other state actors not involved in the racket (Snyder and Durán-Martínez 2009; Dewey 2017b; Flom 2018; Valdés Castellanos 2013). These protection arrangements have two primary dimensions, Snyder and Durán-Martínez assert (p. 255, *italics in original*): "state officials supply selective non-enforcement, that is, *protection from the state itself*. . . . [T]hey also supply selective enforcement against rivals, that is, protection *from competitors*." The dissection of the transactional world of collusion we present below provides fresh empirical evidence on these two dimensions of protection. We also show how protection from the state and from competitors are talked about and negotiated on the ground and demonstrate that collusive relations extend beyond protection.

Our work thus builds on existing research on clandestine state protection by closely examining the dynamics of structured collaboration between police and drug dealers. First, we extend scholarship that has heretofore inspected relationships between state agencies and criminal organizations by examining interactions between individual police officers and drug dealers. Zooming in on interpersonal interactions not only allows us to consider how protection is actually accomplished but also affords a better view of the various kinds of material and informational resources that circulate within collusive relations. Second, we build on research that has considered collusion primarily in terms of payment for an *absence* of enforcement by analyzing the influence of collusion on the dynamics of the drug trade, the policing of that trade, and the interpersonal violence that (oftentimes, but not always) results. While the term "state-sponsored protection racket" may imply a unidirectional protection relationship (i.e., the state protects), criminologist Federico Varese (2011; 2014) finds that political authorities and criminal networks develop strategic and reciprocal interactions that utilize each other's unique access to resources. This insight will prove crucial as we move into our case studies. In his research on Mafia groups in China, Italy, Russia, and the U.S., Varese shows that while police have the ability to enforce (or not) the rule of law, extra-legal actors have greater freedom to act *outside* that framework. Overall, this literature suggests that collusion relationships are contextual, reciprocal, and contingent. Yet there are few studies that unpack how authorities actually tinker with law enforcement in real time and space, what goods and services are exchanged in those relationships, how they start and end, and what purposes (other than protection) they serve.

Systemic Violence

Before the introduction and proliferation of the highly volatile market for crack cocaine, most research attributed the violence triggered by drugs either to "the physical or psychological effects of drug ingestion or to the attempts of drug addicts to acquire economic resources that are needed to support the habit" (Ousey and Lee 2002:74–75). Paul J. Goldstein's (1985) "systemic violence model" shifted the explanation away from the individual and toward the structure of illicit markets. The use of (or dependence on) drugs ceased to be understood as the main cause of violence. Instead, violence was approached as arising "from the exigencies of working or doing business in an illicit market—a context in which the monetary stakes can be enormous but where the economic actors have no recourse to the legal system to resolve disputes" (Goldstein 1985:116). In principle, because participants in the drug trade cannot rely on authorities to manage their grievances or solve their disputes, they engage in informal (and sometimes violent) forms of social control.[24] Violent disputes between rival dealers, retaliation for stealing or failing to pay for drugs, and punishment for selling adulterated products are common in the urban areas we will visit in the forthcoming chapters, as well as in drug markets around the globe.[25]

Yet the operation of the illicit drugs market does not *always* engender violence. Note, for example, the remarkable differences in drug-related violence across countries that are similarly afflicted by trafficking. As Angélica Durán-Martínez (2015:1378) points out: "Mexico experienced an upsurge in violence despite being home to trafficking organizations for over six decades, and in Colombia violence has declined despite persistent trafficking." Moreover, the frequency and visibility of drug violence is also highly variable within countries. Compare, for example, the Mexican city of Ciudad Juarez, which experienced both high drug trafficking and unprecedented violence in the mid-2000s, with the much lower levels of violence in the cities of Culiacán and Tijuana that were drug-trafficking hubs during the same time frame.[26] These case studies attest that drug violence is neither a straightforward outcome of illegality nor a direct result of the size or profitability of the drug market. Rather, as Durán-Martínez (2017:238) masterfully shows, drug violence is a phenomenon "shaped through interactions between the state and criminal actors." Her work clearly demonstrates that the incidence and visibility of drug-related violence are dictated by the cohesion of the state security apparatus and the amount of competition in illegal drug markets.[27]

Studies of a cocaine enclave in Peru and methamphetamine markets in the U.S. and Japan further demonstrate that "the mere presence of an illicit economy, in itself, does not automatically cause violence" (van Dun 2014b:181).[28] Research overwhelmingly confirms that drug market violence is *triggered or exacerbated by what the state does or does not do*. Rather than being intrinsic to illicit actions, commodities, or markets, the relationship between violence and the illegal drug trade is highly contextual and dependent on varying social and political conditions.[29] The link between narcotrafficking and violence is mediated by, on the one hand, the competitiveness of the illegal market, and on the other, by if, when, and how the state intercedes.[30]

Police Illegal Behavior

In the introduction, we stated that our analytic interest lies in the relationships between actors (police officers and drug dealers) rather than discreet groups or organizations. The image of clapping helps to illustrate our focus: We are concerned with the sound produced from the colliding hands, not with the hands per se. Yet some basic knowledge of the configuration of police forces and drug market organizations is needed to understand the sociopolitical context of these relational dynamics.[31] As anthropologist Ben Penglase (2014:105) reminds us in his analysis of insecurity in a Brazilian favela, the micro-realities we will describe are both "deeply local and yet the product(s) of large-scale forces." To provide a basic outline of these larger forces, this section offers a brief overview of recent work on police forces and drug trafficking in Latin America in general and in Argentina in particular.

Over the past two decades, scholarship on policing in Latin America has blossomed. In general agreement with the court cases we will present in this book, scholars have repeatedly found that illegal behavior is widespread among the region's police forces.[32] Political scientist Markus-Michael Müller (2012a:320) puts it well when stating that in most major cities of the region,

the police are considered to be part of the problem [of urban insecurity] and not the solution: basic rights and individual security are inadequately protected; the police are subject to ineffective controls; they are engaged in corruption and criminal activities; and their everyday practices are marked by arbitrary detentions, and abuses including torture and extralegal killings. The principal victims of these practices, it is widely acknowledged, are the marginalised and socially excluded segments of the population.

Diane Davis (2006), to cite one example, dissected police corruption and (the mostly unsuccessful) police reform in Mexico.

Despite such reform efforts, she finds that criminality "flourished, even among the police themselves" (p. 56). Müller's (2012a:332) study of police-citizen interactions in the district of Iztapalapa in Mexico City documents a situation that parallels our empirical material: "Local residents describe many cases where, in return from monetary rewards, officers pass on confidential information about future police raids, turn a blind eye to criminal activities and guarantee the safety of criminals and their customers." And to cite one more example: Penglase (2014:156) makes a similar point in his ethnographic analysis of violence in a Rio de Janeiro favela:

> [P]olice disorder goes hand in hand with drug-trafficker order. . . . [R]ather than seeing the police and drug traffickers as opposite, one group acting arbitrarily while the other functions according to clear rules, it is more accurate to see the two as symbiotically related, acting together to produce (in)security, which they can attempt to manipulate for their own interests. *Rampant corruption among sectors of the police ensures that at times the lines between organized crime and some sectors of the police hardly exists at all.*[33] (*our emphasis*)

Although the actual content of the clandestine relationships between police forces and criminal organizations has not received much detailed scholarly attention, existing scholarship tends to agree that illicit actors—such as the dealers we meet in this book— not only operate against the state but, oftentimes, are complicit with it.[34]

Security Forces in Argentina

Let us now look more closely at the case of Argentina. Since the end of military rule and the return of democracy in 1983, federal and state administrations have tended to disregard issues of public security. According to Marcelo Saín (2015:10), as a result of this neglect, "a particular form of governance of public security took root based on, on the one hand, political misrule, and on the other hand, on police self-governance." Top political authorities delegated the management of public safety to police institutions, which has given rise to largely autonomous police forces and widespread illegal behavior among police officers.[35]

Mark Ungar (2011:258), for example, notes that officers of the Buenos Aires State Police, which operates throughout the country's most populous province, "have been implicated in drug trafficking, torture, bribery, extrajudicial killings, extortion, trigger-happy shootings, and the 1994 bombings of the Argentine Israeli Mutual Association (AMIA)." Involvement of members of the police force in the business of illicit drugs is hardly a recent phenomenon in Argentina. In their book, suggestively subtitled *The Criminal History of the Police of the Province of Buenos Aires*, journalists Carlos Dutil and Ricardo Ragendorfer (1997) include an entire chapter on *narcopolicías* of la Bonaerense, as the Buenos Aires State Police is infamously known. That same year, human rights activists Alicia Oliveira and Sofia Tiscornia (1997:23) also sounded the alarm about what was then perceived as an emergent development within police forces:

It is public knowledge that the control of clandestine gambling and prostitution has been and continues to be important sources of resources for the [Buenos Aires] State Police and the federal police. . . . However, the presence of a new actor in recent years is transforming the ways in which illegal activity is structured within the police. We refer to the drug trafficking and to the role that the specialized bodies of the security forces have in this respect.

A decade later, Marcelo Saín (2008), one of the foremost experts on police (mis)behavior in Argentina, described two co-existing sources of illegal funding in the police force along similar lines.[36] The first is the "traditional fund" (*caja tradicional*), which includes bribes or fees received from illegal gambling, prostitution, street vendors, and unauthorized brothels or night clubs. The second and more recent is the "dirty fund" (*caja sucia*), made up of funds collected from police agents' participation in drug trafficking, car theft, kidnapping, and human smuggling.

In his most recent work, Saín (2017:165) candidly asserts that in Argentina, "there is no criminal undertaking devoted to drug trafficking that does not have at least some degree of protection or police coverage, or in which the police do not participate as a central actor."[37] He describes this as a "dual pact" that, since the late 1980s, has served to support the clandestine relations that are the focus of our investigation. This "dual pact" involves not only licit arrangements between politicians and state authorities who delegate public security to police chiefs (a "political-police" pact) but also clandestine arrangements between police and criminals that regulate and facilitate illicit acts (a "police-criminal" pact).

Four qualifications to this general argument are in order. First, police self-government and the general involvement of its officers in criminal activities do not take place without complications. For example, conflicts can be triggered by the steady growth of criminal enterprises and their increasing autonomy from police control. Central to the main theme of our book, tensions also emerge out of the "interferences and the investigative actions of some other police force that has no connivance with the drug trafficking business and is willing to dismantle the 'police-criminal pact'" (Saín 2015:13). The court documents we draw upon in the next chapters emerge precisely from such "interferences and investigative actions."

Second, it is important to note that police action should not be reduced to the collusion with drug traffickers or other criminal groups. A body of ethnographic work has documented the many aspects and meanings of police work in Argentina—illegal behavior being just one of them.[38] Yet the dynamics and outcomes of the clandestine relationships between police officers and dealers have not been the subject of much empirical scrutiny. Agustina Ugolini's (2010; 2013; 2016) insightful ethnographic work in a Buenos Aires police precinct is an exception to this lack of firsthand knowledge. She vividly describes the on-the-ground formal and informal relationships of conflict and cooperation between police officers, and the way in which they talk about (and justify) funds obtained from illegal activities. Her work shows that engaging in illegal actions of the kind we will be dissecting in the next chapters is somewhat normalized among police officers, understood as part of a "field of possibilities within the regular course of their functions as police officers" (Ugolini 2013:393).[39]

Third, alongside the clandestine participation of members of the police force in illicit activities, there is another trend that matters for understanding the dynamics of collusion we address in the next chapters. In Argentina, there are four national security forces: the Federal Police, whose purpose is the prevention and repression of crimes considered federal in accordance with the penal code (it is also an auxiliary to the federal justice system); the National Guard, with police functions at national borders and federal routes; the Argentine Naval Prefecture, charged with securing rivers and borders; and the Airport Security Police, with control over aircraft and airports. Each state also has the power to organize its own security force to police crimes not defined as "federal" by the penal code.[40] Over the past two decades, these various security forces have experienced important changes. Prominent among them is the growth and militarization of the National Guard at the expense of both the Federal Police ("la Federal") and the Buenos Aires State Police ("la Bonaerense"). The National Guard plays the key role in the cases we analyze in this book. This is largely due to the fact that internal struggles and a series of political decisions taken by various federal administrations "have mutated [the National Guard] from being a border-patrol force and a force in charge of riot control to one partially devoted to urban policing" at the expense of the state and federal police forces (Hathazy 2016:182).

Fourth and finally, there is significant variation in the ways that each state in Argentina governs its police force and in the ways that those forces regulate the markets for illicit drugs. Political scientist Hernán Flom (2018) provides an interesting comparison between two of the states that will occupy our attention in the chapters that follow (Buenos Aires and Santa Fe). He argues that during the 2000s in the state of Buenos Aires, "the government politicized the police, which then regulated drug trafficking through protection rackets," while in the state of Santa Fe, "the government could not control the police force—either to reform it or to capture its rents from crime," and "as a result, the police regulated drug markets through particularistic negotiations" (p. 2). In Flom's view, this variation explains different levels of criminal violence in the two states:

> In Buenos Aires, the government's capture of police rents from crime enabled the implementation of protection rackets with relatively low violence. In contrast, in Santa Fe, the government's inability to control police corruption—even by appropriating it—destabilized the drug market, with the police engaging in particularistic negotiations with criminal actors and extracting rents for themselves while criminal violence soared. (p. 1)

Our analysis does not focus on the causal relationship between degrees of police-criminal collusion and frequency of violence. Rather, we seek to uncover the direct and indirect links between the clandestine connections between drug dealers and agents of the state security forces and the occurrence of interpersonal violence. How and why are collusive relationships producing interpersonal violence in the areas we examine? In the following chapters, we analyze cases across three different states not to compare regulatory regimes of illicit markets or levels of violence but to find commonalities (and some important differences) in the resources, practices, and processes that constitute collusion.

Drug Trafficking and the Police

Social scientific research has documented a variety of ways that police engagement with illegal activities impacts residents at the urban margins. Based on firsthand observations in the favelas of Rio de Janeiro in the late 1990s, Enrique Desmond Arias (2006a:75) explains:

> [L]aw enforcement officers in Tubarao [a favela] were extremely corrupt and violent. Police, maintaining posts within one hundred meter of a *boca de fumo* (drug selling point), rarely bothered traffickers. Groups of armed adolescents, some of whom appeared as young as twelve, openly dealt drugs at the entrance of the favela and in the street below. The occasional violence the police directed against dealers had little effect on trafficking because they used that violence haphazardly to extort money from traffickers.

Almost a decade later, in her ethnography of violence in Rocinha, another favela in Rio, sociologist Erika Larkins (2015:64–65) offers a similar report: "Police corruption in the favela comes in numerous forms. Many officers participate in extralegal markets through enmeshment with traffickers—trading information about police movements and intelligence for cash, selling arms, or agreeing to look the other way during investigations in exchange for a payout." Similar to the case of Brazil, in contemporary Argentina the involvement of members of state security forces in the drug business is no secret. Referred to as *narcopolicía* or narcopolice, major daily newspapers regularly report on the arrest and indictment of members of federal or state police forces for their participation in

illicit drug distribution.[41] After noticing a spike in the number of
state and federal police who had been arrested for drug-related
crimes (111 arrests between January 2013 and July 2015), *La Nación*
journalist Gustavo Carbajal (2015) observed:

> Until two and a half years ago, it was not common for a
> *narcopolicía* to appear in the news. These were isolated cases that
> occurred in the provinces, especially on the border of the prov-
> inces of Salta and Jujuy with Bolivia—as when four Federal Police
> officers were arrested when their truck carrying 120 kilos of co-
> caine was overturned on a road in Jujuy.[42] However, in the last
> 30 months, the appearance of *narcopolicías* has become frequent.
> Especially among members of the Buenos Aires security force,
> which from 2013 to the present has had 25 agents accused of al-
> leged ties to drug trafficking.[43]

Tracking the changes in la Bonaerense, journalist Cecilia Di
Lodovico (2016b) also noted that between December 2016 and
March 2017, 730 police agents were removed from the force and
1,690 internal investigations were opened. These cases involved not
only police officers who are part of drug trafficking networks but
also those active in extortion, car thefts, and kidnappings.

In a detailed review of the many cases of police involvement
in drug trafficking in Argentina, a 2016 report from Center of
Socio-Legal Studies (CELS 2016:114) concluded, "[T]he sheer
number of police agents involved in these networks of narco-
criminality . . . and the high degree of institutional responsibility
of many of them confirm that this is a serious structural issue."
This same report warned against a common misconception about
the dynamics of the drug trade that is often fueled by mainstream
media and politicians, particularly during electoral campaigns
when punitive populism runs rampant. Drug trafficking organizations that operate in Argentina are not akin to large "drug gangs" (or
international cartels) but constitute "predatory micro-networks."

In fact, most are relatively small groups, in many cases composed of extended families that are based in specific and limited urban areas. Journalist Ricardo Ragendorfer summarizes this point well while also describing recent transformations in these clandestine relationships:

> In Argentina, we talk about drug trafficking as if [it was dominated by] organizations such as the Cartel de Cali or Medellín that flood the North American and European markets with their products. Here it is not like that; this is not a producing country. At an international level, this is a country of transit.[44] Here we have small but growing retail organizations. . . . These organizations have some territorial control. . . . In recent years, these organizations are no longer subordinated to the police. They are now on an equal footing to them. Before they had to pay to exist. The police used to manage those organizations. Now sometimes the police officers end up being the employees of these organizations as happens in the states of Santa Fe or Córdoba.[45]

Agreeing that there are key differences between Argentina, Mexico, and Colombia, María de los Ángeles Lasa (2015) offers a slightly different perspective on the trafficking organizations. She describes two main drug-trafficking routes into Argentina, both of which are linked to different groups and violent episodes. The first is what she calls a large-scale trafficking route ("ruta de macro-tráfico") managed by logistically sophisticated criminal organizations. In operation since 1985, this large-scale trafficking route is primarily used to bring cocaine hydrochloride into the country that is destined for European markets. This is similar to Ragendorfer's characterization of Argentina as a "transit" country. As Lasa notes, "The murder of two Colombian nationals in La Tablada (in 2008), the shooting at the Unicenter shopping mall (in 2008), and the murder of Galvis Ramírez in San Fernando (in 2009) . . . are all related to this large-scale trafficking route" (p. 1). Second, she highlights the existence of a small-scale trafficking route ("ruta de micro-tráfico") that emerged after the country's 2001 economic crisis to smuggle in drugs for domestic consumption:

> Between 2001 and 2010, this route has fostered the emergence of a type of actor that was uncommon to Argentina: criminal organizations that are kinship-based, entire families devoted to the production and trade (of cocaine hydrochloride but mostly of cocaine base paste [paco]) for local consumption). Violent episodes and territorial disputes in metropolitan Buenos Aires, Rosario, Córdoba and Tucumán are linked with this small-scale trafficking route. (p. 1)

Although one of the organizations that we will later examine (Los Pescadores, Chapter 6) operates a route that is absent from this account, the emergence of this small-scale trafficking route has been central to the development of the types of organizations and violence we analyze in this book.

Most local analysts agree that the sustained growth of illegal drug consumption in large Argentine cities favored the gradual formation of a highly profitable retail market. While the production, storage, and distribution of illicit drugs extends throughout the country, emerging networks and criminal groups tend to be located in extremely poor and highly marginalized neighborhoods in and around large cities. The drug market groups we will discuss in the next chapters are different from the armed groups that have been the object of much scholarly and journalistic attention in Latin America. They diverge significantly from groups operating in Brazil, Colombia, Jamaica, and Mexico in terms of their organizational complexity, the extent of their territorial control, and their economic, political, and violent capabilities. We draw on this scholarship not because we think the groups we are studying are drug-trafficking organizations writ small (they are not) or because we believe they are on a path to becoming such. Rather, Argentina provides an opportunity to examine clandestine connections between state agents and illicit organizations that are generally younger, more localized, and less professionalized yet clearly depend on these collusive relations for their survival and expansion.

* * *

This chapter began with a discussion of the forms of state intervention in poor urban areas. Literature on the state's presence in materially and symbolically deprived territories has been dominated by two main images: the state's neglect and the state's harsh and punishing presence. While both images help explain lived experiences at the urban margins, scholars have focused much less attention on the mode of state intervention that *engages* with illegal actors and illicit actions as part of its daily operation. With few exceptions, we know very little about how these clandestine connections form, evolve, break down, and ultimately impact interpersonal violence.

This chapter framed these clandestine relations through a discussion of the *intreccio*—the Italian word that refers to the thick entwining of criminal enterprises and state officials. Within this nexus, the development and negotiation of state-sponsored protection rackets is critical to understanding the relationships between drug trafficking, state actions, and urban violence. Literature on illicit markets has called attention to the systemic violence that results when actors cannot rely on authorities to manage their grievances or solve their disputes. In principle, participants engage in informal (and sometimes violent) forms of social control. The relationship between drugs and systemic violence is well established. Yet it is important to note that rather than being integral to illicit markets, violence is triggered or exacerbated by what the state does or does not do. We concluded this chapter by reviewing literature on police (mis)behavior and trafficking in Argentina to provide the necessary context for the ensuing analysis.

Argentina offers an important case to examine police-criminal collusion. Although the country's democratic institutions have implemented transparency measures and joined regional and international agreements to combat state corruption, Argentina consistently receives poor ratings from international monitors. For example, in 2016 Transparency International gave Argentina a score of 32 (out of 100) for perceptions of corruption, far lower than the regional average of 44.[46] In the specific case of state security forces, widespread police corruption co-exists with constant attempts at police reform.[47] Argentina thus offers a clear case where the state is both engaging in and fighting against police misbehavior and abuse.[48]

Drug market dynamics in Argentina also differ from well-studied cases in Brazil, Colombia, and Mexico, where trafficking groups are older and more sophisticated and have more firing capacity. By looking at a place where levels of violence are comparatively low and drug-trafficking groups are comparatively young, our book provides a window into how drug market organizations operate at a more liminal moment—and in a context in which the multiple layers of power among security agencies seem to make the collusive interactions much more fluid and rapidly changing than in other (more established and structured) contexts.

The next two chapters delve into our ethnographic material. Readers will learn that residents in Arquitecto Tucci repeatedly refer to these clandestine relationships as an *arreglo* (arrangement) or variations thereof—police officers are *arreglados* and dealers *arreglan* with police officers. Suspicions about collusion abound in the neighborhood, but evidence of the actual operation of these arrangements is, for obvious reasons, hard to obtain. After describing the lived experiences of violence at the urban margins, we draw on wiretapped conversations and other material from court cases that largely validate residents' shared understandings of the "wicked deals" made between police officers and drug dealers.

2

Drug Violence in the Streets and at Home

With Mary Ellen Stitt

A few homes, one tree, people walking . . . When asked to depict his neighborhood, this fifth grader who lived in Arquitecto Tucci drew a picture and did not want to leave anything out (Figure 2.1). At the forefront, he depicted what most neighbors defined as their main preoccupation: interpersonal violence. People fight. People shoot at each other ("se tiran tiro"). A police car is parked between the homes and people. It seems to bear witness to the violence but does not intervene. It simply sits there, useless. The drawing captures what we heard dozens of times from neighbors. Most were extremely worried about the widespread and increasing violence—to the point of altering their daily routines. Curfews, strict schedules, walking in groups, and avoiding certain areas had become part of residents' everyday lives.

This chapter describes residents' views of and experiences with daily violence in Arquitecto Tucci by examining how perceptions of their neighborhood have changed over time. We then outline a set of pathways through which drug-related violence travels inside the homes of the neighborhood's poor residents, illustrating the limits of focusing exclusively on the public expression of drug-related violence. The analysis we offer here is important not only on its own merits, but also because it provides crucial contextual information to understand the intricate relationship between

The Ambivalent State: Police-Criminal Collusion at the Urban Margins. Javier Auyero, Oxford University Press (2019). © Oxford University Press.
DOI: 10.1093/oso/9780190915537.001.0001

Figure 2.1 An elementary school student's drawing of his neighborhood, Arquitecto Tucci, 2011.

collusion and violence that will be the subject of scrutiny later in the book.

In this chapter and the next, we will show why residents believed they lived in a "no man's land"—*una tierra de nadie*. This expression has three closely interrelated meanings. "No man's land" refers to a place in which the state does not address locals' pressing needs. It also denotes the place's violent character—an area where "anything goes." Neighbors perceived that illicit drugs were behind much of the violence they suffered—either because addicts committed crimes to finance their habit (what analysts call the "economic compulsive" link between drugs and violence) or because dealers took their market disputes into the streets (what analysts call the "systemic violence" of the drug trade). Lastly, this shared understanding of a "no man's land" points to the core theme of this book: collusion between drug traffickers and law enforcement agents. The "anything" in the "anything goes" points an accusatory finger at that complicity.

Everyday Violence in "No Man's Land"

Arquitecto Tucci sits on the banks of the highly contaminated Riachuelo River[1] and is home to 170,000 people who live and work south of the city of Buenos Aires. During its initial period of growth, Tucci was a working-class area, where rows of brick houses were constructed around a main commercial district. The area has since grown significantly through the expansion of informal settlements.[2] Just blocks from the commercial center, paved streets and sidewalks now transition into muddy dirt roads that weave into squatter settlements and shantytowns. In these areas—many of which are prone to flooding—newer residents have occupied tracts of land and built modest homes that are perpetually under construction (Figure 2.2). Simple concrete houses with corrugated

Figure 2.2 Informal settlements along a waterway near the Riachuelo River, Arquitecto Tucci, 2018. Credit: María Fernanda Berti.

metal roofs are built room by room as residents get access to resources and supplies.

Extreme levels of infrastructural deprivation characterize these settlements. In contrast to the original working-class neighborhood, the majority of the homes in shantytowns and squatter settlements lack access to municipal services like electricity, water, sewers, and garbage pickup (Figures 2.3 and 2.4). In their absence, residents rely on open-air sewers, precariously connected electrical wiring, and imported tanks of water and gas.[3] While residents pay the price for these compounding deprivations, criminals and drug-trafficking organizations take advantage of this relative inaccessibility by locating their bunkers and storage facilities in the area and abandoning stolen cars that have been stripped of their parts and burned to prevent identification.

Figure 2.3 Older homes and paved streets in the working-class neighborhood of Arquitecto Tucci, 2010. Credit: Photography Workshop at local elementary school.

Figure 2.4 Unpaved roads, Arquitecto Tucci, 2010. Credit: Photography Workshop at local elementary school.

From areas that are perpetually flooded, poorly lit, and littered with trash (Figure 2.5), the children of Arquitecto Tucci come together in public schools. But in striking contrast to the clean white smocks that the students wear as uniforms, the local elementary school was in a state of disrepair: the roof had collapsed in areas now off-limits to children, paint peeled off dingy classroom walls, and the school yard (like many of the streets and homes) was often flooded with pungent waters from an adjacent water treatment plant.[4] When asked to depict their neighborhood during a photography workshop organized in 2011, students highlighted not only the lack of basic infrastructure but evidence of drugs, crime, and violence.[5]

A dialogue that took place early on during the fieldwork captures this generalized sense of insecurity, its actual manifestations, and locals' understanding of what lies behind it. In 2010, Agustín, one of our research assistants, talked with Valeria, Mariana, and

Figure 2.5 Street littered with garbage in squatter settlement, Arquitecto Tucci, 2018. Credit: María Fernanda Berti.

Sabrina at a local soup kitchen about his visits to Arquitecto Tucci. Agustín explained, "I tend to be a confident person. Luckily so far nothing has happened here in the neighborhood. But all the same, I come prepared that if they do rob me, they would take a little bit of money and a few things I do not mind losing." He then reminded his interlocutors what they had warned him of before: "You always tell me to 'be careful' because I'm not from here and people do not know me. But, what about when you walk through the neighborhood, are you worried?" Valeria, the coordinator of the soup kitchen, responded, "Yes, you always have to be careful!" Agustín followed up, "But you are from the neighborhood, do you also get mugged?" Mariana, who worked as a cook, chimed in: "My daughter was mugged last week. Tell him about it." Sabrina, her daughter, spoke up, "Yeah, they stole my cell phone." Valeria then provided more details: "The boys get together at the corner, and when they need money for drugs or alcohol, they steal it from you." Agustín asked, "Have you all been robbed?" The women all responded with a vigorous "Yes!" Valeria said, "A kid I know robbed me last week. He took my cell. The next day, his mom gave it back to me."

Fast-forward seven years, from the time of this conversation in 2010 to early in 2017. A former resident, Benito (55), moved out of Tucci a few years earlier when his wife got a job an hour and a half away. Although he no longer lived there, Benito regularly returned to the neighborhood because he was active in politics as a local political broker. As we will see in the next chapter, brokers linked to political parties are important actors in the neighborhood. When we talked about his concerns, he remembered that when he was living in Tucci, thieves robbed his house, taking his TV and other valuables. Reflecting on changing public concerns, Benito observed, "In the 1980s and 1990s, public works was the main issue. Now, it's public safety, *la inseguridad*. . . . Of all my friends from youth, none of them are alive. There's only one who can barely speak. Drugs. Drugs killed them. They were killed while stealing, because the drugs made them steal." The overwhelming majority of the people we spoke with agreed with Benito. They were concerned about the lack of public safety, and many linked the danger experienced in the streets and homes to the presence of drugs. Much like their counterparts in other poor urban areas, residents of Tucci felt they were living in an uncertain, unpredictable, and dangerous state of insecurity.[6]

One of the ways that ordinary people convey their present worries is by contrasting the current state of affairs with a past time—one that may have never existed in quite the form it was remembered.[7] These illustrative comparisons can often indicate the depth of one's present discomfort. When asked about their most pressing problems, residents of Arquitecto Tucci regularly went back to the past, more specifically, a "peaceful" past whose exact location varied according to the age of the person. Twenty, thirty, or forty years ago, Arquitecto Tucci was "very different," we were repeatedly told. Our respondents emphasized similar differences between past and present. Some talked about infrastructure, for example, observing, "[T]he streets were all dirt, muddy, now they are paved," or remembering that "there were little lagoons all around." Others stated that "there were fewer homes," and "there were less people," referencing the changing patterns of housing in the once-rural area. A longtime resident of Arquitecto Tucci, Gabriela (45), remembered her childhood:

> Around thirty years ago, there were few houses and it was all muddy. To walk out of the neighborhood, you had to get dirty with mud. But it was healthier. You were able to walk early in the morning. My parents used to take me to the hospital at dawn, because you had to get a number and wait for quite a long time. You could walk safely here; nobody would do anything to you. I miss that a lot.

Gabriela described a time past when, despite the lack of development (few houses, unpaved roads), Tucci was safe for families.

Around the same time, Fernanda (51) moved to the neighborhood. She described what she thought were the most important changes:

Before, we used to sit down on the sidewalks to drink mate,[8] the kids could play outside. Now, it's dangerous. Now, you cannot sit on the front doorstep, on the sidewalk, because the kids do drugs. People bring the stolen cars here and they burn them.[9] They do that at night. You hear an explosion and you have to get up to fight the fire. The other week, I got all burned, right here on the side of my arm. We had to do something about the burning car because our own car was parked next to it. If the [stolen] car explodes, it will burn ours. *We have nothing and on top of that we would be left with nothing!* [¡*Encima que no tenemos nada, no nos queda nada!*] The first time they brought a stolen car, we called the police and they told us to call the fire department. [While we were waiting] . . . a light pole fell and it hurt a kid. This part of the barrio is a *no man's land.* (*our emphasis*)

Fernanda encapsulated what we heard dozens of times: Residents saw themselves as living in a "no man's land" (*tierra de nadie*). In making this reference, residents were not referring to a space that was vacant or unoccupied but to a violent area in which the state did not respond to the everyday needs of its residents. Note how, in just a few sentences, Fernanda moved from the past to the dangerous present, pointing to what she saw as the two main manifestations of violence (drug-related crime and car theft) and the state's response to them. She also highlighted the effects of one of the least studied but pervasive phenomena among the most deprived: horizontal abuse and lateral animosity, or what we could call poor-on-poor violence.[10] Violence, as we will see, is not confined to drug market participants or the unfortunate bystander, but spills into the neighborhood, affecting many (if not most) of its residents.

Another consistent theme that clearly distinguished the past from the present was the lack of public safety: "Vivimos con miedo" (We live in fear), many expressed. Young and old, male and female, almost every single person we spoke to had direct experience with violence. We met Agustina (18) at a focus group we organized in the local high school. An energetic and chatty teenager, she told us the following:

> Just around the corner [from the local school], they assaulted me. . . . I was walking and I suddenly realized there was a kid with a gun. He stole everything from me. He did it alone but you could see another group of kids that was with him just on the other corner. If you needed to ask for help, forget about it. The police car was not around. Nobody gets involved here, they are super scared.

Nobody in the neighborhood was exempt from actual or potential violence. And we mean "nobody" in a literal sense: None of the three dozen residents and community leaders we got to know well over the years of fieldwork had been spared. For example, the local priest shared one of his recent experiences with drug-related violence in the neighborhood:

> I gave a sermon about drugs in the neighborhood. A few days later I got a phone call. It was someone I had never met. He was asking for advice: "What should I do?" he asked me. "I made a complaint about a drug-selling point and the cops are telling me to withdraw the complaint. What should I do?" I told him that I didn't discuss those issues over the phone, that he should come to the church. He never showed up. Someone was clearly testing me.

The doctors at the local health center also experienced threats and direct violent encounters. As one of them explained:

> These days, safeguarding our physical integrity is part of being a doctor in the emergency room. In the past, nobody would attack us. Now they come armed and demand to be treated. There is now a code [i.e., an implicit pact] between us and those [armed] who come for urgent care. We treat them and once the guy leaves, we call the cops. A few months ago, a patient came in with a gun

injury and a .38 in his belt. I had to report it to the police. The patient told me to wait until he was gone.

As these insights attest, community leaders and local professionals were not immune from threats and attacks.

Our field notes were filled with similar stories of residents' experiences with violence. The following is an excerpt from the field diary of the research assistant who worked at a local school, dated April 2016:

> My student, Daira (10), lives with her mom and three sisters. Her father has been in prison for homicide since 2010. Three weeks ago, Daira, her mother, and two of her siblings were shopping on one of the neighborhood's busiest streets at noon when they heard gunshots. "I grabbed the kids," Daira's mom told me, "and tried to hide somewhere. I then saw that Daira was touching her head, and there was blood on it. . . . I was desperate. . . . [W]e ran to the local hospital with the help of a neighbor." Fortunately, the bullet only grazed Daira's head. At the school, we organized a fundraising to pay for her antibiotics and creams. Her classmates now tease Daira, calling her "leaky head."

Alejandra (35) was not as lucky as Daira. On January 8, 2017, in the adjacent Barrio Obrero (a few blocks beyond of the limits of Arquitecto Tucci), she was killed when a stray bullet hit her in the head while she was walking down the street with her four-year-old son. According to preliminary police investigations, she was caught in the middle of a dispute between two drug-trafficking groups.[11]

Violence in Context

Residents' perception of Arquitecto Tucci as a "no man's land" was a fitting description: The neighborhood was indeed a perilous place to live. In 2013, an overwhelming majority of residents cited crime, safety, theft, and drug dealing as their main preoccupations.[12] In addition to a generalized fear about criminality and victimization among residents, actual experiences with violence abound. In Arquitecto Tucci, murder rates have continued to rise: According to the Municipal Attorney's Office, homicides have quadrupled since 2007. There were 17 recorded murders in 2007, 32 in 2009, 54 in 2011, 59 in 2013, and 65 in 2015 (population growth was roughly 5%). The murder rate (38.6 per 100,000) in the neighborhood is now five times that of the state of Buenos Aires.[13]

Compounding deprivations—including chronic poverty, the lack of well-paying jobs, poor schools, environmental degradation that seriously affects residents' overall health, the absence of efficient social services, infrastructural deficiencies in the form of broken sidewalks, intermittent garbage collection, contaminated water, and lack of adequate street lighting—all help to explain why Arquitecto Tucci is such a violent place. As elsewhere, violence thrives in places where these "structural disadvantages" accumulate and mutually reinforce one another.[14]

Alongside this structural dimension, the presence of La Salada, the largest street market in the country, is another key factor at the root of the de-pacification of Arquitecto Tucci. The area adjacent to the market, which is traversed twice a week by thousands of consumers and traders carrying cash and merchandise, presents poor and unemployed youth various opportunities for what we could call, borrowing from and specifying Max Weber (1946), a *highly clustered form of adventure capitalism*. Instead of raiding foreign countries, unemployed youth assault traders and customers who are likely to have valuables on hand (i.e., cash, merchandise, etc.). Since opening in the early 1990s, the market has provided increasing

opportunities for predatory crime, becoming what environmental criminologists call a "high activity node" (Brantingham
and Brantingham 1993:11).

The growth of the drug trade in and around Arquitecto Tucci
is another key factor in the increasing levels of violence. There is
little doubt that drug trafficking has been expanding in Argentina.
Cocaine seizures (including seizures of paco), for example, have
grown exponentially since 2000.[15] As in the rest of country, "drug
trafficking flourished in Buenos Aires in the mid-2000s. Between
2006 and 2013, the volume of cocaine seized grew by 200%, according to the state Attorney General's Report" (Flom 2018:11;
see also Bergman 2018). Although no official figures exist, anec-
dotal evidence published in newspaper accounts and relayed by
our informants support the claim that the preparation, storage,
and distribution of drugs has also expanded in Arquitecto Tucci
and is now organized by small, competing trafficking groups that
oftentimes solve their disputes in public and quite violent ways.

When they described being mugged or assaulted in the streets or
being robbed of their scarce belongings in their homes, residents
mentioned that the perpetrators were not violent outsiders who had
infiltrated a once-peaceful place, but rather people from the neighborhood. These anecdotes buttress Fernanda's plight described
above: Those dwelling in the same deprived areas are victimizing
their neighbors and divesting them of the few belongings they have.
In most residents' accounts, perpetrators are locals who are compelled into (delinquent) actions by drugs. Many of the violent attacks
were either understood as addicts' attempts to acquire the economic
resources needed to support their habit or believed to be the by-
product of disputes between drug dealers. The testimonies of Valeria,
Sabrina, Mariana, and Benito point to the first ("economic compulsive violence"). Daira's and Alejandra's stories are examples of the
second ("systemic violence"). Yet violence is not isolated to the streets
but also, as we will show, enters the homes of Tucci residents.

Drug Violence Comes Home

The child's drawing presented at the beginning of this chapter does not capture one key aspect of the interpersonal violence in Arquitecto Tucci. Violence not only unfolds in the streets and other public spaces of the neighborhood. It is also present inside homes. Although at first obscure to us, instances of domestic violence are related to and exacerbated by the violence produced by drug use and the drug trade.[16]

Up to this point, we have primarily discussed drug violence in the streets—the kind that put Daira in harm's way, that killed Alejandra, and that neighbors refer to when they report "[T]here are shootouts every single night." Yet we found that this violence also spilled into homes, manifesting in physical fights between families, romantic partners, and neighbors. Researched during the height of the crack epidemic in New York City, Philippe Bourgois's (1995) now classic ethnography, *In Search of Respect*, highlights the fact that, much like in Arquitecto Tucci these days, violence related to the drug trade spread from the streets into East Harlem homes. A range of other ethnographic work[17] and community studies[18] also points to an association between violence related to the drug trade and that which takes place in the domestic sphere.[19] The pathways by which drug market violence travels home, however, are still not well understood. How are these two types of violence, normally labeled "drug violence" and "domestic violence," related to one another in real time and space?

In Arquitecto Tucci, we identified three pathways through which drug market activity triggers violence inside homes. In the first of these pathways, which we call *invasion*, the locus of claims made by drug market participants shifts from public to private spaces, as armed dealers enter homes to demand payments or missing drugs. In the second, *protection*, drug dealers do not physically enter other participants' homes, but their demands do. This begins when individuals take scarce resources from relatives to pay for drugs or to pay back drug-related debts. In the third pathway, *preemption*, parents and relatives resort to violence in an attempt to prevent their children from falling victim to graver forms of violence. Fearing the well-known lethal consequences of participating in the drug market (as street-level dealers, consumers, or, as oftentimes happens in the neighborhood, as both), parents physically punish their children to preempt a trajectory that all too often ends in death. These three pathways, which often co-exist in practice, point to the artificial distinction between "public" and "private" spheres of life, an argument that feminist scholars have long made when theorizing family, work, and the economy.[20]

Invasion

The first way that violence enters the home is by *invading* it as dealers seek payments or track down missing drugs. Often armed and ready to use violence if necessary, they enter private spaces in search of debtors and accused thieves. On occasion, family members become caught in the crossfire.

Mariela has lived in Arquitecto Tucci for many years and raised her children in the neighborhood. Now a grandmother, she had recently decided to take in her daughter's children. Mariela recounted the incident that prompted this decision: Her daughter's home had recently been targeted by a group of dealers. They entered the house when her daughter was away and shot at her partner, apparently in retaliation for missing a payment. Mariela explained, "Four gunshots, and the baby was there. Can you imagine what would happen if they shot baby Briana?" Reflecting on the alternatives, she concluded: "It's better if Briana stays with me."

Over the course of fieldwork, many residents recounted such experiences: The regulatory operations of the illicit drug market can easily injure or kill those in proximity. In those cases, sharing a home with a participant in the drug market poses very real risks.

As we saw in the case of Mariela, these risks can profoundly disrupt and rearrange family members' lives.[21]

In other cases, individuals employed in the drug market stay away from home to avoid being found by perpetrators of violence. Many residents told of encounters with dealers in the absence of their family members who were directly involved. In such situations, relatives become not bystanders caught in the crosshairs but the target of debt collection efforts.

The story of Antonio and his mother, Angélica, captures this form of invasion. When we met Angélica, Antonio had recently begun purchasing paco for other young people in the neighborhood, acting as a courier of sorts. One night, a group of armed youth broke into Angélica's house, where Antonio lived along with his two younger brothers. The intruders explained to Angélica that they had given Antonio money earlier in the day, but by late afternoon, he had not returned with the drugs or the money.

"They looked for him everywhere and they had weapons," Angélica said. "They threatened me and told me that they would kill him because he had kept their money. I told them that I'd pay them. I told them that he didn't know what he was doing. I asked them to please not hurt him."

As the experiences of these two mothers illustrate, individuals' involvement in the illicit drug economy can unleash a sequence of events that results in the invasion of the home, often endangering parents, siblings, and children.

Protection

Family members also use violence as a means to defend themselves, their dependents, and their belongings from loved ones involved in drugs. This second pathway that we call *protection* can be prompted by attempts to acquire resources needed to pay for drugs or to repay the dealers for whom they work. To generate these resources, desperate consumers and petty dealers steal household items such as clothing, appliances, or even parts of the home that they can sell for cash. In the context of extreme deprivation that exists in Arquitecto Tucci, such valuable items can be very difficult to replace. Families save for months and sometimes years to purchase building materials, appliances, and other household items, or they buy them on high–interest, long-term credit. Losing them usually means either going without for an extended period of time or, if an item is indispensable, sacrificing other necessities to replace it. When theft becomes recurrent, family members may respond with violence to protect themselves—a form of "self-help."[22]

Antonio (26) had repeatedly stolen the belongings of others in his extremely poor household, from small but crucial supplies such as pots, pans, and plates to more expensive items like the washing machine and his brother Carlos's name-brand sneakers. His mother had stopped leaving the house, even to take her two youngest children to the hospital for mandatory vaccinations, because she was afraid Antonio would sell the few items that remained. One day, Antonio removed the toilet from the only bathroom in the house and tried to sell it for a few pesos at a local store that catered to similarly desperate vendors. As he haggled for money, his brother Carlos caught him in the act and beat him up. When the police got involved, they took the toilet from the store, but the family could not afford the cab fare to get it back to their house from the precinct.

As this incident suggests, when participants in the drug trade begin selling off household items required for basic survival, there is often no clear recourse for those impacted. Families in Arquitecto Tucci nearly always lack the resources to pay off their family members' debts themselves or to address their addiction by committing them to (the scarce and expensive) inpatient rehabilitation centers. Many thus resort to violence as a final means of shielding themselves against the destructive actions of their loved ones.

After a particularly difficult week with her son, Leandro (16), Ana (32) told us, "I hit him with the broom. I hit him everywhere, arms, legs," her voice shaking and eyes full of tears. "He has stolen everything from me," she told us later, again weeping. She went on:

> The first time I beat him was when he sold a cell phone he stole from us. . . . I beat him really badly; I grabbed his fingers, and told him that if he did that again, I was going to break his fingers one by one so that he couldn't steal again. He never took a cell phone again, but he stole sneakers, T-shirts, socks. . . . He steals stuff from me and resells it for 20 pesos so that he can pay for drugs. . . . And I don't want to hit him anymore, for him, for me, for my daughters who see everything.

Ana, like many others, explained being driven out of desperation to use violence against her son.

Susana shared a similar experience when describing how she confronted her son who was addicted to drugs: "I can't, I can't do anything else other than beat him." She explained her reasoning: "He steals from us, he comes home [high on drugs] all dirty and aggressive, and he steals from us. . . . I really don't know what else to do." Over and over, residents told similar stories about the loss of crucial household items and of the eventual and painful decision, in the absence of other recourse, to turn to physical violence to defend themselves, their belongings, and other family members from further victimization.

Preemption

The artificial distinctions that define forms of violence in the scholarly literature are troubled by the pathways of invasion and protection described above. The third pathway we identified refers to the ways that the drug trade can de-pacify homes by triggering violent forms of discipline as parents attempt to *preempt* their children from experiencing the often deadly consequences of involvement in the illicit drug trade. Recall Carolina's story with which we opened the introduction of this book, in which she said that her "biggest fear was to find [her son, Damián] stabbed or shot because of the drugs."

Rather than engaging in the tortured search for her child that Carolina and many others described, Mónica (38) chose to keep her daughter inside by force. "I chained her to the bed so that she doesn't go out," she told us. "I'm scared. What if she gets killed?"

A few months before we interviewed Ana about her troubles with her son Leandro, her eldest son, Matías, was killed in an attempted robbery. Dying, he had been abandoned in front of the local hospital, presumably by his partners in crime. Surrounded by many other examples of early death, Ana now feared that Leandro would meet a similar fate unless she intervened. He had, in fact, already been shot in the leg several weeks before we met her. "What if [Leandro] is the next one to die?" She asked. "I'm really anguished. . . . I can't do anything else other than beat him, because he doesn't understand me, because I've spoken to him and he never listens."

Over and over, distressed parents—mostly mothers—told us about their reliance on fists, kicks, sticks, brooms, and chains to keep their children away from "malas compañías" (friends thought to be bad influences) or, if they had "already fallen" into bad company, to try to control their involvement in the drug economy.[23] Although we cannot evaluate whether these disciplinary tactics contributed to or detracted from their children's well-being, many hours of listening to residents describe these acts repeatedly affirmed their shared belief that violence was their only recourse, the only means left to them to protect their children. Violent physical discipline was, in this sense, perceived as a last-resort tool of care. Under certain circumstances, parents justified it as the only perceived means available to them to keep their children safe and end the cycle of young death in their community. Parents often arrived at this belief not only by observing sequences of events in their neighborhood but also through personal experiences with their children's risk-taking and, in some cases, other deaths in their families.

"There are drugs everywhere here," Valeria (31) said. "Right around the corner, there's someone selling. And there's another one on the other corner, and another one two blocks from here. Everybody knows where they are. The cops go by and don't do anything. They know where each *transa* [dealer] is more than we do." She then told us about how she reacted when she learned that her sixteen-year-old son was smoking marijuana: "When I found out Pablo was smoking, I began to follow him. I took him to school. I told him not to hang out with this or that friend. One night, I saw him smoking right across from our house. I was sewing shoes at the time, and I began to throw shoes at him." She followed with a description of how she disciplined her son after she caught him using drugs: "When I saw him [smoking weed], I hit him really hard and I talked to him. I threatened him. I told him I was going to lock him up, I was going to send him to rehab. . . . He goes to school, he gets good grades, but he smokes. 'Don't do this to me,' I told him." In addition to her threats, Valeria reminded her son about the fatal consequences of getting involved in the drug trade: "I told him about my brother, who also used to do drugs and he died because of them. He used to steal, and one day, drugged, he shot himself. I use him as an example." Valeria made the stakes clear to her son: "Your uncle died because of drugs."

* * *

Drawing on long-term ethnographic fieldwork in the neighborhood of Arquitecto Tucci, this chapter began by describing residents' everyday experiences with violence and examining the structural factors that have increased the presence of drugs and violence in the neighborhood. We detailed how drug dealing has shaped interpersonal violence in Tucci, as consumers commit crimes to finance their addiction and dealers use violence to resolve market disputes. We then analyzed three pathways through which drug-related violence enters the home and impacts social relationships among poor families. We moved beyond a compartmentalized view of violence that isolates different types of interpersonal physical aggression to certain (gendered) spheres of life. In contrast, we presented a more complex picture of drug-related violence, showing how violence invades homes, how family members resort to violence to protect their scarce material possessions, and how parents use violence to preempt what they perceive as more dangerous forms of violence that their children may confront on the street.[24] As we move to our up-close examination of illicit relations between state agents and drug dealers, we ask readers to keep these pathways in mind as they will help to better understand how collusion shapes not only the interpersonal violence in the streets but also inside homes.

The decision to take matters into their own hands is supported by the shared understanding of the area as a "no man's land," where residents report that "people shoot at each other," and they "can't find help." As we explained, a "no man's land" where "anything goes" also refers to the perception that drug dealers who are seen as responsible for most of the violence are in cahoots with police agents: the "anything" insinuates this complicity.

"[A]nyone who has experienced on an embodied level the mystery of 'addiction,'" writes anthropologist Philippe Bourgois (2018:387),

whether personally through uncontrollable emotional cravings or manic ecstatic/soothing epiphanies followed by torturous withdrawals, or through the loss of a family member or a loved one, knows how seriously one has to take the pharmacological power of drug effects. Socio-cultural and political-economic "determinants" of drug effects are much harder to see. When one does ethnographic work in settings dominated by drug trafficking and drug use, the everyday emergency and high stakes of money, violence and damaged health can overwhelm one's capacity for [a] larger, longer term perspective.

Ours is neither a study of addiction nor based on the kind of long-term, deeply embedded ethnographic work for which Bourgois is well-known. But we encountered a similar epistemological obstacle. Constructing a scientific object[25] out of stories of death, injury, and domestic violence required us to build a different perspective—not only one that moves beyond previous analytic distinctions between "public" and "private" forms of violence, but also one that emphasizes the (clandestine) political underpinnings of the maelstrom of suffering witnessed on the ground. In the next chapter, we continue this task by detailing the widespread suspicion that drug dealers are either protected by law enforcement agents or are one and the same ("[L]a policía es toda transa," in Carolina's words). As we will see, concerns about living in a "no man's land" where "anything goes" acquires a more sinister meaning, one that shapes residents' suspicions of law enforcement in the area.

3

Collusion and Legal Cynicism

Let us now focus our attention on the actions of the lonely police car sitting in the middle of the fifth grader's drawing with which we opened the previous chapter (see Figure 2.1). Its presence raises a question central for any political sociology of urban marginality: How does the state respond to the increasing interpersonal violence, expansion of crime, and growth and consolidation of drug trafficking in the neighborhood? The state's repressive forces intervene in the neighborhood in highly intermittent and contradictory ways—one day with massive police presence on the streets, the next with none; one day going after some drug dealers, the next protecting others; one day raiding a drug kitchen, the next distributing drugs from the precinct. Two examples illustrate the state's visible use of force against traffickers—or, paraphrasing Foucault's (1977:9) description of Damien's 1757 public execution—what we could call the "public spectacle" of policing.

In March 2013, the Buenos Aires state police seized almost four tons of marijuana from a warehouse close to a local elementary school where our research assistant, María Fernanda Berti, worked as a teacher. The marijuana had been transported to Arquitecto Tucci from the north, arriving from the province of Misiones in a truck camouflaged by wooden planks. Police sources noted that the cargo was also covered in sawdust to block the pungent odor of the drugs. Authorities estimated that the confiscated drugs had a commercial value of about ARS$30 million (US$6 million). The discovery was largely due to luck: Police found the shipment while investigating the murder of a 22-year-old woman (and the daughter

The Ambivalent State: Police-Criminal Collusion at the Urban Margins. Javier Auyero, Oxford University Press (2019). © Oxford University Press.
DOI: 10.1093/oso/9780190915537.001.0001

Figure 3.1 A police truck parked near a squatter settlement in Arquitecto Tucci, 2018. Credit: María Fernanda Berti.

of a member of the National Guard) during an attempted robbery of the high-value truck. Four people were arrested.

Soon after, the governor of Buenos Aires, the minister of justice and security, and the chief of the Buenos Aires Police spoke at a press conference organized at the site of the raid. "We do not want trafficking organizations to take root in this area of the province," the governor asserted. "One by one, we are putting all [members of] these organizations in prison. . . . This confiscation is one of the most important that we have executed during my administration." He continued, explaining that "we must recognize the work of our police" and that "today more than ever we must commit to our society to continue fighting these groups."

Four years later in June 2017, more than 500 police agents publicly seized an impressive quantity of drugs from another bunker in Arquitecto Tucci. In a single day, officers discovered over 20,000 doses of paco, 220 bushels of marijuana, 70 packets of cocaine, a 12/70 caliber shotgun, and a .9 mm caliber FMK3 machine gun presumed to belong to the leader of a drug-trafficking group. As the drugs were removed from the premises, the Buenos Aires state minister of security addressed a crowd of journalists and photographers: "This fight against drug trafficking and organized crime must be permanent and ongoing. We are going door to door informing neighbors so that they can call a safe line to continue denouncing the drug trafficking events that take place here." Referring to police corruption, he added: "We are going to tear down the drug trafficking wall; the complicity network has just stopped working. . . . We have detained 360 police officers, every complaint is followed in Internal Affairs." As he concluded his statement, the cameras turned from the state official to the bunker itself as a bulldozer demolished the site where the drugs and weapons had been found.

Such theatrical demonstrations of state power—or "festivals of punishment," in the words of Foucault—co-exist with a less visible reality alluded to by the minister. Clandestine state action is not "a more subtle, more subdued" form of penalty (Foucault 1977:8) but one that collaborates with those deemed criminal. Beyond its authoritative statements and visible demonstrations of power, the state's quotidian practices reveal a much more ambivalent stance.

How do these contradictory behaviors impact residents at the urban margins? In this chapter, we draw on a combination of archival records and ethnographic evidence to examine residents' perceptions of police practices in Arquitecto Tucci. We begin by presenting evidence of police misconduct culled from a court case that resulted in the indictment of the local police chief and four other police agents on counts of corruption. This case shows that while residents may be objectively constrained and continually victimized, there are also real efforts to expose and identify individual acts of police wrongdoing. Despite such efforts, residents continue to confront what we call, in a twist on Charles Tilly's (1985) famous formulation, "disorganized organized crime": *disorganized* because residents do not see any predictable pattern in the deployment of police action in the area, and *organized* because they suspect that illegal activity is coordinated from within a highly hierarchical and well-defined institution.

In navigating this social world, residents report widespread cynicism toward law enforcement, sharing a belief that its agents are "illegitimate, unresponsive, and ill equipped to ensure public safety" (Kirk and Papachristos 2011:1191). Different from the extensive research on legal cynicism,[1] we find that mistrust of police emerges not simply out of the perceived unavailability or bias of law enforcement agents but also out of the felt *complicity* between police officers and criminals. This is made clear when residents refer to their neighborhood as a "no man's land" where "anything goes."[2] Officers are perceived as either traffickers themselves (called *transas* or *polinarcos*) or in "arrangements" with them (*arreglados*), and these common beliefs inform the ways that residents respond to their circumstances. As we will see, people concerned with or directly affected by violence often do not contact the local police but turn to alternative outlets and sometimes even take matters into their own hands.

Extortion and Protection

Paola and her husband, Yaolín, moved to Argentina from Peru in 2008.[3] They settled in a small house in Arquitecto Tucci, setting up a textile shop in their home where they manufactured T-shirts to sell in La Salada. Since money was tight, they also operated an informal kiosk out of their house, selling soft drinks and beer to neighbors and passersby.

In 2013, Paola and Yaolín were frequently visited by police agents from the local precinct. The agents threatened to close their illegal textile shop and kiosk, warning the couple that they could face deportation. In exchange for turning a blind eye, the agents demanded money: "Seven thousand pesos and we'll leave you alone," they once told Yaolín. On that occasion, neighbors helped them pay the bribe. Another time, Yaolín remembered, a police agent yelled, "I want 3,000 pesos or I will tear your shop down."

Over time, Paola became tired of being extorted by the police and watching much of the little money she made end up in the police officers' pockets. So on the night of March 5, 2013, unlike other occasions, Paola refused to pay the bribes. When the police agents showed up at her home, she told them that they were "not going to give them any more money." In response, the police raided the house, arresting both Paola and Yaolín not only for their unregistered businesses but also for drug possession and distribution. With the help of the district attorney, the case involving Paola and Yaolín exposed a series of illicit practices undertaken by the police in Arquitecto Tucci. As we will see, what transpired in court testimonies echoed what we heard dozens of times in the neighborhood: Local police routinely extort residents for money. They tolerate illicit actions (in this case, a shop that manufactured knockoff T-shirts and an unlicensed kiosk) provided that the owners pay them for their silence. This case also reveals a darker side of police operations. If residents do not pay these bribes, officers either arrest them or plant evidence to charge them with more serious crimes.

Sworn testimonies show that on the night of the illegal raid, a young man named Juan was walking down the street when police agents stopped him and took him to Paola and Yaolín's home. There, police agents handed him a bag with several doses of cocaine and told him to leave them in the house. While the court case does not provide details on why Juan would have participated, another witness offered more insights. Gustavo told the prosecutor that back in 2013 when he was addicted to paco, he used to hang out around the police precinct because agents would give him leftovers—"noodles, lentils or meat." On the night of the raid, police agents also took Gustavo to Paola and Yaolín's home. Before getting out of the police vehicle, officers showed him two bags of cocaine and told him, "[T]he black bag goes in there [referring to the kiosk]." Police agents then told Gustavo to wait for their call 40 meters away and handed him the cocaine, which he left in the house. Police officers provided Gustavo with not only the evidence but also the story to tell during the raid and subsequent deposition: He said, "[T]hey [the police] asked me to bring the drugs with me and to say that I had bought them there [at the kiosk]." A few hours after the raid, as the officers drove Gustavo home, they reminded him to lie to the prosecutor and say that the drugs were in Paola and Yaolín's home all along. They gave him a dose of paco (*una piedra de pasta base*) in payment for his services.

During oral arguments, it became clear that these extortive practices were not isolated incidents. Local police officers routinely kept drugs they seized during raids and then used them to plant evidence later on. But this time, the police officers involved were caught and eventually brought to trial. Five agents—two officers, two lieutenants, and one sergeant—were accused of several crimes, including conducting an illegal raid, carrying out an illegal arrest, perjury and fabrication of police reports, planting evidence, and unlawful possession of narcotics (this latter charge was eventually dropped). In October 2014, each defendant was sentenced to four years in prison and Paola and Yaolín were cleared of all charges.

Legal Cynicism

The case was likely not a surprise for residents of Arquitecto Tucci. During the trial, one resident told a journalist that officers specialized in "collecting" money from the community. A leader of the Mothers against Paco (a grassroots organization of parents of those addicted to paco) told the same journalist that "cops live off two or three arrested people. They rotate prisoners, and charge for their release. They demand between 500 and 3,000 pesos so that they won't beat or rape them. Sometimes they demand in-kind payments, like a DVD player." As these testimonies suggest, in Arquitecto Tucci police were not simply perceived as incompetent and biased against residents, but were also highly extortive.

In October 2011, Agustín, our research assistant, was riding a bus to Arquitecto Tucci when it was stopped by a checkpoint set up by the National Guard.[4] Seeing this, one passenger on the bus yelled: "They [the officers] are all faggots. The cops and the national guards are all faggots." After the bus went through the checkpoint, one passenger asked another: "Did they pat you down as well?" The passenger responded, "Yes, they all put us against the wall. . . . [T]hey didn't find anything on us. . . . Fuck! They took my cigarettes. Fuck! They do this so that they can take our stuff. They take your sneakers to see if they can find drugs on you." And drawing on an intuitive understanding of the difference between low-level street leaders and high-level traffickers (a distinction that is crucial in the dynamics of collusion to be analyzed later), he added: "They always find one person that sells paco or weed, but they never get the big guys [*los pesados*]. They never fall." A third passenger chimed in on the conversation. "[It's] because it's all arranged [*arreglado*]," he said. "Those guys pay the cops and the cops never bother them. The cops don't care if the big guys keep selling. Here, they do their raids to justify their work, to come up with numbers, to make their stats." The first passenger then concluded this illuminating impromptu exchange: "And for each one of the guys that gets arrested, a whole family gets screwed."

In many direct and indirect ways, residents reported that they had repeated negative interactions with state forces. For example, we spoke with many who had directly experienced violence or extortion (or both) at the hands of either the local police or members of the National Guard: "I was driving my motorcycle and the cops stopped me," Juan (18) told us one day. "They took all my money. You have to give them money, otherwise they take your motorcycle. They want free money [*quieren unos mangos de arriba*]," he explained. Reflecting on her adolescent son's interactions with the police, Marcela (43) explained: "My son came running home one day. The cops had hit him really hard. He now sees the cops or the national guards and he runs away. I tell him not to do that because they might suspect something. But he is really afraid of them." For Marcela, along with most of the residents we spoke with, abuse and misconduct defined local law enforcement: "Police agents rough kids up. They insult them. My son was at the park and he was carrying a girlfriend's lipstick. The cops took it away and began yelling at him: 'What are you, a faggot? Faggot, do you put that in your ass?' . . . Cops also plant drugs on kids . . . and some kids work for the cops [stealing or dealing drugs]. Cops protect drug dealers."

Many other accounts of police action merged descriptions of violence, extortion, and incompetence with those focusing on their illicit relations with criminals. Much like the residents of Mexico City described by sociologist Diane Davis (2006:57), almost everyone we talked to in Arquitecto Tucci saw "only a fine line separating police from criminals." For example, Romina and Cata, who both had previously worked as street-level drug dealers, confidently reflected on drug dealing in Tucci. Cata explained, "[B]eing a dealer [*transa*] is less risky than being a thief. You always have a cop protecting you. It's quite easy. They come to pick up the bribe. Cops go to a pizza place and they get two pizzas for free. They go to the butcher and they get two chickens for free. And they go to the bunker and they get 500 or 600 pesos every night." Anticipating what we find in the next chapters, Romina added that police officers also charged money to release people from jail, levying an under-the-table bail. "For the petty thieves, they charge you 500 pesos," Romina explained. "For the important ones, at least 1,000 pesos. . . . [O]nly those who don't have money go to jail."

Two more field note excerpts capture residents' understandings of law enforcement, indicating a widespread sense that although police are present, they are not there to shield them from violence but rather to protect criminals and especially those working in the drug business. Police officers, from the local point of view, are "arreglados" (arranged) who facilitate the operation of illicit markets and line their own pockets in the process.

Field note excerpt, March 2011
"Half a block from my house," Elena (35) said during a conversation on the street outside her home a few blocks from the local elementary school, "there's a bunker where they sell paco. Everybody knows that you can find it there. The cops know, but nobody does a thing. Neither the neighbors nor the cops do a thing about it. . . . Nobody wants to get in trouble." Not missing a beat, Valeria (in her 30s) added, "[T]he cops have their deals. They know everything. But they only do something when it is in their favor, or when someone else benefits . . . you know what I mean?"

Field note excerpt, April 2011
Joni (18) got his Rivotril pills from a local political broker,[5] his mother told us during a conversation near her house in Arquitecto Tucci. In exchange for the pills, he played the drums at political rallies. Graciela, Joni's mother, once confronted this

political broker. Her friend Valeria told us this encounter was useless. Reflecting on Graciela's options, Valeria said, "Do you know what would happen if you go to the cops to denounce him [the broker]? You will be forced out of the neighborhood. . . . Just look right here, right to the kiosk out there. Next to it, they sell drugs. At night, there are tons of cars coming to buy. The cops don't do a thing. They get 5,000 pesos per month. They know fully well who sells and who doesn't."

As these accounts suggest, mistrust of police was fueled by suspicions about state agents colluding with traffickers. Residents consistently reported widespread cynicism toward law enforcement. In addition to the shared belief that police agents were illegitimate and unresponsive, mistrust of police was rooted in this perceived *complicity* between police officers and criminals.

Action and Inaction

Court cases filed in Arquitecto Tucci and a close reading of the local news confirm that residents' suspicions of collusion were not unfounded. Years after the resolution of Paola and Yaolín's case, residents continued to experience the negative effects of collusion. In May 2017, Guillermo and his neighbors told the local police chief that their block had become a "very busy" drug-selling area. A few weeks later, traffickers fired machine guns at the entrance of Guillermo's home, filmed the event, and then sent him the video via WhatsApp. The clip was later broadcast on national television and reproduced in Argentina's daily newspapers, a cautionary tale of retaliatory dealers. In response to the attack, the governor of Buenos Aires pointed to the "connivance" between authorities and participants in the drug trade: "Gangs feel the impunity." "Turning a blind eye" or looking the other way has a price, and it is known in the neighborhood as *la prote*—short for *la protección* (the protection), that is, the bribe that dealers pay to the local police.[6]

While instances of extortion and corruption were shared through social networks and published in the local news, others were vocalized when residents came together to solve common problems. At a community meeting one of us attended in February 2013, Alicia, one of the leaders of Mothers against Paco, brought up the issue of police complicity with dealers: "Cops know where dealers are but they don't do anything." Another resident, named Elisa, whose son had recently been murdered, clearly elaborated the problem residents were facing:

> My son was killed because of a fight between two trafficking groups that wanted to control the area. We all know who killed him, but the state prosecutor wants witnesses. And who is going to be a witness? The kids are afraid because they know that police officers are complicit with the dealers. Nobody wants to talk. Nobody wants to report. Everybody knows who killed my son, but nobody talks.

Other attendees expressed similar distrust of the police: "Everybody knows where the dealers live, and everybody knows that the police are in cahoots with them . . . and we are afraid that if we report the dealers, we'll suffer the consequences."

At the community meeting, residents repeatedly used the phrase *zona liberada* (liberated zone) to describe their neighborhood, conveying both widespread local knowledge of police complicity and a generalized feeling of living in an unprotected space, a "no man's land," as Fernanda characterized it in the previous chapter. As the meeting came to a close, attendees agreed to organize a rally to protest in front of the local police precinct and decided on their main public claim: "We want the police and the courts to fulfill their role. No more liberated zones. Those who consume should not go to jail, dealers should be imprisoned." The flyers publicizing the rally, reproduced in Figures 3.2 and 3.3, further summarized their point of view. Figure 3.2 asserts: "Enough drugs and deaths in our community. No more liberated zones." Figure 3.3 offers a telling graphic: "Drugs are equal to death, exclusion, delinquency."

The widespread conviction that police officers and drug dealers collude sometimes translated into collective actions such as the one described above. Oftentimes, however, this widespread perception of police-criminal collusion manifested in inactions such as the refusal to speak up or to go to the police to make a complaint or report a crime. For example, Cintia (18) told us about a time when her house was robbed and then asked rhetorically: "Why would you call the police? What for? They don't do anything. You make the complaint. They take the complaint and they file it away." Melissa (16) put it this way: "You call them [the police] fifty times. . . . They never come. And when they come, they ask you a bunch of questions and don't do anything." Mabel (38) summarized police ineffectiveness in this way: "The cops are always late . . . to collect the body if someone was killed or to stich you up if you've been raped." The hesitancy to call the police was rooted not just in their perceived ineffectiveness but also in the fear of retaliation. Residents said things like, "It's better if you don't make a complaint at the local precinct. You will get in trouble" and "You will be forced out of the neighborhood."

Avoiding the police did not mean remaining passive in the face of danger. Cynicism with respect to law enforcement sometimes motivated residents to take matters in their own hands. Rosa, a local political broker, was a case in point. She told us about an episode that took place a few months before we interviewed her involving a group of young people who had squatted in a house on her block and were using it to sell drugs. "What could we do about it? Those kids were quite aggressive," Rosa said. "And the cops knew them. There is no point in reporting them to the police." She then explained what happened at a

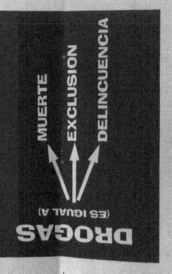

MARCHA VECINAL

BASTA de DROGAS y MUERTES en nuestros Barrios

(NO MÁS ZONAS LIBERADAS)

Vecinos Autoconvocados

BASTA DE ZONAS LIBERADAS EN EL BARRIO

¡¡¡ PAZ, TRABAJO Y JUSTICIA !!!

DROGAS (ES IGUAL A)

MUERTE
EXCLUSION
DELINCUENCIA

BASTA DE ZONAS LIBERADAS

BASTA DE ZONAS LIBERADAS

Figures 3.2 and 3.3 Flyers for neighborhood protest against drugs and "liberated zones," Arquitecto Tucci, 2013.

community meeting that she called to address the squatters and their activities:

> We had meetings with the neighbors about the drug problem. The police chief came. And so did the son of the trafficker, the wife of the trafficker. . . . All those who attended the meeting got threats. One of the neighbors told the chief the location of the selling point and she received a death threat. Her house was stoned. That meeting was a sham, the chief and the street cops are complicit with the dealers. . . . If they put 10,000 police cars on the streets, half are going to be complicit with them.

Sensing the lack of formal alternatives, Rosa organized a group of neighborhood youth to forcibly remove the occupants. "It was pretty rough. . . . We took all the things from inside the house. . . . It was violent . . . but we got rid of them." A few months later, her daughter's purse was stolen. A kid riding a motorcycle snatched it. Rosa knew the thief: "[H]e sells drugs for a dealer who has an arrangement with the cops." Again, she took matters into her own hands rather than calling the police: She went with her husband to his house and demanded the purse back. As Rosa's experiences suggest, residents resorted to alternative ways to maintain social control, sometimes organizing collective action to solve community problems (as in the small group she gathered to evict the dealers) and other times relying on self-help to address their grievances (as in her husband's threats to retrieve the purse).

Excursus: Political Brokers

Rosa was one of a handful of political brokers who worked in Arquitecto Tucci. Many like her provided residents personalized access to public goods and services in the neighborhood.[7] Residents counted on them to solve the daily problems—from "speeding up" the waiting time at a state agency to obtaining vital material goods like medicine or food. Known as *referentes*, brokers run community services, including soup kitchens, health clinics, and sports centers that are funded by political parties or state agencies.[8] In addition to these services, brokers coordinate the delivery of state welfare programs.

The variety of goods and services that *referentes* provide their followers in poor areas such as Arquitecto Tucci is quite extensive. Note the list offered by Rodrigo Zarazaga (2014:33), the foremost expert on the contemporary workings of these networks in Buenos Aires: "jobs, workfare programs, food, medicine, clothes, shoes, coffins, school materials, appliances, bricks, zinc sheets, cash, marijuana and other illegal drugs." Among the goods distributed by brokers, the last two items should not come as a surprise. Recall what we heard from Graciela, Joni's mother, who told us that the local broker gave her son prescription drugs in exchange for his attendance at political rallies. This was hardly a far-fetched claim. In previous research on patronage networks in nearby Villa Paraíso, one of us observed how brokers' close collaborators distributed marijuana to youth before rallies.[9] Of course, not all brokers distribute illicit drugs. In fact, we found that many vehemently opposed this practice and identified a direct link between drugs and de-pacification in their neighborhoods.

The five brokers we spoke with in Arquitecto Tucci shared this widespread concern about the lack of public safety, its relationships with drugs, and their deep distrust of the police. "The cops are closer to the crooks than to the common people," one explained to us during an interview. Another boldly asserted things like "[T]he worst of la Bonaerense [the state police] is in Tucci" and "[T]here are no honest cops." They all agreed that police-criminal collusion was something beyond their control. As one seasoned *referente* told us, "Trying to do something about that is like swimming against the current." Although they noted the magnitude and complexity of the issues, as problem-solvers they did not passively observe the daily drug-related violence. Despite feelings of impotence, many also believed that something could be done about the issue of drugs. The general consensus among them was similar to that of the parents we presented in Chapter 2. To address violence, they needed to preempt the drug trade by "keep[ing] the kids off the street" and "contain[ing] the youth."

What specifically did these well-connected problem-solvers do to "contain" young people? We found that they folded these efforts into their attempts to solve other pressing concerns. One broker, Patricia, was organizing a cultural center to sponsor sports and the arts for local youth. Another, Benito, made sure that the municipal office he managed in the neighborhood employed young people "to keep them occupied." The brokers were willing to try anything that could, one told us, to "remove youth" from what they saw at the main incubator of misbehavior: "the streets."

Betraying What's Right

Residents, grassroots activists, and political brokers all shared a sense that the police had not so much abandoned the neighborhood but were instead there to protect and profit off drug traffickers. Police, from the local point of view, were not only idle, incompetent, or biased, but constantly betraying what was right by actively protecting traffickers who generate much of the daily suffering.

In *Achilles in Vietnam*, psychiatrist Jonathan Shay (1995:3) compares the combatants of Homer's *Iliad* with Vietnam War veterans suffering from post-traumatic stress disorder under his treatment. Shay writes, "Agamemnon, Achilles' commander, wrongfully seizes the prize of honor voted to Achilles by the troops. Achilles' experience of betrayal of 'what's right,' and his reactions to it, are identical to those of American soldiers in Vietnam." Shay uses the phrase "what's right" to capture the common assumptions that were violated by "holders of responsibility and trust" in Vietnam. These

normative expectations, conventions, and shared social values—
captured by the Greek word *themis*—make up a moral order. Shay
continues: "When a leader destroys the legitimacy of the army's
moral order by betraying 'what's right,' he inflicts manifold injuries
on his men" (p. 6).

Listening to residents of Arquitecto Tucci—directly in interviews, casual conversations, and meetings, as well as indirectly in
news reports—repeat time and again, in many different ways, that
they suspect, know, think, and have seen that the "cops are with
dealers," that the officers are *arreglados*, that they are "in cahoots
with the dealers," we could not help but think about the notion of
"the betrayal of what's right." True, Arquitecto Tucci (or any urban
"community" for that matter) is not the unified "moral world" of
the kind described by Shay. But shared ethical expectations do exist
among residents of Arquitecto Tucci. Prominent among them is the
expectation that the police should protect them and not break the
law. In the hearts and minds of residents, withholding protection
from ordinary folks and violating the law amounts to a betrayal of
what's right. No amount of familiarity or proximity to collusion or
daily life in a "no man's land" has normalized these arrangements. If
anything, it has triggered a generalized resignation to a state of affairs that residents see as hard to avoid and unlikely to change.

* * *

Beyond the actual presence of drugs, street dealers, and traffickers
in the neighborhood, residents in Arquitecto Tucci believed that
the police were part of the problem. In this chapter, we analyzed
different expressions of this shared belief about the presence of
police-criminal collusion, explaining how police officers were seen
not only as abusive and extortive but also as actively complicit with
criminals. This, we argued, has bred a deep collective distrust in
the police force and contributed to a shared cynicism toward the
law that pervades everyday life. When they became the victims of

crimes, residents did not call the police, but instead chose either not to act or to solve their problems through alternative channels or collective action.

In this and the previous chapter, we have drawn on our ethnographic data to provide a thick description of life in Arquitecto Tucci and how residents think and feel about state action in their neighborhood. Foreshadowing the chapters to come, we also presented evidence of police misconduct by showing the corrupt and extortive practices of local police. In the chapters that follow, we begin to unpack the relational dynamics of police-criminal collusion using court cases indicting both civilians and police officers for their participation in criminal activity. We will begin in Arquitecto Tucci to learn about how specific "arrangements" are established between the police and a drug-trafficking organization. We then move to different locations throughout Argentina to analyze how clandestine relationships between state agents and drug dealers operate, evolve, and sometimes break down. Through an up-close investigation of actual clandestine interactions, we find that collusion involves more than just the exchange of protection for money. We find that police officers and drug dealers also develop relationships based on the regular exchange of goods and information, from guns, ammunition, and drugs to information about law enforcement and competition, among other things. Participants in collusion also engage in a series of common practices. From engaging in surveillance to modifying work routines and manipulating bureaucratic procedures of the state, relationships of collusion meaningfully impact the ways that state agents, police, and drug dealers conduct their illicit business. Finally, despite constant improvisation and maneuvering that characterizes the clandestine interactions documented in court cases, we analyze relational processes that help explain the patterned nature of police-criminal collusion.

4
Establishing the "Arreglo"

In 2016, eleven people were indicted for a series of drug-related charges in Arquitecto Tucci. This case included nine civilians (three women and six men) and two members of the Buenos Aires State Police who were working with a group that we call "Los Vagones" (The Train Cars). Court documents confirm that at least five more people were likely involved (but not indicted) and that this small group had just two contacts in the State Police. The group's illicit activities were well documented, providing insights into not only the organization's internal operations and clandestine relationships but also the link between collusion and the violence that plagues residents of the neighborhood.[1]

The case of Paola and Yaolín with which we opened the previous chapter provided evidence about police misconduct beyond residents' hearsay.[2] In this chapter, we examine additional court cases that offer a direct window into the actual exchanges between drug dealers and police officers, showing how participants establish such arrangements or "arreglos" and how they impact interpersonal violence in the neighborhood. The subsequent chapters extend from our field site to locations across Argentina in order to unpack the relational dynamics of police-criminal collusion. Beyond paying police to turn a blind eye and cease to enforce the law for certain actors or in certain places, we will show that relationships of collusion are highly patterned and they have important effects on those involved, changing the way they access goods and information and how they navigate their social worlds.

It is not uncommon to suspect an overall "master plan" behind the relations of collusion we describe here. But as we will learn in

The Ambivalent State: Police-Criminal Collusion at the Urban Margins. Javier Auyero, Oxford University Press (2019). © Oxford University Press.
DOI: 10.1093/oso/9780190915537.001.0001

the pages that follow, relationships between police and drug dealers are made and unmade through incessant, oftentimes last-minute improvisations marked by constant mistakes and corrections. Together, the forthcoming chapters offer a view of a world of ongoing and joint maneuvering that helps us better understand what collusion is and does.

One warning is in order: All the testimonies, wiretapped conversations, informants' accounts, and investigative reports that we analyze contain a plethora of information that is not necessarily central to our substantive focus. Instead of presenting all the aspects of the cases, the upcoming chapters provide *analytic reconstructions* that highlight the different interactions, meanings, and consequences of the clandestine connections between members of the state's repressive apparatus and drug market participants.

Most of the court proceedings we accessed document the operation of drug market organizations and their ongoing connections with police agents as they are already fully functioning. They typically do not capture the early stages of those relationships. Before presenting the case of Los Vagones in Arquitecto Tucci, let us first describe another case, which was brought to trial in Máximo Paz (in the state of Buenos Aires) that illuminates the initial activation of clandestine connections.[3] The details extracted from this case provide evidence of what we call "foundational negotiation," the initial moments in which relationships of collusion are born and police officers have the upper hand.

Foundational Negotiation

One early evening in May 2016, police agents in a neighborhood of Máximo Paz raided the home of Alcira Mazzeo.[4] Around 8:30 p.m., as the police agents were searching for drugs in her house, Alcira called Mariano and told him that to avoid being arrested, "the cops want 500,000 pesos." Mariano told Alcira that he only had 200,000 pesos available (less than half of the US$33,000 requested).[5] "No," she replied. "He [the police agent] wants 500,000." In what could have been a scene from a movie, a male voice, presumably that of the police officer standing with Alcira, added: "[You have] one hour."

Over the next two hours, Mariano and this police officer negotiated the amount of money to be paid to prevent Alcira's arrest and how they would exchange the funds. "Listen," Mariano told the officer, "I was able to gather [*rescatar*] 300,000 pesos [US$20,000]. . . . I couldn't get more. Please, the woman [Alcira] has children, don't wreck her life [*la mina tiene hijos, no la arruines, porfa*]." "Okay," the police officer responded. Mariano asked for forty minutes to get the money. An hour later, Mariano and the officer talked again. The officer told Mariano that he was doing him a "big favor" (*una mano grandísima*). Without the money, the officer implied, he would have to arrest Alcira and also detain her daughter.

The exchange that followed clearly illustrates the moment in which a relationship of collusion begins and one way it can proceed. Before delivering the money, Mariano wanted to know if Alcira would be able to "keep working." The police officer replied that they would arrange that later; all he wanted at that moment was the money and he promised to "disappear" immediately. When Mariano asked him who he should talk to in the future, the police officer was vague, ensuring that they would be in touch to arrange that later.

Paying ransom to avoid arrest is not unique to drug dealers in Buenos Aires.[6] Note the similarity of Alcira and Mariano's predicament with that of drug traffickers in Tubarao, one of the favelas in Rio de Janeiro, Brazil, where Enrique Desmond Arias (2006a:76) conducted fieldwork in the late 1990s and early 2000s:

> One resident, closely tied with traffickers, told the story of how a police officer who showed up for work one day in a bad mood shook down a group of minor traffickers. He walked around the

favela angrily looking for some low-level drug dealers to bother. Not finding any, he went to the nearby beach where he located the dealers and, finding narcotics, forced them to come up with some money to ransom their own freedom. The traffickers went off and got the money by borrowing or stealing.[7]

Immediately after they agreed on the amount, Mariano negotiated its delivery. Not wanting to bring the bribe in person, he asked the police officer if he could release Alcira's daughter to pick up and deliver the money. The officer replied, "I can't release any-body, it makes too much noise [*levanta mucha bandera*]." He then added: "You can trust me. I tell you one thing and I deliver. This is a 'touch and go.' I won't even look at your face. Do you understand? I grab what I have to grab and that's it." Mariano agreed but, still wary, decided not to deliver the money in person. "Okay, I'll send someone [with the money]," he replied.

These court documents capture the initial interactions between a police officer and drug dealers in Máximo Paz. But many questions are left unanswered. While we can assume that the money was de-livered, what happened between the police officer and Mariano is beyond the scope of the indictment. In fact, investigative docu-ments explicitly note that they did not confirm the identity of the officer on the phone and call for further investigation into the transaction. Moreover, while law enforcement identified Mariano and recommended "pursu[ing] legal action," to our knowledge, no further steps have been taken.

Despite these gaps, this case clearly illustrates one sequence through which a clandestine relationship begins: When a dealer is detained, a police officer demands money, forcing the dealer to call on their illicit business partners to negotiate their release with the officer. Two previously unrelated actors become linked—forming the kind of new boundaries and connections that constitute the empirical object of this and the next three chapters. This case shows that at the moment of inception, police officers use the authority of the state to establish the upper hand. It also indicates how, early on in an illicit relationship, actors mistrust each other and proceed hesitantly. Here, collusion looks more like a version of "racketeering": Officers produce both "the danger (i.e. an arrest) and, at a price, they shield against it" (Tilly 1985:170). But as we will see in the next cases, a kind of provisional trust develops as clandestine connections evolve and power dynamics become more negotiated and reciprocal.

Back to Arquitecto Tucci

Los Vagones was a drug market organization that operated in the southern province of Buenos Aires. Although it occasionally smuggled marijuana from Paraguay, the organization primarily obtained drugs from larger trafficking groups that operated out of slums in the city of Buenos Aires.[8] According to court documents, the organization sold 10 kilos of marijuana and even more paco per day. The organization not only brought marijuana and paco into the Conurbano but also sold those drugs to petty dealers and users from a network of selling points called "bunkers." The most important ones (and the target of the court case) were in an area of Arquitecto Tucci near a train station known as "the Tracks" (Figure 4.1). Although Los Vagones never operated in the open, members of the organization guarded the streets around these bunkers, surveilling for threats and intimidating residents so that they would not report their activities to the police.

Los Vagones had a hierarchical structure with clearly differentiated roles. It was led by a man named Pepe, who worked with a handful of other leaders to oversee the illicit operations. Most of these leaders were in their 30s and 40s and had some family connections to each other. The rest of the group consisted of lower-level affiliates in charge of transportation (preparing vehicles and moving drugs), storage (of drugs, weapons, and other assets), and

Figure 4.1 The "Tracks," Arquitecto Tucci, 2010. Credit: Photography Workshop at local elementary school.

sales (to other dealers and consumers). Leaders also controlled a security network made up of lookouts called "spies" or "satellites" (*mirillas, satélites, punteros*) and guards called "hitmen" (*sicarios*), who, according to the indictment, primarily threatened and, in two documented cases, even killed their competitors.

This court case relied heavily on wiretapped phone conversations among dealers, many of whom were very explicit about their activities. That said, members of Los Vagones also took precautions against surveillance: They constantly replaced cell phones and SIM cards and sometimes referred to drugs and people with fake names. For example, "Lucho" was the pseudonym used for the male police officer indicted in the case, and "La Morocha" (an informal term for a woman with dark hair and skin) was what dealers called the female police officer. The court case also relied on an informant we call Mateo, who provided information about the group's membership to police in exchange for safety under witness protection.

Finally, the indictment against members of Los Vagones drew on videotaped meetings of police and drug dealers, including one that was leaked to a national television station, which we will discuss in more detail below.

The transcripts of wiretapped phone conversations show that members of Los Vagones spent most of their time discussing drug distribution, payments, and security among each other. Pepe and his subordinates regularly talked about securing new suppliers— what they called "lines" (*líneas*)—when one of them failed to deliver. At the time this group was being surveilled, demand for drugs in and around Arquitecto Tucci was booming, and the group sometimes struggled to keep up with demand unless they constantly added new "lines." For example, one of the leaders said to another, "See if you can get ten kilograms for tomorrow, or five. If not, I can go to Flores [where a slum is located in the city of Buenos Aires] and get some more." In another conversation, a dealer shared information about a delivery: "La Tía just left with the burgers [*patys*]." In this conversation, the speaker referred to drugs as *patys*, a brand name–turned-slang term for hamburgers in Argentina. The dealer continued, "[G]et the people ready so that they can receive her. She is bringing 251 *patys*. Organize where to put them." In addition to these orders to prepare for La Tía's arrival, the dealer also gave directions about what to do with the delivery: "Take 51 and leave them on the soccer field, and keep 200 for tonight."

In addition to drugs, dealers regularly discussed money over the phone, including how much they made and what they spent it on. According to court documents, the group made between ARS $50,000 (US$3,000) and ARS $100,000 (US$6,000) per day. But rather than document such totals, these mundane interactions usually detailed the organization's everyday expenses. For example, in one conversation, a dealer called a leader to report on the previous night's work. He said, "[We gave] 300 pesos [*gambas*] to each of the seven lookouts [*mirillas*], 1,000 pesos to Shrek and Tati, and I kept 2,000." In addition to distributing profits and paying for labor, the organization also regularly paid for supplies like the baggies used to pack drugs and snacks for its members ("la picada de los muchachos").

The case involving Los Vagones also highlights the important connection between narco-trafficking activities and what analysts call the "systemic violence" generated within drug markets.[9] In what follows, we will describe this connection in three important respects. First, the case clearly documents the violent tactics used by Pepe and his hitmen to acquire and maintain control over a particular neighborhood by forcibly eliminating competition. Second, it shows how the police engage in and facilitate this violence. Finally, it exposes an important limit of collusion: When business is compromised, fluctuating profits impact dealers' ability to pay for protection.

Evading Authorities, Targeting Competitors

For members of Los Vagones, evading police and federal security agents was a main concern, forcing them to suddenly suspend their activities on certain days, at certain times, and in certain areas due to state presence. In a wiretapped conversation, a drug dealer told a supplier that he could not reach the bunker because the National Guard was on the highway. Because of the state's presence, he temporarily suspended his delivery. In addition to sharing information among themselves, dealers also attempted to infiltrate official communication. For example, one dealer had a radio that picked up police frequencies, which he used to track where they were going and then pass the information to members of Los Vagones. Finally, dealers discussed more quotidian ways to avoid detection; for example, the need to change phones and numbers to avoid surveillance. Even when dealers suspected police surveillance, they discussed plans to quickly move drugs in and out of specific bunkers in great detail.

Using these sources of information, members of Los Vagones carefully monitored their territory and sometimes intimidated local residents in an effort to keep them from talking to authorities. In one phone conversation, a dealer threatened a man (who would later be called to testify against the group) who he suspected had passed information to the police. The dealer said, "We don't want to have any problems with you." He then offered him a job in the organization, making clear he would eventually find out the identity of the suspected snitch.

Overall, members of Los Vagones operated in a constant state of high alert. For example, one afternoon, state police officers raided Pepe's house for drugs and information about the group. Although he was not home, they arrested his wife and brother-in-law. After the raid, Pepe went into hiding and transferred leadership of the organization to his second-in-command, Chato. This raid could have been part of an anti-drug-trafficking effort to catch the leaders of Los Vagones. But wiretapped phone conversations suggest that regardless of the original intent of the raid, it was being used to extort Pepe, not rid Arquitecto Tucci of drugs. In a conversation on a wiretapped phone a few days later, Pepe assured his lawyer that the police wanted to "reach an agreement [*llegar a un arreglo*]." He then instructed the lawyer to deliver half a million pesos (US$300,000) to a police officer named Saborido to ensure his family would be released and the manhunt would be suspended. The court case does not establish whether the money was transferred to Saborido or if Pepe's family members were released from jail. What it does show is the operational and financial capacity of a group that can successfully evade the police and mobilize large sums of money to avoid being caught.

Interestingly, Los Vagones worked incessantly to evade not only police officers but also other illicit actors who targeted their small but profitable business. This case documents the presence of what Randol Contreras (2012) calls "stick-up kids," or groups of young people who attempt to rob dealers. Because of this additional

threat, dealers devoted significant time to ensuring the safe movement of drugs and money. For example, late one night, a dealer in
Tucci decided not to deliver drugs because he didn't feel safe: "I'm
scared because it's late," he admitted on the phone.

Drug dealers also discussed nearby competitors and the need
to eliminate them. One street seller informed Fifi, a leader of the
group, that Raulito was selling drugs in their area. Fifi instructed,
"Go to him and tell him I said that he has 15 minutes to go somewhere else, otherwise his legs will be broken. Tell him Tío and I said
that. Call me back in 15 to let me know he left." As this conversation suggests, leaders of Los Vagones did not hesitate to threaten
the use of violence to maintain control over the drug market in the
neighborhood.

Los Vagones not only verbally threatened competitors but
also armed its members, attacked rival bunkers, and even killed
members of other drug market groups. Wiretapped phone conversations confirm that members of Los Vagones were regularly armed
with lethal weapons. For example, one dealer informed Chato: "At
the train station there's a group [un junta]. I think they are selling."
Chato agreed to send Saverio, a hitman, with a .38 caliber handgun,
and if needed, to let two other hitmen called "Japonés" and "Tigre"
know so that they could "do what they gotta do."

In another conversation, a dealer told Tío about his plan to confront a competitor: "They are there until 11 p.m. We'll visit him
around 9 or 10." Tío replied, "Yes, that's good. . . . [F]ire some shots
[mandenle cohete], break his knees." The dealer informed him that
he also planned to loot the bunker: "They are in the house. We'll get
in and take whatever they have." Tío was adamant that he use physical force, reiterating, "Yes, but break his knees. If not, tomorrow he
will be back doing the same thing" (our emphasis).

In the most extreme example included in the court case, Mateo,
the informant in witness protection, provided information about
members' involvement in a double homicide. According to his testimony, Pepe sent four hitmen to kill members of another drug

market group they had learned were planning to do business in the area. That night, they attacked a new bunker run by what Pepe called "addicts" (*fisuras*). Two men were killed and Pepe forcibly took over the bunker, expanding his business to the new selling points by violently eliminating the competition.[10]

Collusion and Violence

In addition to documenting the tactics of this organization, court documents provide clear evidence that violence was intricately linked with collusive relationships. First, as we will see in other cases, dealers obtained their guns (called "toys," "tools," and "girls") and ammunition from members of the police force. While we may assume that illicit actors use these weapons to commit crimes, this case provides direct evidence of the link between clandestine connections and violence. In the double homicide described above, guns registered with the police department were used by members of Los Vagones to commit the murders.

Los Vagones also bought inaction and information from the police. In addition to non-enforcement, police officers provided the group with specific news about other officers surveilling them. On a wiretapped cell phone, Lucho (the police officer indicted in the case) spoke with Fifi, one of the leaders of Los Vagones. Lucho asked, "Are they [police] bothering you?" Fifi replied: "Yes, [they were] the other day but not yesterday or today." Lucho promised to help Fifi with the problem: "They are someone else's," he promised, indicating that the officers were from another agency. "They are on the other side of the train tracks. I will find out who they are."

In a subsequent conversation, Officer Lucho warned Fifi, "You guys are being marked [surveilled] by the street patrol in Centinela [a nearby neighborhood]." He gave Fifi more details: "Write down the plate number of the car . . . XL5-C94. It's a white Nissan. They were told that people were bringing stuff around where you are."

Information was regularly exchanged between police officers and drug dealers. Police officers passed information to dealers (as we saw above) and also received information from dealers about other illicit actors in the area. For example, a little after noon one day, Fifi called Lucho. "What's up?" Lucho said when he answered the phone. Fifi replied, "The same as usual . . . those fucking smurfs [*pitufos de mierda*, referring to policemen] have been bothering us for a while." To appease Fifi, Lucho explained what he thought was happening: "Okay, let me explain. It [the problem] is not going to be for long, you see? What happened is that they opened a new police station [*habilitaron ahí la base*] . . . and they sent them to put on a show [*hacer un poco de espamento*]. But they aren't going to fuck around . . . for long." Fifi responded, "Okay, we can wait. Hopefully that happens so we can get back to work. *But there is also competition*" (*our emphasis*). "Leave that to me," Lucho assured him. "I'll deal with them. I'll go fuck with them a bit." Fifi emphasized the importance of Lucho's intervention: "It will be a huge win [*un golazo*] if you can mess with them." When Lucho mentioned he was unfamiliar with the area, Fifi went on to provide specific details of where the competing dealers were doing business.

As this conversation shows, drug dealers not only used violence to eliminate competition, but they also relied on their contacts in the police to take out competitors and maintain their market position. Put another way, dealers paid not only for goods and information but also for direct police intervention on their behalf, in this case, to maintain economic control of their territory with police help.

Paying for Protection

The case involving Los Vagones also provides detailed information about how the group paid for protection. Many conversations included detailed descriptions of money exchanged as bribes. For example, in one phone conversation, a dealer documented all his expenses to a leader: "I have 43,150 pesos [left] because I used 400 yesterday . . . for the cops [*cobanis*]." In another conversation, a dealer told a leader, "I need to take 10,000 pesos and send Cesar and Gorda to the place where we give the thing to the cops. I'll send them now because they are waiting."

While many conversations were retrospective like those above, on other occasions, drug dealers discussed future amounts to pay. For example, in a conversation between two leaders, Tío told Chato that "the cops called" and wanted to know if they could "do it today," referring to receiving their bribe money. He then asked Chato about the amount: "Do I give them ten pesos [referring to 10,000 pesos]?" Chato said yes. Tío then told him to meet La Morocha, the female police officer indicated in the case, at 5 p.m. at the "usual place." This interaction illustrates an important detail: Members of Los Vagones not only paid bribes, but they did so regularly (i.e., they met at the "usual place").

Unlike some of the other cases we will examine, the indictment of both police and members of Los Vagones received widespread public attention when a video was leaked to the media. The video, which aired on national television, captured the actual payment of one of these bribes, which was made in the bathroom of a local gas station. A grainy black-and-white video shows the police officer named Lucho arriving at a gas station on a busy corner near "the Tracks." He exited from the passenger side of a gray car driven by an accomplice and walked to a bathroom that was accessible from the outside of the station. On his way in, he took out his cell phone and called Fifi. "I'm here," he told him. Fifi responded, "Okay, let me tell her to approach you." The video then captures a woman entering the bathroom and closing the door behind her. Minutes later, both exit the bathroom—the woman walking with her head down and Lucho jogging back to the gray car. According to court documents, every week in a similar fashion, Fifi paid Lucho between ARS $10,000 and ARS $12,000 for the protection we described.

Profits and Bribes: The Limits of Protection

The clandestine connections between drug dealers and police are not established and negotiated without conflict. Although Los Vagones made large sums of money selling drugs, these profits fluctuated based on many factors, from issues of supply and demand to the variable costs of labor and security. One issue in particular stood out for the dealers: their ability to actually sell drugs. As described in this chapter, dealers responded to information received from police by sometimes fully stopping their activities. They stalled shipments, suspended sales, and ultimately reduced the hours spent making money.

As a result, dealers negotiated their weekly payments for protection based on their cash on hand. For example, in a wiretapped phone conversation, Tío told Fifi, "When your friends [referring to the police officers] call you . . . your little friends who want to be paid . . . tell them that we are not going to give them what we usually give them. Tell them that we are going to give them only eight [thousand pesos]." Tío went on to explain his decision to reduce the weekly payments: "Why?" he asked hypothetically. "Because your friends are not letting us work during the day or at night. We can't work like this. If you want to earn the money you used to, well, I have to earn mine and those people are not letting me do my job. See what you can do about it." As this conversation suggests, interactional dynamics between drug dealers and police change from the moment of foundational negotiations we described at the opening of the chapter. Whereas police agents can hold greater power in these initial meetings, clandestine relationships evolve over time as interactions become more routine. As they developed a provisional trust, drug market participants like Tío leveraged their power against officers, from making strictly economic arguments to negotiate bribe amounts to secretly collecting evidence to blackmail their contacts in the state.

Beyond Tucci

The case of Los Vagones offers insights into how police-criminal collusion works, the kind of material and informational resources exchanged, and the impact of clandestine relationships on interpersonal violence. Yet the collusion that we are now beginning to uncover extends far beyond the geographical boundaries of Arquitecto Tucci. Three vignettes, extracted from national news sources, illustrate that illicit relationships between drug dealers and police officers are present in many other Argentine cities.

Córdoba, September 22, 2013
A former undercover officer described the relationship between the police and *narcos* in the city of Córdoba: "Basically, the dealer tells the cops about other *narcos* that they can raid. Half of the drugs the cops seize goes to the *narco* who gave the tip, the cops keep the other half, and the *narco* they raid goes to jail. The police chief also receives monthly payments from *narcos*, always more than 50,000 pesos."[11]

Rosario, December 31, 2016
The former police chief of the city of Rosario was accused of giving protection to a local *narco* when the latter was under investigation by the Airport Security Police. According to a federal judge, the former police chief, two other police officers, and a local drug dealer organized a joint "criminal enterprise devoted to the distribution and sale of drugs." The specific function of the police chief, according to the judge, was to protect and ensure the normal development of such activity by preventing police action.[12]

Santa Fe, January 13, 2017
Wiretapped phone conversations revealed a series of offenses in the Santa Fe State Police. One agent from the investigative unit

offered protection to local drug dealers in exchange for a monthly bribe. Another agent from the same division was in charge of contacting new street dealers to sell drugs in Santa Fe, Santo Tomé, and other towns in the northern part of the state. This agent was arrested when he was about to exchange 300 grams of cocaine for ARS $30,000. According to court documents, part of the drugs these two agents were selling was supplied by narcotics seizures.[13]

These brief stories—often buried in the next day's news cycle—show that the complicity reported by residents in Arquitecto Tucci and substantiated by the case of Los Vagones is taking place in many other areas throughout the country.[14] They also point to potential sources of data like federal investigations, judicial proceedings, and wiretapped phone conversations that document the relational dynamics of collusion. Much like the inquisitorial trials that offered historians such as Carlo Ginzburg (1989:142) "an unexplored gold mine," these data sources combined with investigative journalistic reports provided us a treasure trove of evidence on the workings of the state and on the impact of collusion on interpersonal violence. The next chapters turn to a detailed analysis of three more legal proceedings that extend well beyond the boundaries of Arquitecto Tucci.

5

Competition, Retaliation, and Violence

> Los Monos built a business that made the members of
> the family fabulously rich . . . without encountering many
> obstacles in the penal system of the province of Santa Fe.
> Neither police nor prosecutors nor judges had bothered
> them. Along with the supplies to install cocaine kitchens,
> control distributors, and pay for the hitmen required to
> extend the business, [the family members] had invested
> regular sums of money to ensure the cooperation of the
> security forces.
>
> De los Santos and Lascano, *Los Monos: Historia de la*
> *Familia Narco que Transformó a Rosario en un Infierno*

In 2012, a young man named Martín Paz, also known as "el Fantasma"
(the Ghost), was murdered in Argentina's third largest city, Rosario
(pop. 1,276,000). Unlike the many crimes that are left unsolved, local
police began to investigate the incident after it sparked a series of retaliatory murders. This string of killings was widely attributed to a
feud between members of a powerful organization called Los Monos
(the Monkeys) and a rival gang. This resulting police investigation,
which included months of wiretapped phone conversations, offers
a snapshot of the frantic activity of Los Monos over a three-month
period. Unlike the previous case involving Los Vagones, which indicted only two police officers, the case involving Los Monos is far

The Ambivalent State: Police-Criminal Collusion at the Urban Margins. Javier Auyero, Oxford
University Press (2019). © Oxford University Press.
DOI: 10.1093/oso/9780190915537.001.0001

more extensive. In 2015, 21 civilians and 12 members of the security forces (including 10 local police agents, an agent of the Naval Police, and a Federal Police agent) were charged with homicide, conspiracy, accessory to a crime, and aggravated obstruction of justice, among other imputations.

One important fact "leaks out" of this and other formal judicial proceedings we examined (Ginzburg 1989:4): With the help of their contacts in the police, drug dealers spend a considerable amount of time and effort avoiding detection and apprehension. Those whom dealers call *los contrarios*—the police officers they perceive as their opponents—are constantly after them. Aware of attempts to surveil their activities and disrupt their drug shipments and sales, dealers are forced to engage in a continual maneuvering in order to conduct their business without being caught. While dealers do develop relationships of collusion with the police and other security forces, *none of them can count on total protection*: If they did, they would not have to spend so much energy in the cultivation, negotiation, and (in some cases) termination of their trusted contacts within the different state forces. And if they did, we wouldn't have access to the data that provide the basis for this book.

Unlike the case of Los Vagones, the members of Los Monos relied on more than one protector within the state apparatus. In Argentina, many state actors are involved in illegal markets, including but not limited to the State Police, the Federal Police, and the National Guard.[1] A variety of factors influence the patchwork of arrangements that illicit organizations develop with state agents, including location and jurisdiction, business activities, and the competitive landscape. Although they do not enjoy exclusive protection, this fragmented arena has some benefits, allowing drug dealers to reduce their "dependence on any single source" of protection and potentially (re)negotiate their power (Snyder and Durán-Martínez 2009:259).

As in Brazil, China, Mexico, and Russia, state actors sell protection (for hefty sums of money) from the actions of the very same state forces to which they belong.[2] They also sell protection in the form of what sociologist Matías Dewey (2017b:124) calls "non-enforcement of the law or *de facto* suspension of it." These protection arrangements have two primary dimensions: "[S]tate officials supply selective non-enforcement, that is, *protection from the state itself*. . . . [T]hey also supply selective enforcement against rivals, that is, *protection from competitors*" (Snyder and Durán-Martínez 2009:255, *emphasis in original*). As we will see in this and subsequent chapters, police officers and drug dealers do much more than simply buy and sell protection in exchange for non-enforcement.

The Content of Collusion

The court cases we present in this and the next two chapters distinguish between three dimensions of collusion. First, we find that the clandestine relationships between state agents and drug dealers are founded on the exchange of both *material and informational resources*. Second, we show that actors involved in collusive relationships engage in common *practices*. Finally, we identify a set of *relational processes* that help us explain patterns of these collusive interactions. Identifying and thickly describing these resources, practices, and processes underscore both the negotiated and provisional character of the clandestine interpersonal transactions, their impact on daily violence, and the *ambivalent* character of state action. Below we present a schematic description of these resources, practices, and processes to foreshadow the arguments that we will make before turning to the fascinating case of Los Monos.

Resources

Collusion involves the exchange of *resources*, including goods, information, and advice (Table 5.1). Beyond bribes, members of drug

Table 5.1 The Content of Collusion

Resources exchanged among drug-trafficking organizations and state agents in Argentina

Goods	Information	Advice
Cash	Police raids	Interrogation
Drugs	State surveillance	Negotiation
Cars	Criminal actions	Retaliation
Weapons	Other state actors	Future actions
	Other illicit actors	
	Loyalty	

market organizations and state repressive forces take part in a variety of seemingly uncomplicated transactions such as the purchase and sale of U.S. dollars and car parts. They also buy and sell weapons and ammunition, as we saw in the case of Los Vagones. Information is a second resource that circulates between drug dealers and police. The exchange of information can be grouped into three general types: *Protective* information serves to shelter dealers from police actions and other state actors; *competitive* information provides insights into the operation of illicit markets; and *retaliatory* information offers data on trust and loyalty among the actors involved.

Most information exchanged is protective in nature and leveraged by dealers to avoid being the target of police action. This type of information involves details about both past police operations but also, and more importantly, about future ones. One of the most important pieces of information that police officers forward to dealers is news regarding imminent police operations such as confiscations of dealers' property, street sweeps, and raids against "bunkers" where drugs are stored or "kitchens" where drugs are produced. In the legal language of the court proceedings, police officers "warn" (*anticipan*) dealers about "measures" (*medidas*) about to be taken. Finally, state actors and drug dealers exchange information about other illicit actors and who can be trusted within the state, and offer advice regarding *where, when,* and *how* to conduct illicit operations and address market competition.

Practices

Collusion also alters the everyday behaviors and practices of those who participate in it. As part of their clandestine relationships, members of security forces and drug dealers engage in a series of common actions. These include (a) modifying work routines, (b) manipulating bureaucratic procedures, and (c) conducting surveillance.

First, all participants alter their work routines as a direct result of the goods, information, and advice exchanged through their illicit connections. As we will describe in detail, everyday decisions about where to patrol and who to target are informed by tips received from drug dealers. Illicit actors also respond to warnings and suggestions received from their clandestine informants in state agencies, often using this information to justify changing shipment routes, suspending sales, and moving supplies and selling points.

Second, all parties engage in what we call "bureaucratic manipulation": intentional efforts to speed up, slow down, or stymie formal institutional processes. While state agents do this directly, drug dealers also play important roles in these efforts. For example, court cases show that police officers negotiate with dealers to selectively report crimes, change arrest records, and plant or remove evidence. In addition to outright modifications and omissions, participants take steps to expedite certain formal forms of recourse. For example, police encourage judges to approve certain search warrants in response to competition in drug markets. Finally, there are also attempts to delay institutional processes. For example, when dealers are arrested, police will extend their detention so that they can negotiate bribe money in exchange for their release.

Third, we find that all participants engage in surveillance, both internally among themselves and externally in their neighborhoods and social networks. Given the importance of being in the know about who is policing, who is dealing drugs, and who is being protected, both drug dealers and state agents practice surveillance to participate in collusion. Dealers watch each other and their employees, competitors, neighbors, and different state agents that intervene in a given territory. Not surprisingly, state agents take similar measures, closely monitoring the actions, financial transactions, and crimes of illicit actors. Yet this surveillance goes beyond the requirements of their everyday job. In addition to focusing their attention on specific groups, they also track the activities of other police agents and agencies. They do this not only to protect themselves but also to generate information that they can later exchange with their illicit contacts.

Processes

Alongside specific resources and common practices, clandestine relationships between state agents and drug dealers enable three relational processes: (a) reciprocal signaling, (b) identity change, and (c) scale-shift. Police and members of other security agencies indicate to dealers where they can sell, which routes they should use to move their products, and which areas they should avoid. Drug dealers signal to police forces where their competitors are selling— information that can be used to extort or capture these actors and/ or obtain drugs to sell. This process of signaling can occur at a spur of the moment. When state forces uncover an illicit shipment or identify a bunker, drug dealers and their protectors rapidly amend prior routes and close down operations to avoid being caught.

Clandestine connections trigger a second process: identity change, i.e., an alteration in the identities of the actors involved.[3] While drug dealers become protected actors, agents of security forces cease to be enforcers of the law in the areas where the dealers operate. Police officers become not only protectors but also informants—locally known as *narcopolicías* or *polinarcos*.

Finally, as clandestine connections expand and contract, we see a process of *scale-shift* that impacts the range of actors involved in these clandestine networks. Across the cases we analyze, the extent and influence of collusion varies. This variation is dictated by the size and scope of their drug market operations. As highlighted in Table 5.2, larger organizations (such as Los Pescadores or Los Monos) have more contacts with security forces than smaller ones (such as Los Vagones). As we saw in the previous chapter, members of Los Vagones maintained contacts with just two agents in the Buenos Aires State Police to protect their localized operations. Larger groups, we will show, do not rely exclusively on local police; they construct what we call a "patchwork of protection" provided by members of different state agencies at the local, state, and federal levels. This variation is a matter of not only the group's size but also its internal differentiation. As we will see in the next chapter, organizations such as Los Pescadores, which are involved in more dimensions of these illicit supply chains (import, distribution, and sales), have more diversified contacts within security forces. As clandestine connections expand, we see a process of scale-shift at work that leads to a broader network involving a wider range of actors. In the remainder of this chapter, we delve into the "complex web of interdependencies"[4] between state security agents and members of the drug market group called Los Monos to *show* (different from exclusively *telling*) how collusion works on the ground.

Los Monos

Los Monos was one of the most (in)famous drug market organizations operating in contemporary Argentina. Active since the early 2000s, Los Monos produced and distributed cocaine and marijuana

Table 5.2. A Comparison of Drug Trafficking Organizations

Overview of the locations, operations, and relationships of collusion among drug-trafficking organizations analyzed.

Organization	Location	Scale	Drug-Related Activities			Relationships with State Actors			
			Smuggling	Production	Distribution	State Police	Federal Police	National Guard	Others
Los Vagones	Buenos Aires	Neighborhood			√	√			
Los Monos	Rosario	Municipal		√	√	√	√		
Los Pescadores	Corrientes	Inter-state	√	√	√	√	√	√	
La Banda de Raúl	Buenos Aires	Neighborhood	√						√

in Rosario, the third largest city in the country. The group imported coca from Bolivia and then refined it into cocaine and paco in a network of "kitchens" located in the poor neighborhoods of Las Flores, 17 de Agosto, and La Granada. At the time of the investigation, Los Monos was led by a man we call Murray who worked with a close group of associates—all of whom were related by family ties—to coordinate an extensive network of managers, producers, and street-level dealers.[5] Murray oversaw every aspect of the group's operation, from high-level issues involving the drug supply chain and security to managing the details of everyday communication (phones and radios), materials (e.g., the plastic tubes to pack the cocaine), and even the shifts of each seller.

Murray also made and maintained the group's clandestine relationships with security forces, acting as the primary point of contact who then channeled information to others. According to court documents, many of his subordinates (street-level dealers called "soldiers" and "satellites") were not even aware of these relations, although they were the ones who most directly confronted the threat of arrest. Murray had a particularly close relationship with a police officer who we call Belporto. An officer of the local police force, Belporto worked as a "data processor" for Los Monos (De Los Santos and Lascano 2017), passing information to Murray about planned operations, surveillance, and weapons and ammunition, as well advice about when and where it was safe to do business.

Over the past two decades, members of Los Monos have been associated with at least 50 murders. Yet according to journalists Germán De Los Santos and Hernán Lascano (2017:1272), "neither police nor prosecutors nor judges bothered them."[6] Although state agents may not have "bothered" Los Monos, court documents attest that they participated in a network of clandestine relationships that was clearly linked to the group's use of violence.[7] The following event—extracted from wiretapped phone conversations and supported with reports by investigative journalists—highlights the blatant use of violence by Los Monos.

In the middle of the day, a man named Demarre was targeted by members of Los Monos in a drive-by shooting. On a wiretapped phone, Murray called Belporto to find out whether he was dead: "Demarre is in the hospital, check to see how he is doing." The night before, the former leader of Los Monos, "Pájaro" Cantero, was murdered at the bar called Infinity Night. Members of Los Monos thought that Demarre, who was the bar owner, was involved in the plot to kill their leader. As one asserted on the phone, Demarre had "agreed to meet with Pájaro at the bar and, once he arrived, called the hitman who killed him." Based on this suspicion, a member of Los Monos attacked him in broad daylight as he and his wife picked their children up from school. A few minutes after that first call, Officer Belporto called Murray back. He said about Demarre: "Seven shots. He is done."

The death of Pájaro unleashed a series of retaliatory killings. After Demarre died, members of Los Monos turned their attention to finding the person responsible for murdering their leader. Reporting on the events that ensued, one of Argentina's national newspapers ran the ominous headline "The Night When the War Began." Over the next 48 hours, Los Monos targeted the family of Milton César, the person thought to be Pájaro's actual assassin. They killed his mother, brother, and a friend. At least four more people were murdered in direct connection with the assassination of Pájaro over the next couple months.

Discussing Demarre's murder later on, Officer Belporto kept Murray informed about the progress of the police investigation. The car used in the drive-by shooting of Demarre had been seen by dozens of witnesses and its image captured by the street surveillance cameras. According to Belporto, that was the only piece of information the police officers had. He advised Murray: "Make that car vanish, understood?" A few hours later, wiretapped conversations suggest that the car was taken to a body shop and transformed into a used black and yellow taxi that was later put up for sale at a car dealership in a neighboring province.

Developing the "Arreglo"

Like gang leaders in other parts of the world, the top leadership of Los Monos are busy people who deal with matters both internal and external to the organization on a daily basis.[8] Like members of Los Vagones, they spent a lot of time talking about the logistics of their operations, including the purchase, production, transportation, and storage of drugs and weapons and the transfer and lending of money. For example, one dealer asked a leader, "How much do I give to Esteban?" The leader responded: "Give him ten thousand in small bills." They also talked about more mundane details of their operations, including vehicles used for various criminal activities and the need to charge and change phones and radios.

Members also exchanged information among themselves about police activity near their drug selling points ("bunkers") and their affiliates ("kids," "satellites"). As one member of Los Monos told another in a wiretapped phone conversation, "Don't worry, I took all the merchandise and the kids out of the bunker."

In many more conversations, drug dealers and police agents shared information about planned raids. In one set of exchanges, police officers gave Murray details about their plans. One said, "I just talked to Pedele [another officer], and he tells me that either tomorrow or the next day, there's going to be some 'noise' [police action]." Another officer told Murray, "If I see that they [the police] are going towards there [your way], I'll let you know. . . . If I don't call you, it means that we are not going there." On still another occasion, a police officer offered advice for Murray to pass along to his "kids" on the street: "Tell your kids not to have anything strange on them. There are cops stopping cars, checking trunks, everything. It's on 12th Avenue. . . . It's a huge police operation . . . fifty cops on each side of the street."

As in Arquitecto Tucci, security agents also provided dealers with information about ongoing state surveillance operations, from the identity of unmarked police cars roaming nearby to the likelihood of their phones being wiretapped. For example, Murray called a police officer named Pedele to ask about "a white Volkswagen Gol, plate ZPQ-134." Officer Pedele told him it could belong to the "green bugs," referring to the Airport Security Police. Another officer named Dastin told Murray that he learned from a friend in the National Guard that "they had wiretapped a few phones and there are going to be raids tonight. You have to be careful, I don't know whose phone is being tapped.... Just in case, be careful tonight."

In another brief conversation, Officer Belporto informed Murray that agents were surveilling the organization and that he should be careful where he went. They then agreed to meet at "the usual place." As these private conversations attest, police and drug dealers regularly exchange what we call *protective* information: information that serves to shelter dealers from police actions and other state actors. For example, in 2014 the National Guard planned a large-scale, coordinated operation in Rosario targeting Los Monos. Journalists Germán De los Santos and Hernán Lascano (2017:1146) documented what transpired:

On April 4, 2014, Sergio Berni, Federal Secretary of Security, gathered 2,500 national guards on a property in San Nicolas, sixty kilometers from Rosario. They disguised the impending operation as a seminar on climate change for the security forces. A few hours later they disembarked without warning in Rosario. Suddenly, Rosarinos saw patrol helicopters flying through the sky and vans from the National Guard patrolling the streets. That afternoon, federal forces raided sixty-nine bunkers. They were mostly empty. A few hours before, the State Police had leaked the information about Berni's operation.

As this failed operation attests, protective information circulates not only during day-to-day operations but also in anticipation of large-scale events.

Drug dealers and police officers also talked about past raids. Referring to a raid of a dealer's apartment, Murray told Officer Huberto, "The job you guys did on that place on Friday . . . they [the police] stole clothes, the refrigerator, the TV, a motorcycle, they took everything." Huberto replied, "Are you sure it was us? Because the only job we did on Friday was on another guy."

As this conversation and many others illustrate, information flows both ways: Police officers not only provide inside information, but they also rely on information from their illicit contacts. For example, when his sporting goods store was broken into, the owner, who also worked as a policeman, called Murray to find out if he knew the perpetrators: "Do you know those guys who own a blue Ford? They robbed my store. I have the plate number. They took jackets, sneakers, some other clothes." Murray told him he would look into the matter.

Although court documents do not chronicle the foundational negotiation that established these clandestine relations, they do clearly show the exchanges that are at the heart of interactions between drug dealers and state agents. As we will see, the *arrangement* that develops over time between state actors and extra-legal organizations like Los Monos—for example, the relationship between Murray and Officer Belporto—is both provisional and reciprocal.

Competition and Retaliation

Clandestine relationships involve more than just the early warnings gleaned from the exchange of protective information. Los Monos also regularly exchanged *competitive* information about the local drug market with their contacts in state agencies. For example, Murray not only learned about impending raids to his drug bunkers, but he also obtained details about those doing business close to him. If drug selling points were not protected by another police agent, police officers would give Murray the green light to "go ahead and take them out." The information provided by police was then used by drug dealers to (violently) remove competitors. This demonstrates one of the ways in which collusion shapes violence on the ground: channeling physical attacks towards specific targets.

This exchange of competitive information is similarly reciprocal. Murray regularly provided police officers with information about drug activity on the part of the group's competitors, such as the location of bunkers not associated with Los Monos that the police could raid. According to court documents, data provided by dealers were then exploited by the police to increase the number of raids and arrests.

Police officers also provided dealers with what we call *retaliatory* information that served purposes other than to evade apprehension or reduce competition. For example, police officers talked to their illicit contacts about which police officers could be trusted. For example, in one exchange, an agent from the National Guard named Gardenal asked a leader of Los Monos if he knew Officer Belporto. The leader replied, "Yes, yes, he's cool. You can trust him. He's like you, take it easy. He's for real. He's cool, and he delivers." Discussions about trust and loyalty were useful not just to protect the group's leaders and its operations but also to fuel retaliation. For example, police officers passed along the names and home addresses of law enforcement agents who had been involved in raids or were part of ongoing investigations so that dealers could strike back against those involved. Security agents used such discussions of loyalty as an opportunity to reassure dealers of their own trustworthiness and dependability: "You know that if it [a raid] comes from my side, I'll let you know immediately," "Anything you need, you let me know," "Do you need help with anything? Count on me, whatever you need." Phrases like these sprinkled throughout the wiretapped conversations highlight the fact that sharing insider information was also used to maintain collusive relationships between police and drug dealers.

Interestingly, these conversations also addressed the organization's own members. Some of this information appeared neutral. For example, police informed the leaders of Los Monos about the health status of a member in the hospital (or as we saw above, an "enemy") and the legal status of another who had been arrested. On other occasions, however, police officers passed along more sensitive information, for example, informing leaders about people who talked too much or too fast. For example, on a wiretapped call, Officer Belporto told Murray that a police officer was not to be trusted, saying that he was "pointing fingers at your people." Murray, already cognizant of the matter, responded, "I know that he pretends to be our friend and he then stabs you in the back."

In a different conversation, Officer Pedele told Murray, "That guy of yours [referring to a member of Los Monos] is kind of a big-mouth. He told the cops everything, who he talks to, who he works for, who he doesn't work for. . . . He is a snitch [*vigilante*], he is use-less. . . . He gave up names, numbers, everything."

A fascinating aspect of this exchange suggests another way that relationships of collusion operate. In addition to exchanging goods and information, police officers give drug dealers *advice* on how to behave in the future. For example, Pedele offered a piece of advice to Murray so that he could pass it to his subordinates. When discussing police interrogation, he said, "When they start talking, I punch them once so that they talk, and twice so that they shut up. . . . It's important that they have this in mind. I don't care [if they talk] but you're my friend, I tell it to you like it is." In addition to providing practical advice on interacting with the police, officers also occasionally acted as representatives of the drug market groups when dealing with state authorities or other extra-legal actors, for example, when leaders of Los Monos had to negotiate the amount of bribe money with the police chief or when they needed to resolve territorial disputes with other dealers.

The Killing of Hueso

Late one night in May 2013, 32-year-old Hueso and his friends were hanging out on a street corner in Luján, a poor barrio on the southern outskirts of Rosario. Two men and two women quickly drove by on two motorcycles and shot at the group. One of Hueso's friends fired back at the attackers. In seconds, two were shot—Hueso and Pepe, one of the attackers. Hueso died hours later in the hospital. Four days later, Hueso's nine-year-old nephew was injured in another drive-by shooting while he was playing on his computer inside his house in the same neighborhood—apparently in retaliation for Pepe's injury.

Local news outlets portrayed these shootings as the outcome of a long-standing familial beef (*bronca*) that was unrelated to drug trafficking in the area. Hueso, residents told reporters, had never been involved in any sort of illicit business. He used to "package and sell kitchen towels," residents said. If anything, they joked, "he was a towel trafficker." Residents referenced a "problem" between Hueso and his attackers, and without citing any particular source, the local news reported that the Murallón siblings were the perpetrators of the attack.

A close examination of the wiretapped phone conversations during this period, however, offers far less certainty about the series of events. Wiretappings reveal that Hueso was indeed a member of Los Monos and one of Murray's foot soldiers. Conversations between Murray and his right-hand man, Negro ("the man who manages the business," as Murray put it in another phone conversation), captured the aftermath of the shooting. In one, Murray himself speculated about the origins of the attack and suspected it was connected to the recent seizure of the attackers' bunker. In another wiretapped conversation, Murray asked a contact in the police force about whether this previous raid was related to this particular attack.

While illuminating, these conversations do not allow us to adjudicate between different versions of what happened to Hueso and why. For example, we cannot know for sure whether the shooting was related to drug activity or an interpersonal feud. Rather, a detailed examination of the sequence of these conversations reveals how clandestine relations between drug dealers and police officers operate as they navigate this contested terrain and high-stakes business. In what follows, we present lightly edited dialogues between Murray, members of Los Monos, and police officers right after Hueso's murder. These exchanges show the attempts to find out who the attackers were and where they went in the immediate aftermath. They also demonstrate the interactional process leading up to a violent retaliation. As the events unfold, we also learn what happens when bribed police officers (mis)behave in ways that are unexpected to dealers.

We begin with the conversation between Murray and Negro at the moment when Murray found out about the shooting:

MURRAY: Negro?

NEGRO: Listen to me, asshole. They drove by here [the drug selling point] and they shot at Hueso.

MURRAY: Who drove by?

NEGRO: Those [dealers] whose business was busted a while back. They drove by and shot him in his torso.

MURRAY: Who were they?

NEGRO: Those [dealers] who had that bunker that got shut down....

MURRAY: But, whose business was that?

NEGRO: I don't know! They shot at him, dude.

MURRAY: Well, take him to the hospital . . . but whose business was it?

Without any answers, they got off the phone. A few minutes later, the conversation continued:

NEGRO: Hey.

MURRAY: Listen, what were the shooters driving?

NEGRO: Motorcycles.

MURRAY: And did Hueso see them? Did he know them?

NEGRO: No, no.

MURRAY: Oh, so maybe it has nothing to do with the business. . . .

NEGRO: Yes, it might have been Roberto. . . . It seems like it was him. . . .

MURRAY: Did he have a beef with Hueso?

NEGRO: No, no, no. Hueso was just there . . . and then pum pum pum pum pum, they shot ten times. And our kid who was guarding [the bunker] shot back a couple of times. . . .

MURRAY: But did he shoot into the air? He should have shot at them!

NEGRO: Yes, he broke his arm. . . .

MURRAY: The other's [guy's] arm?

NEGRO: Yes, you have no idea how he was screaming. . . .

MURRAY: Ah, okay, so Hueso is injured and so is one of them. . . .

NEGRO: Yes, but in his arm. Hueso got hit in his stomach. . . . We are at the hospital. The bullet went in right under his belly button.

MURRAY: Surgery?

NEGRO: Yes, he went through Emergency. . . .

MURRAY: Okay, keep me updated. Close the bunker for a while.

While Negro took Hueso to the hospital, Murray immediately activated his networks within the local police to find out who attacked his bunker. He first called police officer Belporto to ask him to find out whether anyone had checked into a local emergency room. Over the phone, Officer Belporto reassured him that he would pass word to his contacts in the police force to find out. He then asked Murray if he knew who the attackers were. Murray told him he would find out and let him know.

After a few hours, Negro called Murray again to check in.

MURRAY: Negro?

NEGRO: Listen, can you talk there?

MURRAY: Yes, tell me.

NEGRO: The kid died.

MURRAY: Hueso?

NEGRO: Yes.

MURRAY: Okay, and what's up with his family? Does he have a mother or something?

NEGRO: He has a mother, a brother, a girlfriend.

MURRAY: Okay, listen, did you talk to any of them?

NEGRO: Yes, I know them. They live there in the neighborhood. . . . I am going back to the hospital.

MURRAY: Who took him [Hueso] to the hospital? Was that you? Be careful, because the cops are going to be there. They are going to ask you questions. . . . If the family needs anything, if we have to pay for the funeral, just pay for everything.

NEGRO: Okay, stay calm, I'll take care of everything.

MURRAY: Okay, find out who the attacker was.

NEGRO: Yes, they told me it was Roberto.

MURRAY: Find out if they injured him too.

NEGRO: Yes, yes, he is injured, because he screamed out loud.

Immediately after this conversation, Murray called Officer Belporto and told him the name of the attacker. Belporto asked for the last name, and Murray promised to get back to him with the information. He called Negro:

NEGRO: I am listening.

MURRAY: What's Roberto's last name?

NEGRO: Marionetti.

MURRAY: Marionetti? Ahh . . . Is he one of the Marionettis?

NEGRO: Yes.

Murray then contacted Officer Belporto to pass along the last name of the attacker. Belporto knew the suspect, responding, "[H]e is a dickface [*cara de verga*]." Murray then reminded him, "[I]f you find out that he is in a hospital, let me know." "Yes, for sure," Belporto said, "stay calm."

The phone calls between Murray and Officer Belporto continued as they received more information about the shooting.

BELPORTO: Murray?
MURRAY: I found out there were four of them.
BELPORTO: [On] two motorcycles?
MURRAY: Yes. [It was] Camisa, Roberto, Besito and another one that I don't know.
BELPORTO: Well, so far, nobody has shown up [at a hospital]. You will have to solve this issue yourself. That guy [Roberto] is a rat.
MURRAY: We'll get back at them. We need a few days so that things cool down a bit.
BELPORTO: Yes, those kids are good-for-nothing.
MURRAY: Okay, let me know if one of them checks into a hospital.
BELPORTO: Yeah, as soon as that happens, I'll let you know.

Over the next few days, Negro was detained by police officers in Luján's local police precinct. According to court documents, he threatened the mother of Hueso's alleged killer to extract information about her son's whereabouts. Murray called Officer Belporto to explain what had happened: "He was about to pay for the funeral and they detained him," Murray said before asking if he had a contact in the Luján precinct. Murray's own contact, the local police chief—Chief Abarca—was unresponsive. "[He's] not picking up the phone. He is an asshole. . . . I want to face him and let him know that . . . *if we pay [bribes], he has to respond*" (*our emphasis*).

Officer Belporto promised he would look into it and warned Murray that the homicide division would soon be on the scene of Hueso's murder, so he should close his bunker for the time being.

Negro was later released without charges or explanation. Murray speculated why he had been detained. On the phone with Officer Belporto, he wondered if officers at the precinct detained Negro to "extort him" (*luquearlo*). Agitated, he insisted that Chief Abarca "has to respond. . . . [T]hey shouldn't detain my guy. Abarca pretends he is a fool and I asked him if he thinks I'm an idiot. I pay him. How can he arrest my guy? This is the guy that manages my business. And you don't pick up the phone, and I have to pay again. . . . I am no idiot."

"Smear the Chief"

While leaders of Los Monos tried to untangle what had happened to prompt the series of drive-by shootings, residents of Luján expressed their concerns about the local police to media outlets. To a reporter, one resident explained, "What happened last night [the night of Hueso's murder] is normal. The motorcycles pass by and just by looking at them they shoot you." He added, "They do that because it's arranged with the local police station. It's simple: those who fuck up [can] put down some money and leave." Seizing the opportunity created by these brewing complaints, Murray decided to act on his own grievance against Chief Abarca. But rather than use violence or stop paying bribes, he staged a rally at the local police station to protest police incompetence and complicity with criminals.

On the day of the rally, wiretapped conversations between Murray and Negro captured their discussions about logistics ("We are preparing the fliers") and attendance ("Did a lot of people show up?"). They also brainstormed the messages they wanted convey to the media:

MURRAY: If you talk to *La Ciudad* [the local paper], tell them that Hueso had nothing to do with the business. He was just drinking with his friends on the corner.

NEGRO: Yes, yes, that is all settled. I told them he was a street vendor.
MURRAY: Good. Make them throw dirt at the Luján police station.
NEGRO: Yes, and they know him [Chief Abarca]. He is dirty, dirty, dirty.

In these exchanges, Murray and Negro even discussed the reasons why neighbors were distressed. Developing what social movement scholars would call a "diagnostic frame," they agreed on the following slogan for the protest: "Smear the chief."[9]

While the protest was clearly orchestrated by leaders of Los Monos, nothing in the brief newspaper report describing the protest suggested that participants or the media were aware of this.[10] What this protest shows is that the balance of power in these clandestine relations shifts over time. While Chief Abarca had worked with (and allegedly received payments from) Los Monos, the breakdown of this provisional but still patterned relationship gave Murray the upper hand. This was confirmed a few days later. In a conversation with another police contact, Murray explicitly used this public protest to threaten other officers who failed to deliver: "You better behave. You don't want me to organize a rally there." To this threat, the officer responded by reasserting his trustworthiness: "I have a friends' code, I behave well, I deliver [*Yo tengo códigos de amigos, yo me porto bien, yo cumplo*]."

* * *

Longtime producers and distributors of illegal drugs, Los Monos ran a violent operation that had extensive contacts in various state security agencies in the city of Rosario. This chapter described the reciprocal exchange of goods, information, and advice between members of the group and police officers. Whereas scholarship has documented the presence of these clandestine relations in many Latin American countries, this chapter detailed the actual content of police-criminal collusion. We focused on the particular type of *engagements* between state and criminal actors[11] by scrutinizing the exchange of protective, competitive, and retaliatory information. We also illustrated some of the relational processes that unfold between drug dealers and officers engaged in clandestine relationships. We saw how identities shift: Police officers become not only protectors but also advocates, representatives, and informants of drug market groups (*infiltrados*, or "our cops," as they are referred to by Los Monos).[12] We also saw how the parties signal to each other: *Polinarcos* indicate where it is safe to conduct their illicit business while dealers attempt to get rid of competitors by forwarding tips on their location and operations to the police.

The next chapter analyzes two additional cases that shed light on the nuances of these clandestine relationships. The first part takes us to Argentina's northern border, where an organization that we call Los Pescadores smuggled drugs to distribute throughout the country. We analyze how Los Pescadores, a larger, more extended organization, created a patchwork of protection and responded to political pressure. In the second part of the chapter, we return to Buenos Aires to analyze La Banda de Raúl, a smaller group operating in a crowded drug market in greater Buenos Aires that relied on a broker to mediate its clandestine relationships with the State Police. These two cases add important dimensions to our close inspection of the dynamics of collusion, providing additional evidence of a locally grounded form of state ambivalence.

6

Patchworks of Protection

> Traffickers have all arranged with people from the Naval
> Police, the National Guard, the Federal Police, and the
> local police. . . . When they go out on patrol, they let eve-
> rything go. . . . [Traffickers] make arrangements with the
> police chief: If there is no money, they cannot go through.
> That's why they have to pay: so that they can sell drugs.
>
> Testimony of a protected witness

In May 2014, the Federal Police opened an investigation into drug dealing in a shantytown in the city of Buenos Aires. The investigation identified a town in a northern province as the source of the drugs. After a three-year investigation, in March 2017 authorities launched a massive police operation involving 600 national guards who conducted 47 simultaneous raids in three different provinces. Twenty-eight individuals were arrested, among them several political authorities in the small town of Yapurá. According to news sources, the scandal shocked the general public but not the local residents. They were well aware of the local authorities' participation in drug trafficking: "The people of Yapurá were the least surprised," wrote one reporter. "Everyone knew of the alleged links. Such well-oiled illegal system was a source of income for many inhabitants." It was, as another news report put it, a "major blow against narcopolitics."[1]

Clandestine relationships between police and criminals are not simply economic transactions where cash is exchanged for

The Ambivalent State: Police-Criminal Collusion at the Urban Margins. Javier Auyero, Oxford University Press (2019). © Oxford University Press.
DOI: 10.1093/oso/9780190915537.001.0001

protection or inaction. Rather, as we have shown, they involve a complex exchange of goods, information, and advice that shape the interactions and practices of those involved. In the previous chapters, we reconstructed cases that exposed collusion between state security forces and members of Los Vagones in Buenos Aires and Los Monos in Rosario. Investigative reports and particularly wiretapped phone conversations allowed us to metaphorically go behind the scenes in order to examine the actual micro-dynamics of collusion. Police officers and illicit actors buy and sell cars, guns, and ammunition from each other. They also share different types of information, from the insights that help both parties shelter themselves from detection (protective information) to those that illuminate the operation of illicit markets (competitive information) and offer insights into trust and loyalty (retaliatory information). By unpacking the content of collusion, we seek to show that the state acts in very ambivalent ways. In some instances, the state enforces the law, while at other times in the same territories and among the same destitute populations, it breaks it. Moreover, these clandestine relationships are contingent, volatile, and reciprocal arrangements. Mistakes happen, last-minute improvisations take place, and relations break down and then are repaired, all of which shape violence on the ground.

In this chapter, we analyze police complicity with two additional drug market organizations. The first case examines the organization that we call "Los Pescadores" and illustrates how trafficking groups piece together protection from multiple state agencies, including not just police but also politicians and judges. The second case of La Banda de Raúl highlights the important ways that *arreglos*, or arrangements between drug traffickers and state agents, can be mediated by third parties and how these fragile connections can unravel. Each of our analytic reconstructions excludes many details about both the court cases and the individuals who were indicted. We focus here on what these cases add, complicate, and clarify about the relational underpinnings of collusion.

Los Pescadores

In 2017 in the small town of Yapurá (pop. 8,000), 28 individuals were charged with conspiracy in relation to their involvement in an organization that we call Los Pescadores, or The Fishermen. Based in the province of Corrientes on Argentina's northern border with Paraguay, Los Pescadores traffics marijuana into Argentina, supplying drugs to distributors across the country, including to members of Los Monos in Rosario. Nearly 10 tons of marijuana were seized during a series of arrests that led up to the indictment. While much of this was found in homes, bunkers, and cars, other hiding spots were more creative. For example, one investigation of the National Guard in 2016 discovered over 760,000 kilograms of marijuana by raking the shallow waters near the banks of the Paraná River. Of those charged, seven were high-ranking members of security forces, including a commander from the National Guard, an agent from the Naval Police, two officers from the Federal Police, and three from the state police, most notably, the chief of the local precinct. In addition, two high-ranking local politicians—the mayor and deputy mayor—were also indicted.

Unlike the previous two cases, in the months preceding the arrests, members of Los Pescadores were very aware of the likelihood that their phones were tapped and their movements were closely monitored. Their short conversations and text messages constantly referred to the need to be careful about what was being said and to anticipate possible failures: "We cannot talk about these things on the phone. . . . [T]he National Guard and Naval Police listen to all the calls and they can implicate us"; "This is not a subject to speak about over the phone"; "We can't talk on the phone because it's mortal poison." After a high-ranking drug trafficker was stopped (but not detained) by the Naval Police, he called the deputy mayor of Yapurá, saying, "Tomorrow, I'll stop by your place and we'll talk, because we can't talk much over the phone."

As a result of the accurate assessment that their phones had been wiretapped, members of Los Pescadores almost never referred explicitly to the purchase, storage, transportation, or sale of drugs. Rather, they used a coded language that drew from the main activity of their town: fishing. Varieties of marijuana were named after certain types of fish (*dorado* or *surubí*); purchases were referred to as "fishing" (they "go fishing" in Paraguay); shipments were called "horses"; and subsequent transportation and distribution were discussed as things to be "moved" and "unloaded."

Los Pescadores imported marijuana into Argentina from Paraguay, maintaining an extensive transnational transportation network. The testimony of an informant in witness protection described their trafficking route in detail: "[F]rom Paraguay, it [drug shipment] comes from the large plantations of Pedro Caballero. That is a village in Paraguay, in the north of Paraguay. They bring it by truck to the shore and then across by boats to Corrientes." The court case notes that the group sought the use of minors to move drugs across the border because they were able to "disguise the real motive of the trip." Of those indicted, one was a local teenager.

The group was especially active along the banks of the Paraná River, where traffickers navigated a fleet of boats through the murky brown waters: "They are in the water from Monday to Monday, fifty fishing boats, all motor boats, all with new engines," the informant testified. Once in Argentina, Los Pescadores used ground transportation to move shipments from their storage facilities in Yapurá to different destinations across the country. As the informant explained, "From the boats, they pass to the Argentine coast. . . . From there, [drugs] are loaded into vans or they pass directly to the houses along to the Paraná River. From there, they . . . distribute it, they take it to the destination. I understand that they go to Rosario, to Santa Fe . . . to Buenos Aires."

Whereas the other organizations we have analyzed primarily sold drugs to petty dealers and end-users, Los Pescadores dealt in much larger quantities. As the informant explained, "Each boat carries more or less five hundred or six hundred kilos of marijuana." Court documents revealed that the organization often paid for drugs with cash, but it was not uncommon for Los Pescadores to exchange drugs for cars and boats. For example, in one conversation between traffickers, one said, "I exchange[d] 'the animal' for a Honda Civic 2005." In fact, according to court documents, members of the organization even owned a car dealership in a nearby town and used the business to launder drug money.

Like the other cases we have examined, Los Pescadores operated a hierarchical organization, and many of the members were related through family ties. In addition to a small group of leaders (many of whom were indicted in this case and went to prison), the organization also relied on boat drivers; "bellhops" (*maleteros*), who unloaded drug shipments from boats to trucks; and truck drivers (*fleteros*), who transported drugs to different destinations. Drivers were also assisted by "pointers" (*punteros*), who traveled ahead of the shipments to watch for police. As news reports indicated, many poor youth in the small town made a living by working in this illicit economy.

Because members suspected their conversations were being surveilled, the exchanges captured on wiretapped phones were short and never as explicit as in the cases of Los Monos or Los Vagones. Rather, the conversations were almost always used to arrange face-to-face meetings. Having said this, the 665-page indictment contains ample (but often coded) information that both confirms the existence of clandestine connections between drug-trafficking organizations and members of state security forces and adds a new dimension to what we already know about their operation. First, given the extent of their operations, Los Pescadores diversified their connections with various security forces and included within their protective network elected officials and, apparently although he was not indicted, a judge. Second, the protection afforded to Los Pescadores was geographically uneven. While Los Pescadores enjoyed nearly complete protection within the town where it stored its products, protective arrangements became more fragile and less predictable beyond those boundaries.

Securing Home Base

What does such a comprehensive and predictable protection network look like? In the town of Yapurá, Los Pescadores counted on the full protection of the local police. The court case provides a detailed description of the relationship between traffickers and a man named Sergio, the local police chief, as "fluid and permanent," allowing Los Pescadores to store marijuana within city limits without much trouble. As in other cases, traffickers regularly discussed "the price of fish" (i.e., drugs) and the amount to pay to Chief Sergio among themselves. In one wiretapped conversation, traffickers referred explicitly to the bribe (*punta*) paid to the police chief for services rendered. As one trafficker stated on a wiretapped phone, "[C]all the police [and tell them] to go to town, to the entrance of the church. . . . [H]e doesn't know who they are but [Chief Sergio] will take the bribe." In Yapurá, this money clearly bought non-enforcement, where local police were told "to let things be" (*dejar hacer*, in the language of the court case) so that members of Los Pescadores could "sell [drugs] in peace." As a result, traffickers relied heavily on Chief Sergio and his officers to conduct their illicit business. As one member said to another on the phone, "Look, you're putting a lot of faith [in him]. Everything is crazy, everyone has weapons, 9mm, etc." The speaker was referencing the other clandestine organizations conducting business out of Yapurá. As the court case attests, local police officers also turned a blind eye to illegal gambling and horse racing within city limits.

Court documents confirm the exchange of goods between traffickers and the police. For example, Los Pescadores sold drugs directly to Chief Sergio. "Do you have *dorado* or *surubí*?" the police chief asked a trafficker on a wiretapped phone call. This type of transaction may help explain the marijuana that was later found in the local police station. Although we can only speculate, these drugs may have been used to plant evidence on others, sold for profit, or intended for personal consumption.

This protective network was also effectively endorsed by the two highest local politicians, who also maintained relationships with members of Los Pescadores. As court documents attest, both the mayor and deputy mayor helped to coordinate the movement of narcotics in the town and ensured members act with impunity. When these connections were exposed, the media used the term "narcopolitics" to report on this case. In many respects, elected officials acted as eyes on the streets for the organization. Traffickers referred to the deputy mayor as a *chajá* or *campana*: someone who would signal to members the location of security forces. In one phone conversation with a trafficker, the deputy mayor explained, "[T]he National Guard agents are driving a gray [Ford] Focus and are taking pictures of your house. I'm letting you know in case it's useful." While there was no talk of direct payment to politicians, one informant under witness protection testified that Los Pescadores had financed the mayor's electoral campaign.

The court case refers to the group's protective network as a "connivance of different members of the local police, the Federal Police, the National Guard, and those at the local municipality." Evidence gathered for the trial shows the central role of not only politicians but also members of the judiciary. For example, a lawyer indicted in the case was said to be in charge of "arrangements" made with a judge and paid for by the traffickers. Another informant confirmed this collusion, testifying about a lawyer who engaged in bureaucratic manipulation, paying a judge to quickly release those who were arrested. In a wiretapped conversation, a trafficker referenced the same judge: "He is really cool. If you give him some money, he makes arrangements [*le tirás unos pesos y se arregla*]." Another informant clarified how this manipulation took place: "Judge Tirón and also his secretary, Jorge Garcia . . . They make arrangements when narcos fall. After two days, they [the narcos] can leave, so to speak. They give them cash, money in hand. The lawyer is in charge of this. He is the lawyer for all the narcos there. There are also other lawyers that work with him and do the same thing." As the informant suggests, key actors in the judiciary collaborated with members of Los Pescadores (and potentially other illicit actors) to keep their members out of jail.

Patchworking Protection

Despite this near-complete protection in Yapurá, Los Pescadores encountered ongoing threats from other security forces. Given the centrality of long-distance transportation in their operations (over water from Paraguay and via ground into the provinces), clandestine connections between elected officials, members of security forces, and traffickers served mainly one purpose: to avoid detection from the security forces that monitored borders and interstate traffic. Together, these forces were called "bad bugs" (bichos malos) or "ugly bugs" (bichos feos). For Los Pescadores, controlling roads and highways was essential, as federal agents like the National Guard, Naval Police, and Federal Police sought to intercept trafficking routes.

Los Pescadores relied on a patchwork of contacts in different state agencies to avoid detection. According to the informant (arrepentido), traffickers had "arranged" or "fixed" (arreglados) relationships with certain members of the Naval Police, National Guard, and police at the state and federal levels. He explained, "[I]f there is no money, they cannot get through." Conversations among traffickers also referenced the various "contacts" that they had with members of the security forces to allow shipments to pass without disruption.

Most of the time, traffickers exchanged information among themselves about the presence of security forces in the areas where they were "working" or "fishing." "The greens are at the toll booth," one trafficker warned another, referring to members of the National Guard, also known as the "parrots" or "lettuce" because of their green uniforms. Other traffickers gave directions to the truckers, saying things like "Take a detour" or warning them, "The boats of the Naval Police are there." On other occasions, lookouts shared information about when to move drugs and how to prevent mistakes: "Do not unload, the military has arrived"; "Put it back, it's not safe to cross now. . . . I'll let you know when things go back to normal." Although local police rarely interfered with their activities in Yapurá, these conversation excerpts suggest that other security agents regularly forced traffickers to modify their work routines beyond the city limits. One trafficker made this explicit: "[W]e didn't work because the parrots were around all night."

In addition to sharing information among themselves, Los Pescadores leveraged their local protection network in Yapurá to gather information about policing beyond the relatively secure confines of the town. Chief Sergio, for example, not only "look[ed] elsewhere" in exchange for his bribe, but he also provided intelligence about the locations of other security forces. Wiretapped conversations recorded Chief Sergio telling traffickers that "Federal Police are on the road" or warning them of "procedures" (i.e., drug raids). In addition to this protective information, conversations document traffickers asking the local police to *actually intervene* on their behalf. For instance, on one occasion, traffickers asked Chief Sergio to stop members of the National Guard who were patrolling roads that they used for their shipments.

Traffickers also cultivated a web of contacts to access information from within regional and national security agencies. For example, Perez, a sergeant from the Federal Police, informed traffickers about the presence of "ducks" (Naval Police) and "greens" (National Guard) who were "going around right where you have to leave [on the road]." He added, "[T]he greens are listening to us." Another sergeant named Juarez—this time from the State Police—also provided important logistic information. "Are the feds coming to town now?" a trafficker asked. The sergeant replied, "Nothing. If there's something, I'll let [you] know." Later, he told the trafficker, "There's a group [of state forces] at the crossroads." On a different occasion, a trafficker asked the same sergeant if they could "move around tonight." He responded, "Yes, no problem." Court records also document a series of text messages sent by this sergeant to traffickers detailing the location of patrolling security forces and the need to make last-minute adjustments to a prior itinerary. "Greens are being a plague," he warned via text. In a similar fashion, Los Pescadores obtained information about the targets of raids planned by the state police from a commander of the National Guard. In reference to this contact, one trafficker assured another on the phone, "[He] charges money to let things go by."

Information gathered from security forces was often intertwined in complex exchanges of goods and advice. For example, Perez, the sergeant from the Federal Police, would not only warn traffickers about impending raids but also negotiate his "cut" of their activities, in the form of drugs, vehicles, or the amount of money required to release members from jail. Text messages between traffickers and this sergeant attest to the close coordination they maintained. In one conversation, the sergeant wrote, "*Che*, I still have that present." The trafficker replied, "I need 300 for tomorrow . . . nice fish! Come [and] you can see." In another set of text messages, they discussed packets of narcotics as "girls" (*chicas*). In broken writing with no punctuation, the trafficker wrote, "How many girls are there?" The sergeant responded, "A hundred are pretty." This particular sergeant also teamed up with Los Pescadores to steal drugs from other trafficking groups. He told traffickers: "We have to play today. . . . I already told my players. . . . Tomorrow there won't be anybody around on the field." In this statement, the sergeant explicitly referenced planned raids on other groups. Every now and then, this sergeant would also conduct a counter raid targeting Los Pescadores, as he described it, to "keep up appearances."

Alongside the regular exchange of information, members of security forces, as in Arquitecto Tucci, also sold guns and ammunition to members of Los Pescadores. One day, a trafficker asked Juarez, the sergeant of the State Police: "Do you have bullets for my toy?" He responded, "Yes, a box is 1,200 pesos. If that's okay, stop by to pick it up." While some of these goods were seemingly exchanged fairly, there is also evidence of extortion. For instance, security forces opportunistically detained traffickers and asked for money to ensure their prompt release. These extortive practices involved not only people but goods: Court documents provide evidence that members of the Naval Police would seize vehicles from traffickers and then give them back in exchange for money.

Using the information passed through their clandestine connections, Los Pescadores often successfully evaded detection. But, as with Los Monos, these evasions did not always go as planned. Court documents also include details of mistakes that were made and rectified. For example, one afternoon the National Guard followed a truck carrying 200 kilograms of marijuana. Along the route, the truck was unexpectedly intercepted by the local police (who were in cahoots with traffickers). On the side of the road, members of local police told the National Guard that they had a court order to stop the truck. When asked for documentation, they became defensive, pointed their guns at the other agents, and then left the scene with the truck. Later on, the national guards who had witnessed this erratic behavior found the truck and its illicit cargo abandoned on the side of the road. This botched intervention ultimately resulted in traffickers "losing" their valuable shipments to security forces.

Political Pressure and the Problem of "Too Much Attention"

Los Pescadores enjoyed the most extensive local protection arrangement of all the groups we have examined in Argentina. Yet even these well-established *arreglos* were put to the test. Yapurá was not always a safe haven for members of Los Pescadores: The court case mentions an episode that disrupted the clandestine connections in the group's home base.

In July 2016, a 23-year-old man was killed in front of a local carwash. Just as the State Police began to investigate the scene, a car was mysteriously torched and another one was found nearby with a trunk filled with marijuana. Apparently, the murder was a "score settling" (*un ajuste de cuentas*) between Los Pescadores and another trafficking group operating in the area.[2] Following this dramatic series of events, the local police chief wanted to resolve the case quickly. With no suspect in custody, he began to pressure his contacts in Los Pescadores, who he thought were hiding those involved in the murder.

In the meantime, the small town began to receive increasing (and unwanted) scrutiny from the media and state authorities, something that not only drew attention to the drug activity in the region (as they speculated about whether the violence was drug-related) but also spotlighted the role of local authorities. In a wiretapped conversation after the murder, the mayor told a trafficker, "[T]hey are pressuring me from all sides [*Me están apretando por todos lados*]." According to the court case, Chief Sergio was also "receiving political pressure from the Governor to capture the killer. . . . The reason for the pressure was that the murder was framed by the media as a drug crime." In a text message sent to a trafficker, he wrote, "[They] have asked me to pass the list [of suspects] to the Minister."

With increasing attention on the town, Chief Sergio threatened to interrupt his provision of protection and prevent drug traffickers from "working quietly" until they handed over a suspect. In frantic conversations, traffickers discussed the difficulties they confronted in the aftermath of the murder when their protective arrangements broke down. Highlighting the negotiated and unstable character of protection, Chief Sergio sent the following text message to a trafficker: "You are always asking favors and when I need something, you're nowhere to be found. . . . [T]he thing is simple, ONCE [the murder suspect] APPEARS I WILL GO BACK TO DOING YOU FAVORS." The court case reiterated that until a fugitive was in custody, "the directive of the superiors of [the police chief] would be to allow no illicit activity—either drug sales, gambling or illegal horse races carried out by them." Under pressure, Chief Sergio ultimately followed through on his orders by sending police officers into the town and organizing a raid against Los Pescadores. He hoped that by seizing 700 kilos of marijuana, he would "send them a message": He would not allow trafficking until he had a fugitive in custody.

La Banda de Raúl

In 2015, six Buenos Aires State Police officers were arrested and accused of protecting an organization that we call "La Banda de Raúl." Far smaller and less powerful than Los Pescadores, this group was loosely tied to a larger network of traffickers devoted to the purchase, production, and distribution of illegal drugs.[3] This final case takes us back to the outskirts of the city of Buenos Aires, where La Banda de Raúl operated out of one of the approximately 33 informal settlements located in San Martín.[4] Court documents from this case corroborate our analysis of the resources, practices, and processes at the heart of police-criminal collusion. It also highlights the important ways that *arreglos*, or arrangements between drug traffickers and state agents, can be mediated by third parties and how these fragile connections can unravel.

La banda de literally translates to "the gang of." In this case, this drug trafficking organization was run by a man named Raúl. Like the previous groups we have analyzed and many others around the globe,[5] the organization had a hierarchical structure and many of its members were blood relatives. Its leader, Raúl, worked closely with his business partner, Nélida, and two of his children, Mica and

Diego. According to the indictment, this small group was "devoted to the trafficking of narcotics" and used its well-established connections with different police units to sell marijuana, cocaine, and paco to residents in the informal settlements of San Martín.

In terms of its location, size, and business operations, La Banda de Raúl may not seem distinct from the other cases we have presented thus far. Yet this case highlights an important way that power is negotiated at the urban margins. In addition to his family members and business partner, Raúl employed a man named Primo who worked as a broker between the organization and various state agencies.[6] Wiretaps of Primo's conversations with new dealers shed light on how relationships of collusion begin and how their actual form is shaped by incessant maneuvering, mutual concession, and limits imposed by other parties.

Brokering Collusion

Unlike the other cases we have discussed, the relationships of collusion between police forces and La Banda de Raúl were frequently mediated by a man named Primo, an intermediary with well-oiled contacts in state agencies. According to court proceedings, Primo would even "simulate being a cop" by hanging out at the local police precinct.

Although much about him remains unknown, Primo played a central role in facilitating the illicit business of La Banda de Raúl. First and most importantly, he coordinated the bribes that traffickers paid to the police. This involved negotiating the exact amount and timing of the payments, including both the weekly fee known as *el canon* (the tax) and the entry fee known as *la llave* (the key).[7] In addition to this administrative role, Primo also collected the bribe money from the organization and distributed it among his contacts in different units and branches of the police, making sure to save enough for his own cut of the fees.

Primo worked closely but not exclusively with La Banda de Raúl. Court proceedings registered three instances in which Primo offered his contacts to other dealers and put a price on the protection police could offer for them to continue doing business. When talking with a man who wanted to start selling drugs in the area, Primo explained, "You will have to pay them [one agency of the police] 500 dollars [US], half of what you pay us [another agency]." The man responded, "Okay, that sounds great." "Spectacular!" Primo replied. "A little bit of money [*una monedita*] for everybody and everything will be okay."

In another wiretapped phone conversation, Primo talked to Gastón, another dealer who was starting his business in the area. "Listen, this week you have to be discreet," Primo told him. "I'm arranging with the local precinct and with La Brigada[8] . . . so that you pay one sum to both and they can divide it up. If not, they are going to ask you for a lot of money. This week, don't stay in the same place. Try to change places. Be discreet. I should have news for you over the weekend. Everything is going to be alright." Primo also offered advice about the limits of his contacts: "We are not the only ones on the streets. I cover your ass with us. I can't cover your ass with everybody."

A dialogue between Primo and Raúl illuminates the extent of their clandestine connections, but also the potential conflicts involved in them. During one call, Primo told Raúl that he could make an arrangement with police officers from "La Casita," the Narcotics Division in San Martín, so that Raúl could distribute drugs in the area provided that he pay *la llave* and *el canon*. "Sure," Raúl told Primo. "Talk to them [at La Casita] but I don't want them to kill me [ask for too much money] because I am just starting up again. . . . I can't pay 500 dollars [US] per week for at least a month. . . . I'll be ruined." In exchange for this connection, Raúl provided Primo with information about a cocaine dealer to pass to the police officers so that they could "intercept" him.

When they spoke a few days later, Primo told Raúl that the officers from La Casita did not believe that he was just "starting up." Primo told him that the police officers knew he had already been working for a month. He pointed out to Raúl, they "haven't bothered you" at all during that time. Primo went on: "They want 600 dollars [US] for you to start. They want to be clear. They don't want any trouble. If after the end of the year, you have more work, it [the weekly *canon*] is going to go up." Primo and Raúl then agreed on the amount and on the time and place to make the payment.

Similar to Los Vagones, who we discussed in Chapter 4, bribes were negotiated based on not only what the police demanded but also the profits that dealers were making on the streets. But in this case, the police knew well what was happening in their district, including who was working, when they started, and what profits were being made (presumably through illicit connections with other traffickers).

Interestingly, although traffickers like Raúl agreed on the protection money with some police officers, this did not prevent other officers (from the same precinct or the same district) from making additional claims. In other words, although protection was somewhat reliable, it was never comprehensive. Brokers and protectors could not assure dealers that other units or agents would not enforce the law against them. The result was a constant and mutual monitoring of who was protecting whom, for how much, and for how long. Clandestine relationships were, we reiterate, precarious and subject to many concessions and conflicts.

A few days after Primo and Raúl agreed on the amount, agents from La Casita approached Raúl for more money. He then contacted Primo, saying, "I just don't want them to come and bother me." Primo replied, "Don't trust anybody and don't talk to anybody until I say so." Primo then contacted the chief of La Casita directly in an attempt to clarify who (and how much) needed to be paid to ensure protection.

On this occasion, going to the boss effectively resolved the dispute over the payment to La Casita. But it did not address other problems that would soon emerge. For example, when approached again for money, Primo told Nélida, "It must be people from La Brigada . . . because they also want money." Primo, it was quite clear, could not "cover their asses" with everybody.

In addition to negotiating the bribes, Primo also channeled information and acted as an advocate for the trafficking organization. For example, he informed dealers about future police operations and gathered intelligence about dealers' competitors while simultaneously informing police about where drugs were being sold. He also mediated the sale of confiscated goods to members of La Banda de Raúl. The weed and cocaine that were seized in raids of other drug dealers were sometimes reintroduced in the market by police agents. The term used was *capiar* (i.e., procure drugs in either legal or illegal ways and sell them to a third party). "[I'm] at the office," Primo told one of the dealers, "and we have a bag of stuff. . . . [D]o you want it?"

Another time, Primo told Raúl about the quality and price of the *tizas y piedras* (cocaine and weed) confiscated by the police. "We did a job with the people, and we have seven kilograms of the green stuff. Do you want it?" When Raúl expressed interest in the drugs, Primo then asked for "three *lucas* [US$3,000]" and assured Raúl that the drugs were "even better" than the "stuff" he had sold him previously. The conversation concluded with Primo saying: "I'll bring it to you at night. Please have all the money ready."

Broken Negotiations

As this description of brokered collusion indicates, despite his many contacts, Primo was not able to control the many actors in the field. Police officers, it is important to note, did not always go through Primo to make arrangements with dealers. They would directly collect protection money from dealers themselves and then "liberate" certain areas so that the traffickers could work without being bothered. Brokered or not, maintaining clandestine relationships was an ongoing and tumultuous process that could sometimes break down.

The constant demand for more and larger bribes created difficulties for La Banda de Raúl. Court documents make clear that the group was sometimes unwilling or unable to pay its different protectors on time. "When are you going to have the money ready?" Primo asked a dealer. "The Enano [nickname for a police officer] tells me he needs his money." On another occasion, Raúl told Primo he did not have all the money because, so he claimed, he had to first make a payment to La Brigada.

Still other times, negotiations would fully collapse. This could lead to collective action (as we saw in the case of the rally to shame a police chief organized by Los Monos that we described in Chapter 5). It could also trigger a reconfiguration of either the terms of the *arreglo* or the partners involved in it. The following conversation between Primo and Raúl illustrates an instance in which a clandestine relationship broke down altogether.

PRIMO: What happened?

RAÚL: That Aguirre guy [a police agent] is a faggot. He is driving me crazy. . . .

PRIMO: Who? Aguirre? Aren't you paying him? [*¿No la estás viendo a la gente esa?*]

RAÚL: Yes, I do pay them, because he is in the CPC [Comando de Prevención Comunitaria, a division within the local police], but I don't know what he wants now. He began bothering me last Saturday. . . . [T]he thing is that this faggot used to keep the money for himself. He didn't want to arrange with me and I have to arrange with his boss. Now he wants more money, and I won't give it to him. . . . He is an asshole [*un cachivache boludo*].

As this exchange suggests, Officer Aguirre was demanding bribe payments in addition to his supervisors, who had supposedly promised to control members of their unit. In a prior communication, Aguirre's superior had explicitly told Nélida, "Cut off Aguirre . . . he is not going to work here anymore. You have to arrange with me." She replied, "Okay, but if I see that they keep bothering us, I won't pay anymore. Money is not a gift. I have to work for it and I pay every week."

As the incident with Aguirre illustrates, La Banda de Raúl had to navigate shifting internal arrangements among state actors, which had material impacts on its business. When Aguirre's supervisor told Nélida to channel bribes directly to him (effectively cutting out Aguirre), Nélida responded to this reconfiguration of state power. But she did not simply acquiesce to the change. She warned the supervisor that her allegiance was contingent: If he could not ensure that his officers stop "bothering" her operations, she would stop paying the bribe.

Nélida's "Little Problem"

La Banda de Raúl operated out of an informal settlement in San Martín where it stored and sold cheap marijuana, cocaine, and paco. But it was not the only illicit operation in an area known for being a hotbed of drug market activity. In 2014, Cheko started competing with the organization for a share of the local drug market. Fed up with the drop in business, Nélida picked up the phone one night and called José Luis, the local police chief.

NÉLIDA: I am really sorry to bother you this late, José Luis.

JOSÉ LUIS: What's up, Nélida? Is everything okay?

NÉLIDA: Did you guys do a raid in [the villa] where Andrés was killed?

JOSÉ LUIS: Yes, in [two other informal settlements].

NÉLIDA: So I was told. Did you guys get [i.e., arrest] anyone?

JOSÉ LUIS: I think so. The Investigative Unit [did the raid]. But we didn't get that one [referring to Cheko]. We will catch him though. . . . Stay calm, we are following him. But we don't yet have a warrant. I have to talk to the state prosecutor tomorrow because I need a warrant . . . otherwise I can't arrest him. . . .

NÉLIDA: He [Cheko] is now in charge [of the drug business] there.

Immediately after this exchange, Nélida called Raúl to tell him that the police officers already knew where Cheko lived. Eleven days later, she called the district chief again to inquire about Cheko.

NÉLIDA: I was wondering about my little problem. . . .

JOSÉ LUIS: We don't have a warrant yet. I'm waiting for the state prosecutor to issue one. . . . It's not easy. We have warrants for others, but not for him. He was a little soldier, but a really wise one. . . . But stay calm, everything is going to be okay, you have to be patient, Nélida. . . . We have to do this carefully. If you rush it, it may go wrong.

A month later, Cheko was still dealing drugs from one of Nélida's former selling points. She decided to take matters in her own hands instead of waiting for his arrest. Nélida concluded that the only way to recover her bunker would be to forcibly evict Cheko "because it seems that there [at the precinct], you don't do anything," she told the district chief. Acknowledging the delay, José Luis offered two officers to help her with the eviction. Through this collusive relationship, Nélida collaborated with her contact in the police to manipulate the law enforcement efforts: in this case, to target her competitor. Yet when this bureaucratic manipulation failed, they agreed on other measures.

In October 2014, the eviction took place. Members of La Banda de Raúl along with the off-duty police officers exchanged gunfire with Cheko and successfully took back the bunker. The next day,

Nélida called the district chief to thank him for sending his agents. Following this event, wiretapped phones provided another interesting piece of evidence: Nélida had been in contact with Cheko for an unknown length of time. After the eviction Cheko texted Nélida, accusing her of being protected by the police (*la gorra*).

This incident confirms and extends accounts of how violence operates in illicit markets. In the absence of formal channels to resolve disputes, extra-legal actors like Cheko and Nélida turned to alternative, sometimes violent methods to resolve their conflicts. This is a prime example of what analysts call "systemic violence." Yet this incident adds an interesting dimension to our understanding of drug-related violence. José Luis, now acting as a *narcopolicía*, negotiated not only when and how a violent resolution might occur, but who would conduct it by ultimately offering up his officers to help. Collusive interactions thus shaped and directed the violent eviction that took place. The solution of Nélida's "little problem" illustrates one of the ways in which collusion impacts on the deployment of violence at the urban margins: *Protection directs when and where violence is used.*

The Price of an Arrest

As discussed in Chapter 3, many residents of Arquitecto Tucci believed that local police put a price tag on those arrested. In Chapter 5, we learned that members of Los Monos had "friends" inside the police force who altered the names and identities of those arrested. Something similar occurred between La Banda de Raúl and the police officers in San Martín. In January 2015, one of the leader's brothers, Pey, was arrested while attempting to steal a car with a group of friends. When she heard about the arrest, Mica, a member of La Banda de Raúl, immediately began to negotiate Pey's release with her contacts in the police force. In a wiretapped conversation, an officer at the local precinct asked Mica for US$1,500 in exchange for Pey's release. Mica told the officer that she didn't have the money and asked for more time. Interestingly, in the subsequent negotiations, Mica acknowledged the appearances that the police needed to maintain: She said that she understood that someone from the group needed to stay behind bars. Mica then asked the officer to place Pey's gun onto someone else so that he wasn't charged with possession of a firearm.

As this incident attests, dealers like Mica negotiated directly with the police officers to manipulate formal institutional processes, for example, by changing arrest records, releasing people from jail, or planting or removing evidence. At other times, Primo would go to relatives of those arrested to help secure money to pay bribes. When the mothers, fathers, or partners of those arrested did not have enough money, police officers would keep those arrested in the precinct. On one such call, a relative of someone who had been arrested told Primo that she could not come up with the requested money: "I didn't collect anything.... Tell him I love him."

* * *

This chapter presented the cases of Los Pescadores and La Banda de Raúl to deepen our understanding of the micro-dynamics of collusion and the ambivalent ways that the state operates at the urban margins. The case involving Los Pescadores offered insights into how collusion relationships extend beyond local actors. Due to their deep pockets and extensive operations, Los Pescadores constructed a near-complete protection network in their home base, the small but strategically important town of Yapurá. It also maintained protective contacts well beyond the town's geographic limits, including not just local, regional, and federal security forces but also politicians and judges who benefited from these illicit arrangements. The case of La Banda de Raúl illuminated a different configuration of an *arreglo*—in this case, when collusion is mediated by a broker like Primo or undermined by a low-level police agent like

Aguirre. Despite their very different collusive arrangements, both groups were susceptible to external pressures. For members of La Banda de Raúl, their reliance on a broker generated uncertainty in an often-shifting terrain of clandestine relations. In the case of Los Pescadores, their protection was threatened by political pressure to "solve" a case that was attracting unwanted attention to the town and its leaders. This pressure illustrates and supports our claim about the relational underpinnings of collusion, which are based on contingent and precarious arrangements of reciprocity. As we saw, in these social worlds mistakes were frequent and relationships were strained. The following chapter draws together our findings to provide a synthetic discussion of the content of collusion and how it impacts violence at the urban margins.

7

Unpacking Collusion

From the outskirts of the cities of Buenos Aires and Rosario to the country's northern border, drug market organizations in Argentina take many forms. Some, like Los Vagones and La Banda de Raúl, are local entities that sell drugs to petty dealers and end-users. Others are involved in the larger supply chain of illicit drugs, trafficking marijuana and cocaine across borders like Los Pescadores and producing highly addictive paco in drug kitchens, as in the case of Los Monos. Despite myriad differences in size and scope, the cases of Los Vagones, Los Monos, Los Pescadores, and La Banda de Raúl share several common features. The organizations are all hierarchical and led by tight-knit and often blood-related leaders who have established and maintained connections with members of state security forces. Street-level dealers at the bottom of the pyramidal structure are, as far as the evidence shows, not fully aware of the *arreglos*. This serves the leadership well because they can "give up" some of their employees when the police need to "put on a show" or "make numbers" (i.e., make arrests). Most importantly, all these cases confirm that these clandestine connections are integral to their operations, aiding in the acquisition and preparation of illicit drugs for sale, the elimination of market competitors, and the strategic avoidance of the police.

Drug market organizations pay police officers and other state agents to selectively enforce the law. In some cases, state agents allow and facilitate illicit activity, and in other cases, they intervene and punish those involved. Political scientist Alisha Holland documents a similar form of state action. In her detailed and insightful study of the politics of informal welfare in Santiago de Chile,

The Ambivalent State: Police-Criminal Collusion at the Urban Margins. Javier Auyero, Oxford University Press (2019). © Oxford University Press.
DOI: 10.1093/oso/9780190915537.001.0001

Chile, Bogotá, Colombia, and Lima, Peru, Holland (2017:3) argues that politicians strategically turn to what she calls "forbearance," making decisions to not enforce the law "when welfare policies are inadequate and they need the poor's support to take or retain office." Forbearance, in her account, "functions as a form of informal welfare provision that politicians manipulate to improve the lives of those who violate the law and to signal their commitments to poor constituents more broadly" (p. 3).

Members of state security forces engage in a variation of the forbearance described by Holland, exhibiting an "intentional and revocable government leniency toward violations of the law."[1] With the exception of Los Pescadores, the main actors involved in collusion between police agents and drug traffickers are not politicians,[2] and the purposes of non-enforcement are not precisely "redistributive." Although actors and intentions are different, court cases indisputably show that the three components that define forbearance—"capacity, intention, and revocability"[3]—are present in the decisions made by security agents. Enjoying a monopoly in the use of force, police have the ability to "look elsewhere" when it comes to enforcing the law; they willingly and knowingly do so (planning meetings, exchanges, making calls, etc.); and their decisions can be altered (as we saw in both the cases of Los Monos and Los Pescadores, where police officers and state officials changed their forbearing practices). In this book, we have shown that collusion between police agents and criminal actors involves more than forbearance on the part of the state. Indeed, beyond turning a blind eye to certain illicit activities, we have described a rich and multi-faceted transactional world where participants in collusion build provisional trust networks that meaningfully impact both policing and drug markets.

The previous chapters delved into the complexities and particularities of a series of documented cases of collusion in Argentina. This chapter will provide a synthesis of our empirical findings. It draws out common features across cases, highlighting the patterned character of the transactional world of collusion, as well as the mistakes and last-minute improvisations that abound in the clandestine connections between drug dealers and the police. We then examine the relationship between police-criminal collusion and the localized interpersonal violence we described in Chapters 2 and 3.

Micro-dynamics of Collusion

Through an in-depth analysis of hundreds of pages of court documents, we distinguish three dimensions of collusion that advance our understanding of these clandestine arrangements. First, we find that the clandestine relationships between state agents and drug dealers are based on the exchange of material and informational resources. Our cases show that drug dealers and members of state security forces regularly share protective, competitive, and retaliatory information. Much of this information is protective in nature, warning illicit actors about planned actions of law enforcement. Yet wiretapped conversations also show that information about the dynamics of local drug markets abounds in these clandestine networks, providing much-needed insights into competition and police action. Across the four sites, participants also rely on each other for resources to which they have unique access. In a context of strict regulation, where only licensed adults who undergo a background check can own certain types of non-automatic firearms, court cases confirm that drug dealers acquire guns and ammunition from police.[4] "Do you have bullets for my toy?" one member of Los Pescadores asked a state police officer. He responded, "Yes, a box is 1,200 pesos. If that's okay, stop by to pick it up." In addition to buying and selling U.S. dollars and car parts, actors also exchange illicit drugs, both those held by drug market organizations and those that were previously confiscated by the police.

Second, we show that actors involved in collusive relationships engage in common practices. As we learned, all participants in collusion alter their daily actions as a direct result of the information exchanged through clandestine relationships. Police agents avoid certain territories (the well-documented form of inaction to "liberate an area") and, at other times, flood the area with their presence. They also target different actors based on information received from extra-legal contacts. For example, in the case of Los Vagones, Lucho, the police agent, assured a dealer that he would intimidate his competitors and "go fuck with them a bit." In a similar fashion, dealers change shipment routes, suspend sales, and move supplies from bunker to bunker based on the information they receive from informants in state agencies. Los Pescadores, the organization that operated extensive distribution networks across the country, did this skillfully, navigating a constantly shifting landscape of protected corridors.

Our cases show that parties also engage in three forms of what we call *bureaucratic manipulation*: They work diligently to speed up, slow down, and stymie formal institutional processes. While state agents do this directly, drug dealers also play important roles in these efforts. In multiple cases, police agents negotiated with drug dealers to selectively report crimes, change arrest records, and plant or remove evidence. In addition to outright modifications and omissions, participants took steps to expedite formal forms of recourse. For example, police encouraged judges to approve certain search warrants in response to competition in drug markets.[5] Finally, state actors delayed institutional processes. For example, when members were arrested, police would extend these interactions to build in time to negotiate bribe money. In all these instances, time was a resource that could be leveraged by manipulating bureaucratic practices.

The following interaction between members of Los Monos and their contact in the local police highlight the power of these behavioral changes. In one call, Officer Belporto asked a drug dealer named Flaco for his whereabouts. Flaco replied by launching into a frantic description of what had just happened: "We lost, really bad. They [the police] let me go. I put another kid in my place. But Cabezón and Sara are still in [detained in the police station], they are trying to see what they can do."

Officer Belporto replied: "It's all been dealt with. That's why I am looking for you, asshole. Go home, I had you released. . . . They are going to put someone else [in jail] instead of Cabezón and Sara." Before hanging up the phone, Belporto instructed Flaco to get rid of the car involved: The car that Cabezón was driving has to "be gone" (i.e., disappear), he said. "Don't worry," Belporto reassured Flaco, "I'm in the middle. Don't worry. . . . There's nothing I could do about the gun. One of the chiefs got to it first."

According to wiretapped conversations, Flaco's release was not an easy negotiation. During this conversation with Flaco, Officer Belporto revealed that he still needed to pay the officers who had released him: "Now I have to go and look for the money. They wanted more money, I have to fight because they wanted to leave you all in the station." As evidenced in this exchange, Officer Belporto negotiated with the police involved in the arrest on behalf of Los Monos while at the same time providing advice to the latter. The conversations soon turned to negotiating the release of those who were still in custody:

FLACO: The cops are asking for too much money [to release Cabezón and Sara].

BELPORTO: No way, they are crazy, they have nothing on them. . . .

FLACO: Can you call them? Cabezón is really mad. . . . The police want 15,000 pesos more. . . .

BELPORTO: They are crazy, they have nothing on them.

FLACO: Well, look into it. . . . If not, we'll see.

BELPORTO: Don't even think about giving them more money. They can only detain them until 8 or 9 a.m. After that, they have to release them. They have nothing on them [i.e., there are no specific charges]. No way, asshole.

FLACO: Well, call them. I can't wait until 9 a.m.

BELPORTO: Well, if they have to wait, they have to wait.... Don't be an asshole, the officers are manipulating them [*sicologeándolos*].... Wait a bit.... Be patient.

In this instance, Officer Belporto became a broker on behalf of members of Los Monos. While he was able to intervene in the bureaucratic practices of these arrests, he also represented the group when individual officers demanded more money. This is similar to the role of Primo, the broker who coordinated the clandestine connections between La Banda de Raúl (and others) and local police.

The court cases also show that participants in collusion *engage in surveillance*, both internal to their groups and external in their neighborhoods and social networks. Drug dealers watch each other and their employees, competitors, neighbors, and the different state agents that intervene in a given territory. State agents take similar measures, closely tracking fellow officers and other security agencies. For example, after a dealer asked about the identity of police agents on the street, an officer working with Los Vagones promised to "find out who they [were]." State agents also closely monitor other illicit actors, including what they do, how much money they make, and the crimes they engage in. This was made clear when the leader of La Banda de Raúl said he could not pay the proposed bribe amount. During that negotiation, police rejected his excuse, saying that they knew how long he had been working and the amounts of money he was making.

Finally, we identify a set of relational processes that help us explain the patterned nature of these collusive interactions. As we introduced in Chapter 5, our cases show three interrelated processes at work: reciprocal signaling, identity change, and scale-shift. Once clandestine connections are established, actors undertake the crucial process of *reciprocal signaling*. By passing information back and forth, state security agents signal to drug market participants the locations where they can sell, which routes they should use to move their products, and which areas they should avoid, while dealers signal to police forces what their plans are and where their competitors are operating.

If sustained over time, clandestine connections facilitate a second process: *identity change*, an alteration in the identities of the actors involved. State actors stop being law enforcers in the areas where dealers operate and become protectors, informants, and even the foot soldiers of drug market groups (*infiltrados*, as they are referred to by members of Los Monos[6]). As one of the leaders of Los Monos once said, referring to the police, "[T]hey are *our cobanis*" (*our emphasis*). Police agents who are no longer loyal to the state become *narcopolicías* or *polinarcos*. For illicit actors, these state agents are no longer seen as opponents or *contrarios* to illicit activity but rather are complicit in it. Drug dealers also go through a change in the way in which they understand themselves and are understood by others; they become protected actors—*arreglados con la gorra* (arranged with the cops).

Finally, there are important variations in our cases in the number and level of connections between illicit actors and members of state security forces. Larger organizations (such as Los Pescadores or Los Monos) are more internally differentiated and have more contacts with security forces than smaller ones. As clandestine connections expand and contract, we see a process of *scale-shift* at work that impacts the range of actors involved in these clandestine networks.[7] Organizations such as Los Pescadores devoted not just to retail sales but also to import and distribution have more diversified contacts within security forces (including not only local police officers but also officers from the Federal Police, the National Guard, and Naval Police).

Maneuvers and Mistakes

Our reconstructions of court cases show patterned ways in which drug market participants and state security agents relate to each other—the kinds of resources they exchange, their shared practices, and the relational processes that show the patterned nature of collusion. Readers may get the impression that a carefully crafted master plan to maximize drug-trade profits and achieve impunity is at work. But when we look closer at the interactions that unfold, we see a social universe filled with errors, unintended consequences, and spontaneous actions, as well as constant corrections and attempts to repair relationships damaged by those mistakes. Instead of a consistent strategy, we find that both security agents and drug dealers take part in incessant, oftentimes hasty maneuvering that includes attempts to sometimes monitor and at other times expand clandestine relations.

In an insightful and provocative essay, sociologist Charles Tilly (1996) uses the image of "invisible elbows" to summarize his understanding of how social life works. "Coming home from the grocery store," he writes,

> arms overflowing with food-filled bags, you wedge yourself against the doorjamb, somehow free a hand to open the kitchen door, enter the house, then nudge the door closed with your elbow. Because elbows are not prehensile and, in this situation, not visible either, you sometimes slam the door smartly, sometimes swing the door halfway closed, sometimes missed completely on the first pass, and sometimes—responding to one of these earlier calamities—spill groceries all over the kitchen floor.[8]

The systematic properties of actors and objects involved in this familiar vignette (door, elbow, groceries) constrain the outcomes of the "attempted nudge." Tilly adds, "Over many trips to the grocery store, which of these outcomes occurs forms a frequency distribution with stable probabilities modified by learning. With practice, you may get your door-closing average up to .900" (p. 594). And therein lies Tilly's key insight: Erroneous interactions and unanticipated consequences pervade social interactions, but so do "error correction and responses, sometimes almost instantaneous, to unexpected outcomes" (p. 595). Collectively, these mistakes and rectifications acquired through learning and practice produce a "systematic, durable social structure" (p. 595), even in the absence of unified, conscious intention.

The clandestine transactional universe we examined in the previous three chapters is not different from this (Mertonian-Tillyian) social world. While our in-depth analysis of collusion illustrates its patterned nature, it also shows a transactional universe marked by mistakes, corrections, and improvisations. Multiple quotidian conversations attest to the ways that drug dealers and police officers change course to monitor others. For example, two suspicious members of Los Monos shared information about surveillance:

MARCELO: A Toyota with tinted windows went by my mother's house and took pictures. I asked [Officer] Belporto and he said it's a vehicle from the federal police.

RAMÓN: I don't have a contact there, do you have one?

MARCELO: Yes, but the cops are no longer there. I think they moved to Seventh Avenue. . . .

RAMÓN: I don't know. . . . I only know what Belporto told me.

MARCELO: Okay, give me a second and I'll let you know.

The two dealers picked up their conversation days later, when one relayed that a contact in the Federal Police confirmed that the Toyota belonged to them.

Drug dealers usually devise complicated schemes to obtain, move, and sell drugs, pay subordinates, and ultimately avoid detection. But these are frequently revised and replaced: Drugs are sent to one location, unloaded at different times, moved to another secret storage place, then re-packaged for street sale. From the vantage point of wiretapped phone calls, these constant modifications appear in the form of frequent communication and changing information.

Mistake amended

Days after the police raided the home of a relative of the leader of Los Monos, Murray called one of his contacts in the state police to demand they reverse course. Apparently, the officers involved didn't know that the home (also used as a drug selling spot) was protected. Murray said to the police officer: "Listen, tell [Officer] Gallo that the cops went to bother my aunt's [selling] spot yesterday, the one that is close to the bridge. Tell him that that spot is ours."

Over the course of exchanges like the one documented above, mistakes are common: Sheltered places are raided, valuable drugs are seized, and protected individuals are arrested. As mistakes occur, so do attempts to prevent and correct them. Drug dealers hastily move drugs out of bunkers in anticipation of a raid; they alert street-level dealers of police action; and they avoid communications because of suspected wiretapping. Police officers, in turn, are asked to give back confiscated goods, clear a record, or target a competitor.

The following conversation between the leader of Los Monos and another dealer captures an attempt to make a correction at the eleventh hour. Upon learning of an imminent raid on their drug bunker, the dealers sprang into action:

DAMIÁN: Sorry to bother you, Murray, but the kids from the store [drug-selling point] are saying that everybody is there, helicopters, national guards walking by. . . . It's all rotten there. I'm now going over there now to pick up the kids and bring them here. . . .

MURRAY: OK, leave the merchandise there, somewhere hidden, in a backyard, or throw it somewhere. And come with the kids.

The two got off the phone and talked again 15 minutes later:

MURRAY: So, what happened?

DAMIÁN: All good, stay calm. I took everything out, the merchandise, the kids, everything. . . .

MURRAY: Who was going around?

DAMIÁN: Three guys from National Guard were there and a helicopter was hovering above.

MURRAY: Where was the raid?

DAMIÁN: They are walking around, doing the rounds here in the neighborhood.

Four hours later, after the security agents had left without finding anything, the dealers went back to business as usual:

MURRAY: Hey, all is calm in the spot. You can open it again. It's over. . . .

DAMIÁN: OK, I'll open it up.

Oftentimes, as judicial documents show, these corrections are made on the spot. This is evidenced when dealers are detained and quickly released without a record (their names frantically replaced with those of low-level dealers), when officers hurriedly inform dealers not to use a particular vehicle spotted during a police operation, or when they tell arrested suspects not to talk to other officers. Correcting errors involves not only logistics but, as we saw in the constant reassurances of trust made by police agents to drug dealers, also attempts at mending marred relationships with the use of threats.

One afternoon, police officers launched a raid on an unassuming home on the outskirts of Rosario. Rather than targeting an active drug bunker or a storage site, police went after someone perhaps more valuable: the mother of the leader of Los Monos. Similar to the way drug violence invades people's homes, as we discussed in Chapter 2, so too do police forces. When police officers found drugs in his mother's house, Murray activated his many contacts to clear her record. He told one of his closest collaborators to call a police officer and threaten him: "I have everything recorded, I recorded the many conversations we had. . . . [If they don't clear her record] we are all going to jail. I don't care." After this unexpected raid, Murray reverted to threats in an attempt to resolve the unwanted police attention.

The patterned character of the clandestine world under investigation is complicated by these error-correcting maneuvers and on-the-spot improvisations. We find that these illicit relationships of collusion are often activated not during the course of smooth transactions and precisely scheduled events but during moments that are filled with mistakes, amendments, and unintended consequences; in other words, a world of invisible elbows.

It is important to point out that these relationships are enabled and constrained by power dynamics within police departments, between security forces, and between the policing and the political fields. The overall working of this patterned universe of manifold illicit transactions cannot be explained exclusively by what takes place between security agents and drug dealers and what the bulk of our interactional data captures. Relations between police forces and state and federal administrations as well as changing patterns of drug production, distribution, and consumption that we described in Chapter 1 are also central explanatory factors in the operation of these illicit links and their violent effects.

Much of this patterned maneuvering can be explained by the lack of democratic control over the police forces. Marcelo Saín (2015; 2017) details the nature of "police self-government," which is made possible by the absence of external controls and of internal accountability.[9] Changes in the production, distribution, and consumption of illicit drugs are another important external condition that make these clandestine relations possible and sustainable. The fact that drug consumption has increased, retail markets have expanded, and the home-grown production of cocaine and paco has escalated (due to what some call the "balloon effect"—i.e., the pressure on narco-traffickers in other countries—but also due to easy local access to the chemical components needed for drug production), plus the sustained profitability of the drug business and its territorial implantation in poor areas,[10] all allow clandestine relations to flourish.[11]

Now that we have unpacked the resources, practices, and processes at the heart of police-criminal collusion and its relational and improvisational character, let us merge the evidence gathered from ethnographic fieldwork with the court documents. This will allow us to inspect the connections between collusion and the legal cynicism we described in Chapter 3 and the ways that collusion relates to the persistence of interpersonal violence at the urban margins we discussed in Chapter 2.

Trust and Cynicism

In *Trust and Rule*, Charles Tilly (2005:12) defines a trust network as a set of "ramified interpersonal connections, consisting mainly of strong ties, within which people set valued, consequential, long-term resources and enterprises at risk to the malfeasance, mistakes, or failures of others." The court proceedings and wiretapped conversations we have presented in the previous chapters suggest that drug dealers and members of security forces are seeking to create such a network. But what they are also co-constructing is a system of diffused and precarious reciprocity—diffused in that the exact definition of equivalence is not very precise and the sequence of events is not narrowly bounded,[12] and precarious in that this is an unstable system subjected to constant re-negotiation, threats, and sudden breakdowns. Within this system of exchanges, trust is a contingent and volatile property.

What drug dealers seek through these exchanges is economic control of the territory where they seek to conduct their illicit business. Depending on the size and scope of their operations, they attempt to gain control over a few blocks (Los Vagones and La Banda de Raúl), a certain area of a city (Los Monos), or an entire town and extensive roads and waterways (Los Pescadores). Using contacts inside the state's repressive apparatus, organizations seek to achieve this control to evade the rules and regulations of the state. For drug dealers, the state is thus *both a resource to be used in their criminal enterprise and a force to be reckoned with and avoided.*

With the evidence of collusion and its inner workings, we could argue that the legal cynicism that we describe in Chapter 3 stems not only from the suspected collusion between police and dealers but also from its *unsteady and volatile* nature—a dual character that makes it so difficult for residents to figure out exactly what is going on.[13] It is not simply the existence of collusion but also its uncertain and unsettled character that makes residents believe law enforcement agents are passive, incapable, and ultimately lack legitimacy.[14] Unpacking the content of clandestine state action thus helps us better understand poor people's cynicism about law enforcement and the grueling position that they face on a daily basis. Given their (well-founded) suspicions about police officers, they cannot fully depend on them for protection from violence. These doubts were made clear when residents questioned the purpose of calling the police: "What for?" they asked. True, not every police officer colludes with drug market organizations. Again, the fact that legal investigations and court records exist proves this point. But residents believe the *arreglo* is real, and if they believe it is real, as William Thomas and Dorothy Thomas (1928) put it a long time ago, it is real in its consequences. In Arquitecto Tucci, there is a widespread suspicion of all law enforcement, not particular officers or specific units. As we have seen, in exchange for money, illicit actors can call certain police officers to release areas from police action while residents hesitate or choose not to call at all. Thus, drug market organizations, paradoxically, have access to the state protection that is unavailable to most poor residents.

Collusion and Violence

Violence is not an intrinsic feature of all drug markets. As we described in Chapter 1, although interpersonal physical aggression is not a given, quarrels between drug dealers, retaliatory actions for disloyalty and theft, and physical retributions for trading in adulterated products show that illicit drug markets can be quite violent.[15] To that volatility, we should now add the actions of police and other security agents described in previous chapters. Extant scholarship has inspected the relationships between drug control law enforcement, violent crime, and public health.[16] Police intervention in drug markets, for example, can be disruptive, pushing dealers into new territories and producing "turf wars" that can increase violence in adjacent areas.[17] Yet the cases we have described in the previous chapters present a type of "law enforcement" different from the one examined in the literature. Police agents make and un-make pacts with drug dealers, "liberate" zones for trafficking, sell weapons and ammunition to dealers, enable physical retaliation, protect certain drug selling points (and allow attacks on others), and in effect, become an armed force protecting one market competitor over others. Once we bring these actions into the picture, it is not hard to understand how and why systemic violence takes the form it does in poor neighborhoods like Arquitecto Tucci. This highlights one of the contributions of this book: that concealed and illicit police interventions in the drug markets are key to understanding the production of violence.

In her illuminating book, *The Politics of Drug Violence*, political scientist Angélica Durán-Martínez (2018:598) states that "[p]olice corruption is often associated with violence and growing criminal behavior, yet most studies do not specify the mechanisms connecting law enforcement and violence." What is the relationship between police-criminal collusion and interpersonal violence? How are these clandestine connections related to the "sudden reversals of fortune"[18] that shake poor people's daily lives? First, drug dealers attack, injure, and kill others with the impunity provided by police protection. Second, such acts of violence are sometimes carried out with the material support and the informational resources provided by state actors. As we described, police agents not only share information with dealers, but they also sell them munitions and even provide personnel to assist in eliminating competition.

Collusion sometimes *supports* violence and at other times, *channels* it. Drug dealers do not and often cannot attack their competitors if they are protected by the police. But when parties are not shielded by members of some state force, illicit actors can—as indicated by the police—"go ahead and take them out." In other words, protection directs where the violence goes by marking targets with no illicit connection to the state. We have seen how this channeling occurs on a few occasions; let us now reconstruct one additional instance that shows the actual process in detail.

Fourteen-year-old Lourdes lived in a modest brick house in the poor neighborhood of Flat Tires. She and her four siblings had been abandoned by their parents. To make ends meet, one of her older siblings, Nicolás, was attempting the impossible: establish a drug selling point out of the family's backyard apartment without the blessing of Los Monos. This particular set of exchanges took place between Murray (the leader of Los Monos), Mario (one of his soldiers), and Officer Delfín, one of their contacts in the state police:

MARIO: Murray, you have competition there, in the Flat Tires neighborhood. They are working really well. . . .
MURRAY: Who does that spot belong to?

MARIO: I don't know. It might belong to Nicolás, he drives a Ford.
MURRAY: OK, I'll find out. . . . Try to look into the exact address.
MARIO: OK, cool. If you support me, we can get rid of them and
keep the little house for us.

A few days later, Mario followed up with Murray about what had transpired: "I sent one of my kids there, and yes, they are working. It's a little house, and you buy the stuff in the back, and they have that Ford that I mentioned." Murray asked for the exact address and, hours later, Mario called him with the information.

With the information in hand, Murray then called Officer Delfín and asked him if that particular address sounded familiar and whether or not the bunker "has a permit [*si está habilitado*], because it is very close to one of ours and if it doesn't, we are going to send someone to shut it down." Later that day, Officer Delfín responded: "Yes, it has a permit, but it doesn't matter, you can go ahead and take it down." Murray wanted to know who issued the illicit "permit" but Officer Delfín didn't know. After consulting with another police contact, Murray told Mario that he could attack: "Go hard on them [*Dale a mansalva nomás*]." A few days later, around 10 p.m., two men affiliated with Los Monos drove by this house and opened fire. One bullet hit Lourdes in the chest. She died on her way to the hospital.

Our joint analysis of court cases and ethnographic material uncovers other intricate and pernicious ways in which police-criminal collusion relates to interpersonal violence. As we described in Chapter 2, drug-related violence makes both streets and homes unsafe. Fear pervades interpersonal interactions: Residents are not only afraid of venturing outside their homes but also, as Carolina's story in the introduction attests, terrified about the uncertain predicament of their loved ones, especially when they are somehow involved with drugs. In Chapter 2, we identified a set of pathways through which the violence of the drug trade travels inside homes, underscoring the artificial division between private and public manifestations of violence. Given their well-founded suspicions about *narcopolicías who regularly betray what is right* and the widespread legal cynicism, why would residents resort to the police? In many cases, we find people take matters into their own hands. In the absence of alternative ways to address addiction, parents use violence against their loved ones in an attempt to keep their sons and daughters from "being killed or raped" because of their involvement with drugs. We are not in a position to say whether they are right in their assessments or whether the violence they unleash on their loved ones accomplishes what they think it does. Rather, what matters is that parents believe the police are "criminals in uniform" and that they have no alternative other than violent discipline. Collusion, like violence, travels inside poor homes and shapes the interactions between family members.

As should now be clear, the relationship between collusion and violence is not unidirectional. Police-criminal collusion does not just shape interpersonal violence. Rather, this relationship is reciprocal: Violence gives form to collusion. The systemic violence of the drug trade—that which transpires when dealers are assaulted, injured, or killed to recoup debts or to eliminate a competitor—encourages actors to seek police protection, not simply to be able to do business but to do it in as physically safe a way as possible.

* * *

This chapter provided a synthetic picture of the dynamics of collusion. We discussed the common resources, practices, and processes at the heart of clandestine relationships and drew the four court cases together to highlight the simultaneous presence of patterns, mistakes, and corrections. A close inspection of the dimensions of collusion served to better explain its complex relationship with the violence that shakes the daily lives of marginalized populations.

8

Conclusions

> Es decir, la policía no sólo dejó hacer, sino que hizo.
> [T]he police not only let it [drug trafficking] happen, but
> they actually engage in it.
>
> Marcelo Saín, *Por qué Preferimos No Ver la Inseguridad*
> *(Aunque Digamos lo Contrario)*[1]

> To ask sociology to be useful for something is always a way
> of asking it to be useful to those in power—whereas the
> scientific function of sociology is to understand the so-
> cial world, starting with the structures of power. (Pierre
> Bourdieu 1993:8–20)

"The cops are all dealers," Carolina told us in her modest home in the poor neighborhood of Arquitecto Tucci. As we described in the opening pages of this book, Carolina struggled not only to make ends meet but also to navigate the rising rates of violence in her *barrio* and the pernicious effects of her eldest son's addiction to drugs. For Carolina, the culprit of these problems was clear: The police allowed illicit drugs and violence to flourish in her neighborhood. As the subsequent pages of this book have shown, Carolina's suspicions of police-criminal collusion were not unfounded. Indeed, it is well known that in contemporary Argentina and many other countries, the police engage in clandestine relationships with extra-legal actors.[2] In his close analysis of three court cases involving *narcopolicías* in Buenos Aires,

The Ambivalent State: Police-Criminal Collusion at the Urban Margins. Javier Auyero, Oxford
University Press (2019). © Oxford University Press.
DOI: 10.1093/oso/9780190915537.001.0001

Marcelo Saín (2017) provides ample evidence that police are active participants in drug trafficking. Focusing on the state side of relational arrangements like those we examined in previous chapters, Saín identifies two different types of police intervention. The first takes place at what he calls the "operational level," which involves the ways the police enable drug market activities, for example, by providing drugs, housing, cars, and other material supports to actors in this illicit economy. Police also intervene at the "judicial-institutional level" to ensure the impunity of drug dealers by "preventing the actions of certain judicial or police sectors" (p. 1821). This involves planting evidence, witnesses, and even corpses; manipulating judges and prosecutors; and creating diversions and false investigative lines. Saín decisively concludes: "[T]he police not only let it [drug trafficking] happen, but they actually engage in it" (p. 1821). The empirical evidence we presented in this book not only confirms Saín's analysis but also extends these findings beyond Buenos Aires to detail the microdynamics of these clandestine relations.

Argentine newspapers continue to report on cases like the ones we reconstructed in this book. For example, a new case was opened in the same area where police agents and members of La Banda de Raúl were indicted in 2015 (Chapter 6). In 2017, 11 members of the security forces, many of them operating in the district of San Martín in the province of Buenos Aires, were accused of protecting drug dealers in nearby shantytowns. Similar to the cases we analyzed, police officers were also blamed for selling illicit narcotics to a drug gang, appropriating drugs seized during police operations, and conducting raids without authorization.[3] The officers indicted were different from those involved in the case of La Banda de Raúl, but the *modus operandi* was similar. It is no wonder why, after reviewing the many cases of police corruption in this district, a report from the Center for Socio-Legal Studies (CELS 2016:122) asserts that in San Martín, "[police] involvement in networks of illegality, especially in the sale of illicit drugs, is a *structural* phenomenon" (*our emphasis*). Even if leadership changes, the report matter-of-factly concludes, illicit activities remain protected by judicial and political actors.

This does not bode well for people like Carolina and the many other residents we talked to during the course of our ethnographic fieldwork. Residents, we found, collectively develop legal cynicism not simply out of the perceived unavailability or bias of law enforcement agents but also out of the *felt complicity* between police officers and those who commit crimes. Given their (well-founded) suspicions about where police loyalties lie, residents could not reliably call on the police for protection from the violence that unfolded not only on the streets but also in their homes. For this and other reasons, residents felt that they lived in a "no man's land" that was not simply the result of the state's absence, inefficiency, or ineptitude, but also a product of its ambivalence.

Through our combination of ethnographic fieldwork and archival data of cases documenting the inner workings of police-criminal collusion, we extended and complemented with fine-grained detail the scholarship on the relationships between criminal organizations and the state.[4] Like much existing academic literature, the analytic reconstructions we presented show protection and concealment at work. But different from explanations that have focused either on the absence of the state or its violent presence, we have argued that by including the clandestine dimensions of state actions into the analysis, the state that emerges is a deeply ambivalent organization. It is a state that enforces the rule of law while at the same time acts as an accomplice to what it defines as criminal behavior.

It is not our intention to add another modifier to the long list used by scholars to characterize the state (carceral, clientelist, failed, neoliberal, patriarchal, penal, just to name a few).[5] We use the qualifier "ambivalent" to typify one manifestation of state action at a specific place and during a particular time. This book provides evidence of a locally grounded form of state ambivalence: one that simultaneously enforces and breaks the law in the same geographical space and among the same disadvantaged populations.

Toward a Socio-political Imagination

Much political analysis in both political sociology and political science is premised on a strict separation between the *political field*, where officials, politicians, activists, pundits, journalists, and others act and interact, and the *sphere of everyday life*, where ordinary folks live, go to school, work, and raise their families. Take a mother like Carolina anguishing over the fate of a son "lost to drugs" and desperately searching for him in the middle of the night. Or the story of a father, like one that we spoke with in Arquitecto Tucci, frustratingly and furiously punching his daughter to "break her drug habit" and keep her away from the "bad crowd." Consider the case of a drug dealer striking a deal with a police officer with an upbringing not so different from his own, relaying suspicions and warnings from the streets to the precinct and then back again. These lived experiences and actions are not (so we are implicitly told) the proper objects of political inquiry; that is, unless those parents, residents, police officers, or dealers happen to attend a rally, cast a ballot, or voice their opinions about this policy or that candidate. Politics thus becomes a pre-eminent pre-constructed object, as the late French sociologist Pierre Bourdieu would say. Actors inside the political field define what politics is and does, and then analysts reproduce these dominant constructions in their inquiries.

The underlying scholarly endeavor of this book was to place politics back where it matters the most: in the daily life of ordinary folks. We sought to build a relational political object by showing that parents' desperation about their child's addiction or residents' suspicions about police complicity with drug dealers is not only mutually imbricated but also intricately related to what the state does (or does not do). This object is not something that was "found" but rather one that was *constructed* in order to integrate those ordinary, seemingly trivial experiences into political analysis.[6] In doing so, we hope to have contributed to furthering the agenda of a political sociology of urban marginality[7] by engaging in what we could call, paraphrasing C. Wright Mills (1959), an exercise of *socio-political imagination*—a quality of mind that links the workings of the state with the everyday experiences of the most marginalized residents.

Our examination of the content and consequences of collusion was also intended to develop a broader political sociology of violence. In order to understand and explain the sources and trajectory of violence at the urban margins, we should keep a close eye on what is taking place in police stations, criminal courts, and prison cells, tallying drug arrests and seizures, and tracking the prison and re-incarceration rates affecting the poor[8]—what Müller (2016:28) calls "the punitive government of urban marginality." We should also closely study police in barrios, shantytowns, slums, and squatter settlements,[9] as well as changing forms of policing[10] and the human rights violations that figure prominently in police action and inside prisons across the Americas.[11]

Alongside attention to these overt state actions, a political sociology of violence must also account for the state's clandestine actions and relations. Police complicity with drug dealers and the resulting impact on urban violence is not exclusive to Argentina. Examining experiences in Argentina, Brazil, Colombia, the Dominican Republic, Honduras, and Venezuela, José Miguel Cruz (2016:392) points out, "The state and its representatives are not the only ones responsible for the upsurge in criminal violence in the region. To be sure, drug traffickers, gangs, petty dealers, and other actors are also to blame for the maelstrom of violence. However, the picture would be incomplete without including the state's contribution to crime and violence." He concludes that police involvement in criminal activity "represents a significant obstacle to the development of sound policies to reduce violence" (p. 392).

Beyond Latin America, there is ample evidence that collusion relationships are active in urban areas. In the United States, major metropolitan areas like Chicago and New York City are often used as examples of police misconduct and participation in drug trafficking.[12] Closer to our current homes in the state of Texas, nine police agents and three drug traffickers were arrested by the FBI in 2012 and later convicted on conspiracy charges for drug trafficking along the U.S.-Mexico border. A subsequent investigation conducted by journalists José Luis Pardoy and Alejandra Inzunza (2014a; 2014b) confirmed that this was not an isolated case. A variety of state officials—from sheriffs and street police to border patrol and customs agents—have been bribed by drug market organizations.[13] A report published by the federal government in 2014 confirmed that nearly 2,000 law enforcement officials in the United States were under investigation for involvement in organized crime.[14] As these ongoing investigations attest, the focus on the state's visible, oftentimes quite public arm should not overshadow attention to the more obscure, often illicit modes of state action, which offer crucial explanatory dimensions of the violence that routinely shakes poor people's lives.[15] Rather than dismissing such acts as aberrant phenomena or denouncing them on moralistic grounds, the challenge for a proper sociological analysis is to incorporate clandestine action into our understanding of the material and symbolic operation of the ambivalent state.

Violence, Stigma, and the Politics of Sight

Like the street violence that characterizes poor neighborhoods throughout the Americas, Carolina's home in Arquitecto Tucci has seen its share of interpersonal violence. As we studied these different forms of violence, we also began to interrogate the modalities of state action in the lower regions of the social and geographical space. The rumors of police-criminal collusion we documented at the site of our ethnographic fieldwork prompted us to expand our scope and to examine other cases in other areas. Zooming in on concrete, face-to-face (or phone-to-phone) interactions, our work—both in the field and in the legal archive—sought to make visible the exchanges, practices, and processes that help us better understand police-criminal collusion and how it impacts the violence experienced by residents.

Sight—what we see and what we don't see about poverty, policing, and violence—has a politics (i.e., it is part of a power struggle).[16] This book makes an intervention into what is being said and seen (and what is being denied and hidden) in public conversations about these important issues. We believe that making collusion visible, dissecting its forms of operation, and examining its hidden connections to interpersonal violence, can contribute to political change. As Timothy Pachirat (2011:255) puts it in his insightful analysis of the modern slaughterhouse, "[A] politics of sight that breaches zones of confinement may indeed be a critically important catalyst for political transformation." But we should be cautious. Shedding light on the dynamics of collusion may also lead to novel forms of concealment—"more effective ways of confining it" (p. 253)—or to public apathy and fatalism about its existence and impact on everyday life.

Exposing the inner workings of collusion at the urban margins may also impact the stigma that befalls marginalized areas. Urban research agrees that dispossessed residents "are discredited and devalued not simply because of their poverty, class position, ethno-racial origin, or religious affiliation, but because of the places with which they are associated" (Slater 2017).[17] Merging Erving Goffman's concept of stigma with Bourdieu's theory of symbolic power, sociologist Loïc Wacquant (2007:67) calls the symbolic denigration of marginalized urban areas "territorial stigmatization," a "blemish of place" that superimposes on "already existing stigmata traditionally associated with poverty." The territorial infamy that squatter settlements, slums, and shantytowns in Argentina have sadly enjoyed for decades[18] is now amplified by their association with drug trafficking—an activity that, as we documented, is conducted with the illicit participation of state actors. In other words, the "wicked deal"[19] between drug market organizations and state actors nurtures the negative symbolic representations of these deprived territories. The same state that, in public displays of punitive power, shows up in televised raids against "narcos" and their "bunkers" is also the one that links with them in clandestine ways.[20] In both cases, the outcome is the same: the perpetuation and amplification of the denigrated reputation of these territories and their residents. Further research should scrutinize not only the changing socio-political production of this territorial stigma but also the ways in which marginalized residents appropriate and contest it.

These days, it is customary for social science research to conclude with a section of "policy implications." While practical and actionable recommendations may seem benign, this mandate implicitly conveys that the value of the social sciences depends on their ability to speak to decision-makers within the state. British geographer Tom Slater relates this expectation to the growing heteronomy of urban scholarship. Social scientists, he writes, are less and less able to (and, early on in their careers, actually trained to not) ask their own questions. Instead, they "[ask] questions and us[e] categories invented and imposed by various state institutions" (forthcoming). Pressure is mounting to show our worth by obtaining external funding. If, when, and how we can pursue social science research tends to be increasingly dictated by success in that (financial) quest. Grant money—some of which comes from the very organs of the state—prescribes research topics and becomes a progressively prominent metric of scholarly merit used to decide, among other things, hiring, tenure, and promotion. As a result, Slater continues, there is a "serious subordination of scholarly to policy agendas, and the rise of policy-driven research at the expense of research-driven policy" (forthcoming).

For better or for worse, neither a funding initiative nor a policymaking imperative triggered the research at the heart of this book. Rather, our shared intellectual and political interests drove our research and writing. We conceived *The Ambivalent State* both as an intervention into public debates about the complicated relationships between the state and its poor citizens and as an attempt to reorient urban scholarship to pay more attention to illicit, clandestine relationships. Lacking the vocation of policymakers or social engineers, we have no recipes to offer to those in government or civil society. We do, however, have a few final words about what we believe the role of social science should be, the need to reorient analysis toward less evident topics, and the possibilities to transform the political reality we have just described.

Focused as it is on the easily visible and conceptually direct side of politics—the one that takes place in government houses, parliaments, voting booths, and that is broadcast through mass media and social media—much political analysis tends to overlook the clandestine connections that we scrutinized in this book. When acknowledged, their existence is often seen as either evidence of the general sordidness of politics and the corruptive influence of power or as a sign of the "backwardness" of less than democratic regimes. Although clandestine connections lack the prestige of a legitimate object of political analysis, we hope to have shown that they constitute a crucial dimension of politics and statecraft that must be empirically dissected and theorized to better understand *routine* state action.[21] We have sought to expose what is hidden from view, unearth relationships sequestered from public discussion, and analyze the collective experience of life in poor areas—or what Loïc Wacquant (2010:199) aptly calls the "mental atmosphere" of territories of relegation—as they relate to this form of state intervention. We approach these issues not as inherent properties of the people living in poor areas but as relational products of their daily encounters with an ambivalent state that routinely betrays what is right.

This type of scholarly work has value in and of itself whether specific policy recommendations are forthcoming or not. It is, first and foremost, an act of recognition for those routinely overlooked or disregarded by the powerful. Didier Fassin (2013:xix) puts it well when he writes:

> [B]y revealing what is generally concealed—or simply ignored—the ethnographer re-establishes citizens in their responsibility to know what is going on and take part in the public sphere, and reinstitutes the individuals and groups affected by these policies in their right to have their experiences acknowledged and their voice heard.

Other than firmly concurring with José Miguel Cruz (2016:392) that "the fight against crime in the region must start by reforming the state and transforming the very institutions that are supposed to guarantee the rule of law," we have no specific advice for those in power. But that does not mean we are eluding our intellectual responsibility; we are rather embracing a specific form of committed scholarly intervention of the kind advocated by Pierre Bourdieu (2000), among others.[22]

Collusion between state and extra-legal actors is a patterned, generalized,[23] and durable phenomenon in Argentina. As elsewhere in the world, it poses a "significant threat to the stability of democratic institutions and to the success of democratization" (della Porta and Vannucci 2012:142). Yet this does not mean that the profound entanglement between drug market groups and security forces is a permanent feature of the polity. Transformation can occur. We engaged in this research project and wrote this book not simply for scholarly purposes but also because we believe change is possible and necessary. But for collusion to be disentangled and eradicated, it will take something more than removing individuals or altering policy. Our shared conviction is that any attempt at political change will need to count on the support of mobilized citizens and grassroots organizations. Glimmers of hope exist. Many of our sources attest to the fact that there are institutional and collective efforts to address and eradicate collusion. Our book has relied on court cases produced by state officials who are, as Marcelo Saín (2015:13) explains, "trying to break up" collusive entanglements between drug dealers and the police. We have also drawn upon official reports that document police illicit actions that have been produced by the Center for Socio-Legal Studies, one of the most prominent human rights organizations in Argentina.[24] In Chapter 3, we referred to the actions of the Mothers against Paco, a group founded by Alicia Romero, whose son, Emanuel, was killed in drug-related violence in a neighborhood near Arquitecto Tucci.[25] Following his death, she organized groups of parents to address addiction in their communities and the organization now has chapters across the country. These groups demonstrate that while poor residents may be objectively constrained and continually victimized, they also engage in meaningful efforts to identify and expose police-criminal collusion.

The example of the anti-Mafia movement in Italy provides an apt model for such an orchestrated effort. A long time in the making, this movement brought together activists with widely different (and oftentimes opposing) political backgrounds who had to "invest considerable time, energy, and patience in building trust" among themselves in order to raise consciousness about morality in politics and denounce the corruption of the state and the party system (Schneider and Schneider 2003:162).[26] Much ink has been spilled in portraying the deep divides that characterize Latin American politics: *la grieta* (the crack) is the term used to describe the highly polarized political field in Argentina. It is up for debate whether this "deep divide" is a new feature of contemporary politics in the region or, as even a superficial look at the extremely fractious history of contemporary Argentina would attest, a somewhat enduring feature of its polity. We argue, following the Italian example, that activists who have few things in common (regarding, for example, their views on the role of the state in the economy or their opinions about reproductive rights, to name a few contentious issues) may find common ground in the fight for transparency, accountability, and decency in politics and policing.

"This is how things are here." We both heard this phrase or variations thereof during the many years we spent in Buenos Aires living and conducting research for this and other projects.[27] The phrase calls for a realistic acknowledgment of durable problems (political and police corruption being just one of them). It is also deployed to dampen any sort of shocking reaction toward the existence of what, from the outside looking in, could be categorized as contemptible behavior. After all, "this is how thing *are* here, get over it" (*our emphasis*). The phrase denotes no small dose of resignation—as if by uttering it, speakers would be stating that this is how things "will always be," no reason to dwell much on it. In this book, we sought to dissect how clandestine connections *are*, but we do not believe in their ineluctability. Things can be different, but it will take much concerted and collective effort (and we suspect no small number of frustrations and setbacks) to transform this state of affairs.

Coda

Since we began this project, the popularity of "tough on crime" policies has been on the rise in Argentina. During the 2015 elections, the presidential candidates from the three major parties all embraced some version of "zero tolerance," from harsher sentences to lowering the minimum age of criminal responsibility. This emergent punitive consensus among dominant actors in the political field structures (and is structured by) dominant common sense on the topic. As we write this, a newly released representative survey shows that 53% of respondents believe that the solution to the lack of public safety (which, after "inflation," is listed as the main problem facing the country) is to provide "more support to the police and harsher sentences to criminals."[28] Interestingly enough, "tough on crime" receives more support from those at the bottom of the social structure: 59.4% of those with only a primary education would like to see harsher sentences and more support to the police as opposed to 42.2% of those with a university education.

As with dominant common sense around other issues (think, for example, about abortion in Latin America or affirmative action and migration policies in the United States and Europe), it takes years and many powerful symbolic interventions to change how people think about the "causes" and "reasonable" ways to address insecurity, *el problema de la seguridad*. These days, the causes of crime are thought to be lax sentencing and weak enforcement. Following this logic, the "obvious" way to tackle crime is with a muscular police force. In the words of Minister of Security Patricia Bullrich, "[W]e have to take care of those who take care of us."[29]

Plenty of scholarship has disproved the effectiveness and indeed troubled the basic principles of "tough on crime" policies. Our analysis provides further grounds to question those punitive policies (and the doxa that feeds them [Wacquant 2009]). Although we have offered no specific policy recommendations, we are certain about one thing: Given the lived experiences dissected in this book, "more power to the police"—that is, to security forces that routinely engage in illegal behavior, govern themselves, and are unaccountable to elected authorities—will do nothing to curb clandestine connections between police and those who commit crimes. In this sense, scrutinizing collusion and making the hidden relationships between police forces and drug dealers visible for the public to see, for the public to know and discuss, is our way of contributing to the long-term political task of disassembling this increasingly dominant common sense about the sources of and solutions to crime and violence in Argentina.

We want to conclude by paraphrasing anthropologist Katherine Verdery (2018:297), who reflected on her remarkable journey into the files that the Romanian security police collected on her while she conducted ethnographic fieldwork. Despite her access to classified files, she observed that she had "scarcely begun to make out what lies in [the state's] shadows. Those shadows are quintessentially the stuff of state-making." After reading and re-reading our legal archive, cross-checking the information with newspaper reports, and returning again and again to our fieldwork material, we had a similar sensation: When it comes to understanding how the state really works, we are still very much in the dark. This project is just a first step. But by scrutinizing the clandestine connections between law enforcement agents and drug dealers, we hope to have shed some much-needed light not only on the ways the Argentine state operates but also on a widespread form of statecraft in the contemporary world.

Notes

Preface and Acknowledgments

1. See also Das and Poole (2004).
2. Bourdieu (2015); Fassin (2015); Jessop (2016); Morgan and Orloff (2017); Schneider and Schneider (2003).
3. Berlusconi (2013); Campana (2011); Campana and Varese (2012); Natarajan (2006).
4. Among them, Ginzburg (1992); Kertzer (2008).

Introduction

1. Unless otherwise noted, all names of peoples and places have been changed to protect their anonymity. Arquitecto Tucci is the same neighborhood where one of us conducted fieldwork for a previous project (Auyero and Berti 2015).
2. Known as *bazuco* in Colombia, *baserolo* in Ecuador, and *mono* in Chile, *paco* is a cheap, highly addictive form of cocaine. On the way in which the spread of paco relates to the transformation of Argentina from a country of transshipment into one of consumption and production of cocaine, see the interesting report by Guy Taylor (2008).
3. Real name.
4. Madres contra el Paco is an organization present in many poor neighborhoods, shantytowns, and squatter settlements in Argentina. They engage in public shaming (locally known as *escraches*) of drug dealers by marching around dealers' houses, publicly denouncing the deleterious effects of the products dealers sell, and demanding court and/or police action against them.
5. On November 28, the bodyguard, a police officer named Alberto Martín Murúa, was sentenced to two years of probation. See "Robo a Oberlin: Condicional al custodio y 5 años al ladron," *cba24n*, November

The Ambivalent State: Police-Criminal Collusion at the Urban Margins. Javier Auyero, Oxford University Press (2019). © Oxford University Press.
DOI: 10.1093/oso/9780190915537.001.0001

28, 2018, https://www.cba24n.com.ar/robo-al-padre-oberlin-prision-condicional-al-custodio-y-5-anos-para-el-ladron.

6. Oberlín's story is not unique. Similar to times of military dictatorships and authoritarian rule, priests working with and for the poor (for example, Enrique Angelelli and José Mujica in Argentina, Óscar Romero in El Salvador, and Juan José Gerardi in Guatemala) are threatened or killed. These days, the victimizers are not only military or paramilitary actors but also drug lords who, in many cases, act in complicity with state officials. For an illuminating chronicle of Girardi's assassination, see Goldman (2007). On the recent killings of Mexican priests José Alfredo López Guillén, Alejo Jiménez, and José Juárez, see, David Agren, " 'Narcos Alone Rule': Mexico Shaken after Three Priests Killed within a Week," *Guardian*, September 29, 2015, retrieved June 1, 2018, www.theguardian.com/world/2016/sep/29/mexico-catholic-priests-killed-drug-trafficking.

7. Bourgois (2015); Koonings and Kruijt (2015); Menjívar and Walsh (2017); Penglase (2014); Larkins (2015); Santamaría and Carey (2017); UNDP (2013).

8. Moser and McIlawine (2004); Rodgers, Beall, and Kanbur (2012); Salahub, Gottsbacher, and DeBoer (2018); Wilding (2010).

9. Kessler and Bruno (2018).

10. Brysk (2012); Cruz (2016); Durán-Martínez (2018); Imbusch, Misse, and Carrión (2011); Morenoff, Sampson, and Raudenbush (2001); Ousey and Lee (2002); Sampson, Raudenbush, and Earls (1997); Sampson and Wilson (1995); Denyer Willis (2015).

11. See also Arias (2017).

12. See also Fassin (2013) and Soss and Weaver (2017).

13. See Davis (2010) and Durán-Martínez (2015, 2018).

14. Given how well-known this group is in Argentina, and in the city of Rosario in particular, we use its real name (Los Monos). We changed the names of all other trafficking groups analyzed in this book. The names and small identifying details of individuals named in the court cases have been changed.

15. The Conurbano Bonaerense is an area made up of 33 districts that surround the city of Buenos Aires. Roughly 14 million people reside in the Conurbano. Although geographically small (just 0.5% of the national territory), 29% of the total population live there, and 40% of its residents fall below the national poverty line (Ronconi and Zarazaga 2017).

16. For exceptions, see Arias's (2006a; 2017) research. On the difference between data collection and theoretically driven data production, see Bourdieu, Chamboderon, and Passeron (1991).

17. Auyero (2013).
18. Dewey, Míguez, and Saín (2017); Jessop (2016).
19. Arias (2006a:75).
20. On descriptions of weak states and "governance voids," see Anderson (1999); Koonings and Kruijt (2007); and Venkatesh (2008). For descriptions of poor neighborhoods as highly controlled by the state, see Goffman (2014); Müller (2016); and Rios (2010).
21. In this sense, our use is closer to Garland's (1996) analysis of ambivalence in British crime control policy. Focusing on the early 1990s, he identifies a "remarkably volatile and ambivalent pattern" (p. 449) in crime control policy, rhetoric, and criminological thinking (i.e., "law and order," "tough on crime," "punitive outbursts," and "demonization of criminals" co-exist with strategies of "normalizing crime," "responsibilizing others," "defining deviance down"). In our case, we are referring to ambivalence in the state's on-the-ground practice and not in crime policy or rhetoric. During the period of this study, Argentina's dominant policy on crime emphasized the criminalization of illicit drugs and dealers and was often accompanied by public displays of force through well-publicized arrests and raids.
22. For overviews of scholarship on the state, see Hall and Ikenberry (1989); Hobson (2006); King and Le Gales (2012); Morgan and Orloff (2017); Nelson (2006); and Weiss (2006).
23. On the symbolic dimension of the state, see Bourdieu (2015); Loyal and Quilley (2017); and Morgan and Orloff (2017). As Morgan and Orloff (2017:449) explain well: "[S]tates concentrate and deploy both material and symbolic powers. Weber was right to emphasize states' control of the means of coercion in specified geographic territories, but he also highlighted the centrality of legitimacy to any form of rule; neither coercion nor legitimacy is a given—they both must be accomplished. State legitimacy requires more than mere force; states also operate through the pull they have on the public consciousness. The subjective element of state power is of vital importance, as states are not mere arenas in which utility-maximizing individuals satisfy their goals. At the very least, states help define those goals, and some would see states operating at a deeper level in constituting subjects and shaping the forms of knowledge out of which public and private action develop."
24. Blanco et al. (2014); Marwell (2016); Morgan and Orloff (2017).
25. For analogous arguments, see Arias (2006b); Arias and Goldstein (2010); Jaffe (2013); Rodgers (2006); and Denyer Willis (2009; 2015).

26. On police repressive actions, see reports from CELS (2014; 2016) and CORREPI (available at http://www.correpi.lahaine.org). On incarceration, see reports in Procuración Penitenciaria de la Nación, accessible at http://www.ppn.gov.ar/?q=node/2586.

27. Perlman's description is similar to Bobea's (2015) analysis of the "criminogenic environment."

28. On legal cynicism, see Kirk and Matsuda (2011); Kirk and Papachristos (2011); Kirk et al. (2012); and Sampson and Bartusch (1998).

29. Emirbayer (1997); Mische (2008); Tilly (2002); Zelizer (2012).

30. For a critique of the approach and its (claim to) novelty, see Burawoy (2017).

31. Auyero (2000; 2007; 2013).

32. For a similar emphasis on interactions in the study of drug-related violence, see Duran-Martinez (2015) and Bailey and Taylor (2009).

33. Further details of that fieldwork can be found in Auyero and Berti (2015).

34. These three federal law enforcement agencies are dependent on the national Ministry of Security and have jurisdiction over the trafficking of illicit drugs.

35. For more on the use of wiretapped conversations, see Berlusconi (2013); Campana (2011); and Natarajan (2006).

36. Campana and Varese (2012).

37. Emerson, Fretz, and Shaw (1995).

38. See, for example, Cavanagh (2014); Tamous (2017); and de los Santos and Lascano (2017).

39. Becker (1958; 1970); Katz (2001; 2002).

40. For descriptions of conflicts within security agencies, see Hathazy (2016) and Saín (2017). For evidence that investigations (wiretappings included) can be manipulated by members of police forces, see the case of the narcopolicías in Entre Ríos. Jorge Riani, "Detienen Por Narcotráfico Al Comisario Que Dirigía Los Golpes Antidrogas En Entre Ríos," La Nación, May 15, 2015, retrieved June 1, 2018, http://www.lanacion.com.ar/1792937-detienen-por-narcotrafico-al-comisario-que-dirigia-los-golpes-antidrogas-en-entre-rios.

41. On money laundering and electoral campaigns, see Casas-Zamora (2013); Ferreira Rubio (2013); and González (2013). In Argentina, research confirms that illicit links extend well beyond low-level security agents. In his comparison between police regulation of drug trafficking in the states of Buenos Aires and Santa Fe, for example, political scientist Hernán Flom (2018:12) reports: "Numerous unconnected interviewees and secondary

sources reported extensive police corruption linked to drug trafficking and other organized criminal activities in various neighborhoods of Greater Buenos Aires (GBA). While there is no evidence of direct political involvement in managing the police rackets, it is doubtful that these could have persisted without political knowledge or protection." For additional evidence of clandestine connections among politicians, state officials, and judges in Argentina, see Saín (2017). Beyond Argentina, a host of evidence confirms the far-reaching character of these links. Based on a close analysis of witness testimonies from three U.S. trials, a report from the Human Rights Clinic (2017:3, 6) at the University of Texas at Austin uncovers a pattern of "state complicity, tolerance, acquiescence, and/or cooperation with the Zeta [drug] cartel" in the Mexican state of Coahuila involving not only low-level state and municipal police but also "city police chiefs, state and federal prosecutors, state prisons, sectors of the federal police and the Mexican army, and state politicians."

42. For detailed descriptions, see the work by CELS (2016); Marcelo Saín (2004; 2008); and Matías Dewey (2012a; 2012b; 2015). See also Ossona (2017).

43. For a description of members of the judiciary involved in drug trafficking networks, see CELS (2016). For a report on politicians involved in cases of drug trafficking, see Di Lodovico (2016a). One of the most notorious cases is that of Judge Raúl Reynoso, who was indicted for charging hefty fees (up to US$350,000) to protect roads from police action so traffickers could move their products and to free dealers caught by the police without charges. See "Procesan a un juez federal acusado de cobrar coimas para liberar a narcos," Clarín, January 12, 2015, retrieved June 1, 2018, https://www.clarin.com/policiales/procesan-federal-acusado-liberar-narcos_0_4yk4IDIVg.html. See also Saralegui (2017).

44. Saín (2017).

45. For a description of politically generated arson, see Auyero (2012). On food lootings, see Auyero (2007).

Chapter 1

1. For a more recent review, see Schneider (2018).

2. This very broad question has been at the center of both classic and contemporary scholarship in the social sciences. Many authors agree that the decline of interpersonal violence in a given territory is the historical outcome of the concentration of legitimate violence by the state (Weber

1978). Norbert Elias (1978:179), for example, argues that the pacification of society—what he describes as the "relatively peaceful collective life of large masses of people"—is intricately related to the state's monopoly of force. The more the state legally hoards the deployment of physical violence, the more peaceful the social spaces in which people interact will become (see Auyero and Sobering 2017). The Eliasian perspective has been adopted by contemporary authors to explain the general decline of interpersonal violence over many centuries across the globe. For an example, see Pinker (2012) and Yashar (2012). For a critique, see Gray (2015) and Malešević (2017). Elias's notion of the civilizing process has several shortcomings and ambivalences, and its applicability across time and space has been questioned. David Garland (1996), for example, points out that the notion of a state presumably "capable of providing security, law and order, and crime control within its territorial boundaries" is nothing more than a myth. High crime rates and the "widely acknowledged limitations of criminal justice agencies," which Garland highlighted two decades ago for the case of Britain, corroded the myth of the sovereign state. Criticisms aside, what concerns us here are the questions raised by this literature about the relationship between the strength and actions of a central power and "the patterning of the whole libidinal economy—drives, affects, emotions, and all" (Elias 1978:239).

3. Anderson (1999); Auyero (2000); Williams (1992).

4. Denyer Willis (2015); Fassin (2013); Goffman (2009); Müller (2016); Rios (2010); Stuart (2016).

5. Anderson (1999); Desmond (2016); Massey (1990); Ralph (2014); Rivlin (2010); Wilson (1996).

6. On punishment practices, see Alexander (2012); Goffman (2009); Rios (2010); Soss, Fording, and Schram (2011); Soss and Weaver (2017); and Wacquant (2009). On the racialized "war on drugs," see Jarecki (2012). On the militarization of domestic police forces, see Kraska and Kappeler (1997).

7. Scholars frequently document how the state breaks the law (Brinks 2008; Goldstein 2012; Penglase 2014). For details on human rights violations, see CELS (2012; 2016).

8. See Arias (2006a; 2017) for nuanced and informative exceptions.

9. Arias (2006b); Arias and Barnes (2016).

10. Saín (2017).

11. Economists, for example, conceptualize collusion as a form of interfirm cooperation intended to suppress competition to increase profits.

What scholars call *explicit* collusion is predicated on two forms of exchange: interfirm communication and the transfer of material resources (Marshall and Marx 2014:6). Research on cartel behavior agrees that the exchange of informational resources is critical to efforts to impact market dynamics (Athey and Bagwell 2001; Harrington and Skrzypacz 2011; Kandori and Matsushima 1998).

12. Our definition is based on existing literature in political sociology, particularly that of Brooks (2016); della Porta and Vannucci (2012); and Rothstein and Varraich (2017).

13. See also Granovetter (2007). For broader definitions of corruption, see Beetham (2015) and Lessig (2013). For a recent review of sociological approaches, see Heath et al. (2016).

14. On the prevalence and misuse of the term "collusion," see Goodman (2017).

15. On the role of exchange in political corruption, see della Porta and Vannucci (1999).

16. This includes illuminating works by historians and historical sociologists (Astorga 2005; Gunst 1995; Roldán 2002; Valdés Castellanos 2013), political scientists (Arias 2006a; Brass 1992; Wilkinson 2004) and anthropologists (Das 1990; Kakar 1996). On what the state is and what it does, see also Arias (2017) and Cruz (2016).

17. For efforts to move beyond the weak/strong binary to understand state action, see Arias (2006a; 2017); Arias and Barnes (2016); Dewey, Míguez, and Saín (2017); Rodgers (2006); and Schneider and Schneider (2003).

18. See also Schenider (2018).

19. Barkey (1994).

20. Similarly, Penglase (2014:113) states that clandestine relations between traffickers and policemen in a Rio favela are conflictive, "dynamic, conflicted, and unstable." See also Arias (2006a).

21. Many a historical example also shows that collusive relations between legitimate powerholders and criminal organizations have been used to repress left-wing activism while turning a blind eye to the illicit activities such as drug trafficking. In the United States, there is a long history of political actors' involvement with organized crime: "the shenanigans of Tammany Hall's party machine, the political sheltering of alcohol smuggling and bootlegging during Prohibition, and the financial contributions by diverse crime syndicates to later campaigns" (Casas-Zamora 2013:2). See also Blok (2001); Chubb (1996); Gambetta (1993); and Varese (2011; 2014).

22. "During the presidency of Ernesto Samper (1994–1998)," Durán-Martínez (2018:1854) writes, "the extensive links between the Cali DTO [drug trafficking organizations] and sectors of the police and the political class came to light; accusations emerged that Samper's presidential campaign had received funds from the Rodríguez Orejuela brothers, drug lords in the Cali DTO (as Chapter 5 describes). The judicial process initiated with these accusations, known as Proceso 8000 (the 8,000 Process, named for the case number assigned to the investigation by the Prosecutor General's Office), linked twenty-one senators and representatives of Congress, hundreds of police officers, private companies, and national authorities such as the general comptroller of the nation and the general procurator, with Cali traffickers. President Samper himself was exonerated, but the scandal seriously undermined his authority." See also Durán-Martínez (2015).

23. For additional research on the Sicilian Mafia, see Gambetta (1993).

24. Violence is oftentimes deployed to resolve contractual arrangements (Andreas and Wallman 2009) or to address disciplinary or succession problems (Reuter 2009a).

25. For descriptions of the use of violence in drug markets, see Bourgois (1995); Ousey and Lee (2002); Reding (2009); Reinarman and Levine (1997); Rodgers (2017); and Venkatesh (2008). For descriptions of systemic violence in the Conurbano Bonaerense, see Di Lodovico (2009a; 2009b; 2009c) and Messi (2003; 2010). For a general assessment of this kind of violence in the city of Rosario, see Font (2011). See also Saín (2017).

26. A similar comparison could be made for the cities of Cali and Medellín in Colombia in the 1990s and 2000s (Durán-Martínez 2018). See also Valdés Castellanos (2013).

27. "State interventions against crime," Durán-Martínez (2018:653) writes, "can shape the criminal market and, in turn, violence. For example, heightened law enforcement can force cooperation among criminals who would otherwise work individually and create pressures for territorial expansion, but it may also force organizations to reduce their size to evade attention. Arrests and enforcement pressures can transform, fragment, or create leadership vacancies within criminal organizations, which can turn into violent market disputes. State action can thus spur competition in the illegal market and increase the quantity of violence."

28. For the case of Peru, see van Dun (2014a; 2014b). On the methamphetamine markets in the United States and Japan, see Friman (2009).

29. See Friman (2009); Naylor (2009); Ousey and Lee (2002); Reuter (2009a); Snyder and Durán-Martínez (2009); Williams (2009); Zimring and Hawkins (1997).

30. Durán-Martinez (2018). For a different perspective, see Resignato (2000).

31. Isaac Martin made us aware of this point during a presentation of an early draft of two of the chapters of this book at his home institution (UCSD).

32. For a review, see Bonner (2014).

33. Put differently, Penglase (2014:20) writes: "Police corruption and the actual involvement of some policemen in the drug trade produce scenarios that are shifting and opaque: the police and the drug dealers can be allies, can work together against other police or other drug dealers, or can quickly switch sides."

34. On this complicity, see Arias (2006a; 2017); Davis (2006); and Ungar (2011). For more on the abuse of power within a branch of the Mexican police, see Garrido and Torres (2011). On community policing efforts in Mexico City, see Müller (2010).

35. On the police in Argentina, see Flom (2018) and Saín (2004; 2008; 2015).

36. For an overview of the historiography on the Argentine police, see Barreneche (2015). For an examination of police abuse and corruption in Buenos Aires during the 1950s and 1960s, see Barreneche (2016).

37. See also Dewey (2012a; 2015; 2017b), whose work provides an empirically rich dissection of what he calls "the clandestine order."

38. For an ethnography of police behavior in Rosario, see Frederic et al. (2013). On police violence, see Glanc and Glanc (2013). On its relationship to notions of respect, see Garriga Zucal (2013; 2016). On the socialization process of new recruits of the Buenos Aires police, see Melotto (2013). On police education, see Frederic (2013). On the relationships between police officers and judges, see Bianciotto (2013).

39. Ugolini's (2016) ethnography of a police station in the Conurbano Bonaerense insightfully describes the highly situational character of what she calls "narratives of legitimation" deployed by police officers. These narratives are used by officers both to define what are considered to be "legitimate" practices and to justify for themselves and for others their illegal behavior.

40. State police departments are made possible by the federal nature of the Argentine Constitution (Barrera 2013).

41. For a review of some of the most notorious recent cases, see CELS (2016).

42. He is referring to an episode that took place in May 2005. See "Detuvieron a cuatro policías federales con 116 kilos de cocaína," *La Nación*, May

10, 2005, retrieved June 1, 2018, http://www.lanacion.com.ar/702998-detuvieron-a-cuatro-policias-federales-con-116-kilos-de-cocaina.

43. Gustavo Carbajal, "Cada vez son más los policías procesados por narcotráfico," *La Nación,* July 12, 2015, retrieved June 1, 2018, http://www.lanacion.com.ar/1809748-cada-vez-son-mas-los-policias-procesados-por-narcotrafico.

44. On the misleading distinction between producing, consuming, and trans-shipment countries, see CELS (2016).

45. Quoted in Facundo Aguirre and Tomás Máscolo, "Ricardo Ragendorfer: 'La Fuga Fue Comprada y La Bonaerense Salió a Marcar La Cancha,'" *La Izquierda Diario,* January 8, 2016, retrieved June 1, 2018, http://www.laizquierdadiario.com/Ricardo-Ragendorfer-La-fuga-fue-comprada-y-la-Bonaerense-salio-a-marcar-la-cancha.

46. On measures of corruption in Argentina, see Heath et al. (2016) and Transparency International (2016). For a comparative perspective on regional and international efforts to combat corruption, see Manzetti (2009).

47. For analyses of the complicated dynamic between corruption and reform, see Dewey (2015); Hinton (2006); Saín (2008; 2017); and Ungar (2011).

48. For a discussion of this paradox, see Johnston (2014:151–55).

Chapter 2

1. The Riachuelo River is highly polluted and has been called "the worst ecological disaster of the country," according to the Federal Ombudsman (Peralta 2003). On the current state of affairs, see "Riachuelo: La contaminación y los riesgos para la salud," *La Nación,* October 2, 2017, retrieved June 1, 2018, https://www.lanacion.com.ar/2068268-la-contaminacion-y-los-riesgos-para-la-salud-para-saber-mas.

2. Residents in the older neighborhood are property owners and generally better off compared to shantytown dwellers and squatters, both of whom experience issues related to their unresolved land tenure.

3. In addition to infrastructural deprivation (Rodgers and O'Neill 2012), many residents are exposed to environmental hazards like poor air quality and contaminated water (Auyero and Swistun 2009).

4. Despite these poor conditions, the state has not entirely deserted residents of Arquitecto Tucci. One public hospital, an urgent care unit (Unidad de Pronta Atención [UPA]), several public schools, the Asignación Universal por Hijo (the largest conditional cash transfer

program, effective since 2008), and many other welfare programs (e.g., Argentina Trabaja, Plan Vida) provide assistance to residents. Of the 100 interviews conducted for previous work (Auyero and Berti 2015), a little more than half of the interviewees (54%) benefited from one or more of these state programs.

5. For more details on this, see Auyero and Berti (2015).
6. In Penglase's (2014) ethnographic account of drug-related violence in Caxambu, a Rio de Janeiro favela, residents expressed similar concerns. See also Larkins (2015).
7. On the issue of memory and the idealized past, see the classic statement by Erikson (1976).
8. Made by an infusion of dried leaves of yerba, mate is a traditional drink in Argentina.
9. This often occurs after car thieves are done disassembling them for parts to sell on the black market. On the market for stolen car parts in Buenos Aires, see Dewey (2012a).
10. Wacquant (2015).
11. We were finished with our fieldwork when this episode took place. Specific citations are not included to protect anonymity of field site.
12. Auyero and Berti (2015).
13. On the geography of homicides in Argentina, see Sol Amaya and Bianca Pallaro, "El mapa de los homicidios en la Argentina," *La Nación*, November 16, 2017, retrieved June 1, 2018, https://www.lanacion.com.ar/2082534-el-mapa-de-los-homicidios-en-la-argentina.
14. Sampson and Wilson (1995).
15. Compare the 113,732.29 kilograms of coca leaf seized in 2015 with the 4,554.13 kilograms seized in 2010 (UNODC 2016). See also Olivia Sohr, "Los Datos Del Narcotráfico," *Chequeado*, November 13, 2013, retrieved June 1, 2018, http://chequeado.com/el-explicador/los-datos-del-narcotrafico and Matías Di Santi and Martín Slipczuk, "Burzaco: 'Estamos En Un Año Récord En Todo Lo Que Es Incautación de Cocaína, Éxtasis y Metanfetaminas,'" *Chequeado*, September 23, 2016, retrieved June 1, 2018, http://chequeado.com/ultimas-noticias/burzaco-estamos-en-un-ano-record-en-todo-lo-que-es-incautacion-de-cocaina-extasis-y-metanfetaminas/.
16. For a review of the relationship between alcohol, drugs, and violence, see Parker and Auerhahn (1998).
17. Bourgois (1995); Contreras (2012); Harding (2010); Jones (2009); Kotlowitz (1991); LeBlanc (2004); McCart et al. (2007); Venkatesh (2008).
18. Brennan, Molnar, and Earls (2007); Clark et al. (2008); Osofsky (1999).

19. In examining the ways that drug violence travels from streets into homes, we want to underscore the need to adopt a more comprehensive understanding of drug violence. Our project dovetails with recent work by Angélica Durán-Martínez (2018:1273), who contends: "The importance of using a broad definition of drug violence is illustrated by examining the violence that exploded in Mexico after President Felipe Calderón declared war against trafficking organizations in 2006. The government initially claimed that most violence involved criminals, but it was forced to start changing this rhetoric after the famous Mexican poet Javier Sicilia, whose son was killed in April 2011, organized a victims' movement called the Movimiento por la Paz con Justicia y Dignidad (Movement for Peace with Justice and Dignity). The massive victim gatherings promoted by Sicilia made evident that drug violence affected many civilians who died as a result of abuses of force by state officials, of extortion, of 'stray bullets' (being in the wrong place at the wrong time), and of a variety of causes that transcended, but were not detached from, trafficking disputes."

20. On the misleading dichotomy between public and private life, see Wilding (2010). An article drawing on a subsection of this data (Auyero and Kilanski 2015) analyzed how residents living in dangerous contexts cared for themselves and their families. Residents adopted two sets of practices aimed at protecting themselves and their loved ones. First, they adopted small, mundane acts to form connections and create order in a chaotic environment. Second, parents taught their children about the nature and use of violence in attempts to protect them from harm.

21. Di Lodovico (2009b); Messi (2003; 2010; 2012).

22. Black (1983).

23. We found that mothers did most of the disciplinary work to protect their children. Our field site is hardly an exception in this respect. U.S. black feminist scholars and others have shown that attempting to keep loved ones out of harm's way—particularly challenging in the context of racism and poverty—is widely understood as women's work (Bryson et al. 2001; Elliott and Aseltine 2013; Hochschild and Manchung 1990; Jones 2009). According to a generalized perception among residents of Arquitecto Tucci, a child or children involved in the drug economy is the result of "bad mothering" (Auyero and Berti 2015). Social scientists have found that mothers feel intense pressure to engage in practices linked to class- and geographically specific understandings of being a "good" mother (Badinter 1981; Collins 2019; Edin and Kefalas 2005; Hays 1996). As a result, mothers (not fathers) are the ones who are blamed if children are injured or killed or have otherwise "fallen" to drug addiction.

24. Not all of the violence of the drug trade travels home, nor can every episode of violence in the domestic sphere be traced to disputes that drift inward. But the more we scrutinized violent events within homes, the more we noted that they were in fact connected to violence generated by drug trafficking. Our examination of this connection helps to clarify an association often documented in social science literature (Bourgois 1995; Brennan et al. 2007; Clark et al. 2008; Contreras 2012; Harding 2010; Jones 2009; Kotlowitz 1991; LeBlanc 2004; McCart et al. 2007; Osofsky 1999; Venkatesh 2008) by identifying a set of pathways through which the public violence of an illicit market enters homes.

25. Bourdieu, Chamboderon, and Passeron (1991).

Chapter 3

1. The term "legal cynicism" was first developed by criminologists to challenge the notion that racial minorities in the United States held subcultural values that tolerated deviance and thus accommodated higher levels of crime. Calling for research to examine neighborhood contexts, Robert Sampson and Dawn Bartusch (1998:782) differentiated between individual attitudes toward deviance and perceptions of the law, observing that "support for what one personally views as 'appropriate' (or normative) forms of conduct does not necessarily imply support for the regulations of the larger society or the mechanisms used to enforce such conduct (i.e. laws, policing)." Scholars have since moved from understanding legal cynicism as a form of anomie or "normlessness" that results from continual exposure to injustice, segregation, and insecurity (Anderson 1999; Nivette el al. 2015) to a cultural frame through which people observe and make sense of their social worlds (Hagan, Kaiser, and Hanson 2016). As David Kirk and Andrew Papachristos (2011:1192) explain, "legal cynicism is cultural precisely because individual perceptions of the law are augmented and solidified through communication and social interaction among neighborhood residents." As a cultural mechanism, legal cynicism is shaped by both structural determinants (and deprivations) and negative interactions with state agents, particularly the police. Legal cynicism among residents has material effects on crime and violence. When people perceive the law as unavailable, individuals are left to resolve their problems independently. Examining the case of Chicago, David Kirk and Mauri Matsuda (2011) find that in neighborhoods with high levels of legal cynicism, residents are less likely to report crimes than in neighborhoods

where people have more trust in the police. High rates of legal cynicism also help explain the persistence of homicides despite declining rates of poverty and violence in Chicago (Kirk and Papachristos 2011).

2. This widespread feeling, we should note, is not exclusive to Arquitecto Tucci. In a representative survey conducted among youth living in informal settlements in Argentina, over two-thirds (68.3%) stated that the police either know about or participate in the drug trafficking taking place in their neighborhoods (UCA 2016). On perceptions of police (in) efficiency and corruption in Santiago (Chile), Lima (Peru), and Bogota (Colombia), see Arias and Tocornal Montt (2018). On perceptions of the police and interactions between police and citizens in Mexico, see Müller (2012a).

3. This is a reconstruction based on the court case, the testimonies transcribed therein, and newspaper accounts about the episode. Names have been modified.

4. Beginning in December 2010, it was common to see the National Guard patrolling the streets of poor areas in the Conurbano Bonaerense. On their deployment in marginalized areas, see Sozzo (2014) and Raspall (2012). On the relationship between their presence and the corruption of the Federal Police force—i.e., its participation in extortion and its protection of some drug "kitchens"—see CELS (2012), especially pp. 107–8, 121–22.

5. Like many others, Joni mixes Rivotril with alcohol. On the risks and highly addictive character of such a mix, see Lizmarie Maldonado, "Concurrent Alcohol and Clonazepam Abuse," *Drugabuse*, n.d., retrieved June 1, 2018, http://drugabuse.com/library/concurrent-alcohol-and-clonazepam-abuse/.

6. Specific citations not included to protect anonymity of field site.

7. For a full description of the workings of patronage politics in contemporary Argentina and the role of brokers, see Auyero (2000) and Auyero and Benzecry (2017).

8. Ossona (2014); Zarazaga (2014).

9. Auyero (2000).

Chapter 4

1. Throughout this book, we describe the drug trafficking organizations in the past tense, acknowledging that each group was impacted in different ways by the outcome of the trials.

2. On hearsay (or "public secrets") about relationships between police and traffickers, see Penglase (2014:122–28).

3. At time of writing, this case has been brought to trial but no arrests have been made.
4. Names of places and persons in this section have been changed.
5. We converted Argentine pesos (ARS) to U.S. dollars (USD) using the average exchange rate for the year in which the conversations took place.
6. Saín (2015).
7. For similar examples in the favela of Santa Ana in Rio de Janeiro, Brazil, see Arias (2006a:114).
8. For details on how drug trafficking organizations use slums and other informal settlements, see Alarcón (2009).
9. Goldstein (1985).
10. Specific citations reporting on these homicides are not included to protect anonymity of the field site.
11. Ruiz (2013).
12. "Hay Fecha para el Juicio Oral al ex Jefe de Policía," *Página/12*, December 31, 2017, retrieved June 1, 2018, https://www.pagina12.com.ar/11728-tognoli-ya-sabe-su-dia-y-su-hora. See also several reports published in www.cosecharoja.org.
13. "Dos Policías de Santa Fe Serán Procesados por Proteger a un Narcotraficante," *La Nación*, January 13, 2017, retrieved June 1, 2018, http://www.lanacion.com.ar/1975400-dos-policias-de-santa-fe-seran-procesados-por-proteger-a-un-narcotraficante.
14. Saín (2015).

Chapter 5

1. For details about collusion at different levels of the state security forces, see Dewey (2015; 2017b) and Saín (2015).
2. On collusion in Brazil, China, Mexico, and Russia, see Arias and Barnes (2016); Flores Pérez (2014); and Stephenson (2017).
3. This process is also documented by McAdam, Tarrow, and Tilly (2001) for the case of collective contentious action.
4. Stephenson (2017:422).
5. For descriptions of these family connections, see De los Santos and Lascano (2017) and Schreiner and Tamous (2016).
6. On the documented murders associated with Los Monos, see also Schreiner and Tamous (2016).
7. The book *Los Monos: Historia de la familia narco que transformó a Rosario en un infierno* by journalists De los Santos and Lascano (2017) provides

a vivid chronicle of the murderous character of this group. The reconstruction of this episode is based on this book and on the following article: Mauro Aguilar, "La noche en la que empezó la guerra: Pájaro Cantero, acribillado a traición," *Clarín*, March 25, 2017, retrieved June 1, 2018, https://www.clarin.com/policiales/noche-empezo-guerra-pajaro-cantero-acribillado-traicion_0_HJybb7Nhg.html.

8. For a comparative analysis of gangs around the world, see Hazen and Rodgers (2014).

9. On framing processes in social movements, see Benford and Snow (2000) and Snow and Benford (1988; 1992).

10. This rally was reported in the local newspaper. It is important to note that not all public protests of police corruption are connected to trafficking organizations like Los Monos. For example, to our knowledge the protests that were planned in the community meeting in Arquitecto Tucci that we described in Chapter 3 were not affiliated with Los Vagones or other illicit actors in the neighborhood.

11. Arias (2006a; 2018).

12. De los Santos and Lascano (2017).

Chapter 6

1. Our reconstructions are based on several articles published in *La Nación, Clarín, La Política OnLine*. Specific citations not included to protect anonymity of town.

2. Specific citations not included to protect anonymity of town.

3. Saín (2015).

4. On the number of informal settlements in Buenos Aires, see Marcos Quintans, "En Argentina hay más de 4 mil villas que en conjunto ocupan una superficie más grande que toda la Ciudad de Buenos Aires," *Infobae*, January 27, 2018, retrieved June 1, 2018, https://www.infobae.com/sociedad/2018/01/27/en-argentina-hay-mas-de-4-mil-villas-que-en-conjunto-ocupan-una-superficie-mas-grande-que-toda-la-ciudad-de-buenos-aires/. On violence, drug addiction, and general lack of trust in the police and National Guard in poor informal settlements, see Navarro (2016).

5. Arias (2017); Gay (2005).

6. The relationship between corrupted and corruptor, Donatella della Porta and Alberto Vannucci (2012:138) write, "may sometimes be made easier by the intervention of a wide range of brokers who specialize in illegal

markets, where expected rewards, as well as risks, are generally higher. Middlemen may establish contacts between the two parties, looking for approachable and receptive partners, they may help conduct negotiations and physically transfer bribes."

7. According to the proceeding, in 2014 Raúl paid US$500 per week to the José León Suarez precinct; US$1,500 per week to the Narcotics Division of San Martín (also known as "La Casita"); US$1,000 per week to the DDI (Dirección Departamental de Investigaciones—Investigations Unit) San Martín; and US$500 per week to the Comando de Prevención Comunitaria.

8. La Brigada is a special unit of the State Police.

Chapter 7

1. Holland (2017:13).

2. Politicians may receive part of the bribes accepted by the police, but they are typically not able to oversee what specific police agents, units, or departments are doing (Saín 2015).

3. Holland (2017:14).

4. For details on gun regulation in Argentina, see "Argentina: Gun Facts, Figures and the Law," *Gun Policy*, n.d., https://www.gunpolicy.org/firearms/region/argentina.

5. On the relationship between police and the judiciary, see Bianciotto (2013).

6. De los Santos and Lascano (2017).

7. McAdam, Tarrow, and Tilly (2001:331). See also McAdam, Tarrow, and Tilly (2008).

8. Tilly (1996:593).

9. See also Hathazy (2013).

10. Bergman (2016); Sain (2015).

11. The diffusion of what Philippe Bourgois (2018:391) calls "addiction markets" to many locations and vulnerable groups in Latin America "has been the product of ratcheting up of state coercion and legal repression generated by the escalation of the US wars on terror and drugs. Traffickers responded to the intensified monitoring of US airspace after 9/11 by multiplying short-legged international transport layovers along diversified airborne, overland, underground and aquatic routes." See also "Southward Marching Powder," *Economist,* November 22, 2013, retrieved June 1, 2018, https://www.economist.com/blogs/americasview/2013/11/drugs-argentina and Mike LaSusa, "Report Maps Regional Differences in Argentina Drug Trade," *InSight Crime,* February 4, 2016,

retrieved June 1, 2018, https://www.insightcrime.org/news/analysis/report-maps-regional-differences-in-argentina-drug-trade.

12. Keohane (1986); Sahlins (1972; 1977).

13. We want to thank Dennis Rodgers for making us aware of this crucial point.

14. Kirk and Matsuda (2011); Kirk and Papachristos (2011); Kirk et al. (2012).

15. Detailed descriptions of such conflicts can be found in Bourgois (1995); Ousey and Lee (2002); Reding (2009); Reinarman and Levine (1997); Rodgers (2017); and Venkatesh (2008).

16. Miron (2001); Shepard and Blackley (2005); Werb et al. (2011). Maher and Dixon (2001).

17. Resignato (2000); Vargas (2016).

18. Elias (1994:450).

Chapter 8

1. Saín (2017:821).

2. Davis (2006); Ungar (2011); Valdés Castellanos (2013).

3. Di Lodovico (2017).

4. Works on relationships between criminal organizations and the state include those by Andreas and Wallman (2009); Arias (2006b; 2017); Arias and Barnes (2016); Denyer Willis (2009; 2015); Flores Pérez (2014); Stephenson (2017); and Williams (2009).

5. Morgan and Orloff (2017).

6. For a classic treatment of the construction of sociological objects, see Bourdieu et al. (1991).

7. Auyero and Jensen (2015).

8. Goffman (2014); Müller (2012a; 2012b; 2016); Rios (2010); Stuart (2016); Soss and Weaver (2017); Wacquant (2009).

9. Fassin (2013); Denyer Willis (2015).

10. Stuart (2016).

11. CELS (2016); Seri (2012); and Ungar (2011).

12. For the case of Chicago, see Kalven (2016) and Hagedorn (2015); for New York City, see Czitrom (2016).

13. This story was broken in the Mexican newspaper *El Universal* (Pardoy and Inzunza 2014a) and later published in English (Pardoy and Inzunza 2014b).

14. U.S. Department of Homeland Security, "Investigation of DHS Employee Corruption Cases," November 23, 2015, https://www.dhs.gov/sites/

default/files/publications/Departmental%20Management%20and%20
Operations%20%28DMO%29%20-%20Investigation%20of%20DHS%20
Employee%20Corruption%20Cases_0.pdf.

15. Auyero, Bourgois, and Scheper-Hughes (2015).

16. Bourdieu, Chamboderon, and Passeron (1991); Pachirat (2011).

17. Penglase (2014); Wacquant (2008; 2010); Wacquant, Slater, and Pereyra (2014).

18. Auyero (1999); Auyero and Swistun (2009).

19. Schneider and Schneider (2008:363).

20. Specific citations referencing local *operativos* not included to protect anonymity of field site.

21. Auyero (2007).

22. As one of us wrote elsewhere (Collins, Jensen, and Auyero 2017), we are well aware of the risks involved in this kind of public social science (Stacey 2004). Still a precarious pursuit facing internal and external pressures, this kind of intervention is not always rewarded within academia (Schor 2004; Vaughan 2004).

23. We assert this based on our evidence and that of others (e.g., Saín 2017).

24. For more information about CELS, see their website: https://www.cels.org.ar/.

25. Alicia Romero described her history and decision to start the Madres contra Paco in an interview with *La Nacion* in 2016. See José Eduardo Abadi, "Alicia Romero, de Madres Contra El Paco: 'Ayudar Nos Saca Un Poco Del Dolor,'" *Clarín*, August 14, 2016, retrieved June 1, 2018, https://www.clarin.com/viva/alicia-romero-madres-paco-ayudar_0_BypCTRDY.html.

26. See also Perry (2018).

27. Auyero (2013); Auyero and Berti (2015); Auyero and Swistun (2009); Sobering (2016; 2018).

28. See "Inseguridad vs. Inflación: Llamativa Encuesta Sobre Las Problemas de Los Argentinos," *Clarín*, January 31, 2018, retrieved June 1, 2018, https://www.clarin.com/politica/inseguridad-vs-inflacion-llamativa-encuesta-problemas-argentinos_0_S1q7zBkIG.html.

29. "Bullrich: 'Nosotros Vamos a Cuidar a Los Que Nos Cuidan,'" *La Prensa*, February 1, 2018, retrieved June 1, 2018, http://www.laprensa.com.ar/461705-Bullrich-Nosotros-vamos-a-cuidar-a-los-que-nos-cuidan.note.aspx.

References

Alarcón, Cristian. 2009. *Si Me Querés Quereme Transa*. Buenos Aires: Norma.

Alexander, Michelle. 2012. *The New Jim Crow: Mass Incarceration in the Age of Colorblindness*. New York: New Press.

Anderson, Elijah. 1999. *Code of the Street: Decency, Violence, and the Moral Life of the Inner City*. New York: Norton.

Andreas, Peter, and Joel Wallman. 2009. "Illicit Markets and Violence: What Is the Relationship?" *Crime, Law and Social Change* 52(3):225–29.

Arias, Desmond, and Nicholas Barnes. 2016. "Crime and Plural Orders in Rio de Janeiro, Brazil." *Current Sociology* 65(3):448–65.

Arias, Desmond, and Daniel Goldstein, eds. 2010. *Violent Democracies in Latin America*. Durham, NC: Duke University Press.

Arias, Enrique Desmond. 2006a. *Drugs and Democracy in Rio de Janeiro: Trafficking, Social Networks, and Public Security*. Chapel Hill: University of North Carolina Press.

Arias, Enrique Desmond. 2006b. "Trouble en Route: Drug Trafficking and Clientelism in Rio de Janeiro Shantytowns." *Qualitative Sociology* 29(4):427–45.

Arias, Enrique Desmond. 2017. *Criminal Enterprises and Governance in Latin America and the Caribbean*. Cambridge, UK: Cambridge University Press.

Arias, Enrique Desmond, and Ximena Tocornal Montt. 2018. "Social Disorganisation and Neighbourhood Effects in Latin America: Insights and Limitations." Pp. 121–38 in *Social Theories of Urban Violence in the Global South: Towards Safe and Inclusive Cities*, edited by J. E. Salahub, M. Gottsbacher, and J. de Boer. Abingdon, UK: Routledge.

Arlacchi, Pino. 1983. *Mafia, Peasants and Great Estates: Society in Traditional Calabria*. Cambridge, UK: CUP Archive.

Athey, Susan, and Kyle Bagwell. 2001. "Optimal Collusion with Private Information." *RAND Journal of Economics* 32(3): 428–65.

Astorga, Luis. 2005. *El Siglo de las Drogas*. Mexico City: Plaza & Janes.

Auyero, Javier. 1999. "'This Is a Lot Like the Bronx, Isn't It?' Lived Experiences of Marginality in an Argentine Slum." *International Journal of Urban and Regional Research* 23(1):45–69.

Auyero, Javier. 2000. "The Logic of Clientelism in Argentina: An Ethnographic Account." *Latin American Research Review* 35(3):55–81.

Auyero, Javier. 2007. *Routine Politics and Violence in Argentina: The Gray Zone of State Power*. Cambridge, UK: Cambridge University Press.

The Ambivalent State: Police-Criminal Collusion at the Urban Margins. Javier Auyero, Oxford University Press (2019). © Oxford University Press.
DOI: 10.1093/oso/9780190915537.001.0001

Auyero, Javier. 2012. *Patients of the State: The Politics of Waiting in Argentina.* Durham, NC: Duke University Press.

Auyero, Javier. 2013. "Born amid Bullets." *Contexts,* February 9.

Auyero, Javier, and Claudio Benzecry 2017. "The Practical Logic of Political Domination: Conceptualizing the Clientelist Habitus." *Sociological Theory* 37(3):179–99.

Auyero, Javier, and María Fernanda Berti. 2015. *In Harm's Way: The Dynamics of Urban Violence.* Princeton, NJ: Princeton University Press.

Auyero, Javier, Philippe Bourgois, and Nancy Scheper-Hughes, eds. 2015. *Violence at the Urban Margins.* New York: Oxford University Press.

Auyero, Javier, and Katherine Jensen. 2015. "For Political Ethnographies of Urban Marginality." *City & Community* 14(4):359–63.

Auyero, Javier, and Kristine Kilanski. 2015. "From 'Making Toast' to 'Splitting Apples': Dissecting 'Care' in the Midst of Chronic Violence." *Theory and Society* 44(5):393–414.

Auyero, Javier, and Katherine Sobering. 2017. "Violence, the State, and the Poor: A View from the South." *Sociological Forum* 32(S1):1018–31.

Auyero, Javier, and Débora Alejandra Swistun. 2009. *Flammable: Environmental Suffering in an Argentine Shantytown.* Oxford: Oxford University Press.

Badinter, Elisabeth. 1981. *The Myth of Motherhood: An Historical View of the Maternal Instinct.* London: Souvenir Press.

Bailey, John, and Matthew M. Taylor. 2009. "Evade, Corrupt, or Confront? Organized Crime and the State in Brazil and Mexico." *Journal of Politics in Latin America* 1(2): 3–29.

Barkey, Karen. 1994. *Bandits and Bureaucrats: The Ottoman Route to State Centralization.* Ithaca, NY: Cornell University Press.

Barreneche, Osvaldo. 2015. "Las Instituciones de Seguridad y del Castigo en Argentina y América Latina: Recorrido Historiográfico, Desafíos y Propuestas de Diálogo con la Historia del Derecho." Research Paper Series 2015-04. Max Planck Institute for European Legal History.

Barreneche, Osvaldo. 2016. "Policías en el Banquillo: La Justicia Penal frente a la Violencia y Corrupción Policial Bonaerense en la Década de 1960." Paper presented at the Jornadas Crimen y Sociedad: Diez años de estudios sobre Policía, Delito y Justicia en Perspectiva Histórica, Bariloche, October 12–14.

Barrera, Nicolás. 2013. "Policía, Territorio y Discrecionalidad: Una Etnografía sobre la Espacialidad en las Prácticas Policiales en la Ciudad de Rosario." Pp. 355–78 in *De Armas Llevar: Estudios Socioantropológicos sobre los Quehaceres de Policías y Fuerzas de Seguridad,* edited by S. Frederic, M. Galvani, J. G. Zucal, and B. Renoldi. La Plata: Universidad Nacional de La Plata, Facultad de Periodismo y Comunicación Social.

Becker, Howard. 1958. "Problems of Inference and Proof in Participant Observation." *American Sociological Review* 23(6):652–60.

Becker, Howard. 1970. *Sociological Work: Methods and Substance*. Chicago: Aldine.

Beetham, David. 2015. "Moving beyond a Narrow Definition of Corruption." Pp. 41–46 in *How Corrupt Is Britain?*, edited by D. Whyte. London: Pluto Press.

Benford, Robert D., and David A. Snow. 2000. "Framing Processes and Social Movements: An Overview and Assessment." *Annual Review of Sociology* 26:611–39.

Bergman, Marcelo. 2016. *Drogas, Narcotráfico y Poder en América Latina*. Buenos Aires: Fondo de Cultura Económica.

Bergman, Marcelo. 2018. *More Money, More Crime. Prosperity and Rising Crime in Latin America*. New York: Oxford University Press.

Berlusconi, Giulia. 2013. "Do All the Pieces Matter? Assessing the Reliability of Law Enforcement Data Sources for the Network Analysis of Wire Taps." *Global Crime* 14(1):61–81.

Bianciotto, María Laura. 2013. "Previsión, Anticipación y Viveza: A Propósito de la Relación entre Prácticas Policiales y Ámbito Judicial en Rosario." Pp. 305–26 in *De Armas Llevar: Estudios Socioantropológicos sobre los Quehaceres de Policías y Fuerzas de Seguridad*, edited by S. Frederic, M. Galvani, J. G. Zucal, and B. Renoldi. La Plata: Universidad Nacional de La Plata. Facultad de Periodismo y Comunicación Social.

Black, Donald. 1983. "Crime as Social Control." *American Sociological Review* 48(1):34–45.

Blanco, Ismael, Steven Griggs, and Helen Sullivan. 2014. "Situating the Local in the Neoliberalisation and Transformation of Urban Governance." *Urban Studies* 51(15):3129–46.

Blok, Anton. 2001. *Honor and Violence*. Cambridge, UK: Polity.

Bobea, Lilan. 2015. "Santo Domingo: Criminogenic Violence and Resilience." Pp. 134–54 in *Violence and Resilience in Latin American Cities*, edited by K. Koonings and D. Kruijt. London: Zed Books.

Bonner, Michelle D. 2014. "Violence, Policing, and Citizen (In)Security." *Latin American Research Review* 49(1): 261–69.

Bourdieu, Pierre. 1993. "A Science that Makes Trouble." Pp. 8–20 in *Sociology in Question*, Pierre Bourdieu. New York: Sage.

Bourdieu, Pierre. 2000. "For a Scholarship with Commitment." *Profession* 40–45.

Bourdieu, Pierre. 2015. *On the State: Lectures at the College de France, 1989–1992*. Malden, MA: Polity.

Bourdieu, Pierre, Jean-Claude Chamboderon, and Jean-Claude Passeron. 1991. *The Craft of Sociology*. New York: de Gruyter.

Bourgois, Philippe. 1995. *In Search of Respect. Selling Crack in El Barrio*. New York: Cambridge University Press.

Bourgois, Philippe 2015. "Insecurity, the War on Drugs, and Crimes of the State: Symbolic Violence in the Americas." Pp. 305–22 in *Violence at the Urban Margins*, edited by J. Auyero, P. Bourgois, and N. Scheper-Hughes. New York: Oxford University Press.

Bourgois, Philippe. 2018. "Decolonising Drug Studies in an Era of Predatory Accumulation." *Third World Quarterly* 39(2):385–98.

Brantingham, Patricia L., and Paul J. Brantingham. 1993. "Nodes, Paths and Edges: Considerations on the Complexity of Crime and the Physical Environment." *Journal of Environmental Psychology* 13(1):3–28.

Brass, Paul. 1992. *Theft of an Idol*. Princeton, NJ: Princeton University Press.

Brennan, Robert T., Beth E. Molnar, and Felton Earls. 2007. "Refining the Measurement of Exposure to Violence (ETV) in Urban Youth." *Journal of Community Psychology* 35(5):603–18.

Brinks, Daniel M. 2008. *The Judicial Response to Police Killings in Latin America: Inequality and the Rule of Law*. Cambridge, UK: Cambridge University Press.

Brooks, Graham. 2016. *Criminology of Corruption: Theoretical Approaches*. London: Palgrave Macmillan.

Brysk, Alison. 2012. "National Insecurity and the Citizenship Gap." Pp. 459–74 in *Shifting Frontiers of Citizenship: The Latin American Experience*, edited by M. Sznajder, C. A. Forment, and L. Whitehead. Boston: Brill.

Bryson, Lois, Kathleen McPhillips, and Kathryn Robinson. 2001. "Turning Public Issues into Private Troubles: Lead Contamination, Domestic Labor, and the Exploitation of Women's Unpaid Labor in Australia." *Gender and Society* 15(5):754–72.

Burawoy, Michael. 2017. "On Desmond: The Limits of Spontaneous Sociology." *Theory and Society* 46(4):261–84.

Campana, Paolo. 2011. "Eavesdropping on the Mob: The Functional Diversification of Mafia Activities across Territories." *European Journal of Criminology* 8(3):213–28.

Campana, Paolo, and Federico Varese. 2012. "Listening to the Wire: Criteria and Techniques for the Quantitative Analysis of Phone Intercepts." *Trends in Organized Crime* 15(1):13–30.

Carbajal, Gustavo. 2015. "Cada vez son más los policías procesados por narcotráfico." *La Nación*, July 12. Retrieved June 1, 2018 (http://www.lanacion.com.ar/1809748-cada-vez-son-mas-los-policias-procesados-por-narcotrafico).

Casas-Zamora, Kevin. 2013. "On Organized Crime and Political Finance: Why Does the Connection Matter?" Pp. 1–21 in *Dangerous Liaisons: Organized Crime and Political Finance in Latin America and Beyond*, edited by K. Casas-Zamora. Washington, DC: Brookings Institution Press.

Cavanagh, Gaston. 2014. "Los Monos: The Drug Gang of Rosario, Argentina's Most Violent City." *VICE News*, August 28. Retrieved June 1, 2018 (https://

news.vice.com/article/los-monos-the-drug-gang-of-rosario-argentinas-most-violent-city).

CELS (Centro de Estudios Legales y Sociales). 2012. *Derechos Humanos en Argentina*. Informe 2012. Buenos Aires: Siglo XXI.

CELS (Centro de Estudios Legales y Sociales). 2014. *Derechos Humanos en Argentina*. Informe 2014. Buenos Aires: Siglo XXI.

CELS (Centro de Estudios Legales y Sociales). 2016. *Derechos Humanos en Argentina*. Informe 2016. Buenos Aires: Siglo XXI.

Chubb, Judith. 1996. "The Mafia, the Market and the State in Italy and Russia." *Journal of Modern Italian Studies* 1(2):273–91.

Czitrom, Daniel. 2016. *New York Exposed: The Gilded Age Police Scandal That Launched the Progressive Era*. Oxford: Oxford University Press.

Clark, Cheryl, Louise Ryan, Ichiro Kawachi, Marina J. Canner, Lisa Berkman, and Rosalind J. Wright. 2008. "Witnessing Community Violence in Residential Neighborhoods: A Mental Health Hazard for Urban Women." *Journal of Urban Health* 85(1):22–38.

Clemens, Elisabeth S. 2016. *What Is Political Sociology?* Malden, MA: Polity.

Collins, Caitlyn. 2019. *Making Motherhood Work: How Women Manage Careers and Caregiving*. Princeton, NJ: Princeton University Press.

Collins, Caitlyn, Katherine Jensen, and Javier Auyero. 2017. "A Proposal for Public Sociology as Localized Intervention and Collective Enterprise: The Makings and Impact of *Invisible in Austin*." *Qualitative Sociology* 40(2):191–214.

Contreras, Randol. 2012. *The Stickup Kids: Race, Drugs, Violence, and the American Dream*. Berkeley: University of California Press.

Cruz, José Miguel. 2016. "State and Criminal Violence in Latin America." *Crime, Law and Social Change* 66:375–96.

Das, Veena, ed. 1990. *Mirrors of Violence: Communities, Riots and Survivors in South Asia*. Oxford: Oxford University Press.

Das, Veena, and Deborah Poole, eds. 2004. *Anthropology in the Margins of the State*. Santa Fe, NM: School for Advanced Research Press.

Davis, Diane E. 2006. "Undermining the Rule of Law: Democratization and the Dark Side of Police Reform in Mexico." *Latin American Politics and Society* 48(1):55–86.

Davis, Diane E. 2010. "Irregular Armed Forces, Shifting Patterns of Commitment, and Fragmented Sovereignty in the Developing World." *Theory and Society* 39:397–413.

De los Santos, Germán, and Hernán Lascano. 2017. *Los Monos: Historia de La Familia Narco que Transformó a Rosario En Un Infierno*. Buenos Aires: Sudamericana.

Della Porta, Donatella, and Alberto Vannucci. 1999. *Corrupt Exchanges: Actors, Resources, and Mechanisms of Political Corruption*. New York: Transaction.

Della Porta, Donatella, and Alberto Vannucci. 2012. *The Hidden Order of Corruption: An Institutional Approach*. New York: Routledge.

Denyer Willis, Graham. 2009. "Deadly Symbiosis? The PCC, the State and the Institutionalization of Violence in São Paulo." Pp. 167–81 in *Youth Violence in Latin America*, edited by D. Rodgers and G. A. Jones. New York: Palgrave Macmillan.

Denyer Willis, Graham. 2015. *The Killing Consensus: Police, Organized Crime, and the Regulation of Life and Death in Urban Brazil*. Berkeley: University of California Press.

Desmond, Matthew. 2014. "Relational Ethnography." *Theory and Society* 43(5):547–79.

Desmond, Matthew. 2016. *Evicted: Poverty and Profit in an American City*. New York: Crown.

Dewey, Matías. 2012a. "Illegal Police Protection and the Market for Stolen Vehicles in Buenos Aires." *Journal of Latin American Studies* 44(4):679–702.

Dewey, Matías. 2012b. "The Making of Hybrid Stateness: Sources of Police Performance in the Conurbano." *Revista de Ciencia Política* 32(3):659–72.

Dewey, Matías. 2015. *El Orden Clandestino: Política, Fuerzas de Seguridad y Mercados Ilegales en la Argentina*. Buenos Aires: Katz Editores.

Dewey, Matías. 2017a. "State Power and Crime." Pp. 1–15 in *The SAGE Handbook for Political Sociology*, edited by W. Outhwaite and S. Turner. Thousand Oaks, CA: Sage.

Dewey, Matías. 2017b. "State-Sponsored Protection Rackets: Regulating the Market for Counterfeit Clothing in Argentina." Pp. 123–40 in *The Architecture of Illegal Markets: Towards an Economic Sociology of Illegality in the Economy*, edited by J. Beckert and M. Dewey. Oxford: Oxford University Press.

Dewey, Matías, Daniel Pedro Míguez, and Marcelo Fabina Saín. 2017. "The Strength of Collusion: A Conceptual Framework for Interpreting Hybrid Social Orders." *Current Sociology* 65(3):395–410.

Di Lodovico, Cecilia. 2009a. "Jefes narcos se disputan el tráfico en la Villa 9 de Julio." *24CON*, July 16. Retrieved June 1, 2018 (www.24con.com).

Di Lodovico, Cecilia. 2009b. "El joven que 'guapeó' a los transas y terminó muerto." *24CON*, August 9. Retrieved June 1, 2018 (www.24con.com).

Di Lodovico, Cecilia. 2009c. "Murió otro narco en el tiroteo de la Villa 9 de Julio." *24CON*, September 2. Retrieved June 1, 2018 (www.24con.com).

Di Lodovico, Cecilia. 2016a. "Narcoestado: Jueces, Fiscales, Dirigentes y Policías Involucrados En Redes Mafiosas." *Perfil*, March 13. Retrieved June 1, 2018 (http://www.perfil.com/noticias/sociedad/Narcoestado-jueces-fiscales-dirigentes-y-policias-involucrados-en-redes-mafiosas--20160312-0061.phtml).

Di Lodovico, Cecilia. 2016b. "En tres meses separaron a 730 policías y se iniciaron cerca de 1.700 sumarios." *Perfil*, March 20. Retrieved June 1, 2018 (http://www.perfil.com/noticias/policia/En-tres-meses-separaron-a-730-policias-y-se-iniciaron-cerca-de-1.700-sumarios-20160320-0066.phtml).

Di Lodovico, Cecilia. 2017. "Zonas liberadas: Acusan a un subcomisario y diez agentes." *Perfil*, May 20. Retrieved June 1, 2018 (http://www.perfil.com/policia/zonas-liberadas-acusan-a-un-subcomisario-y-diez-agentes.phtml).

Durán-Martínez, Angélica. 2015. "To Kill and Tell? State Power, Criminal Competition, and Drug Violence." *Journal of Conflict Resolution* 59(8):1377–402.

Durán-Martínez, Angélica. 2017. "Drug Trafficking and Drug Policies in the Americas: Change, Continuity, and Challenges." *Latin American Politics and Society* 59(2):145–53.

Durán-Martínez, Angélica. 2018. *The Politics of Drug Violence. Criminals, Cops, and Politicians in Colombia and Mexico.* New York: Oxford University Press.

Dutil, Carlos, and Ricardo Ragendorfer. 1997. *La Bonaerense: Historia Criminal de la Policía de la Provincia de Buenos Aires.* Buenos Aires: Planeta.

Edin, Kathryn, and Maria J. Kefalas. 2005. *Promises I Can Keep: Why Poor Women Put Motherhood before Marriage.* Berkeley: University of California Press.

Elias, Norbert. 1978. "On Transformations of Aggressiveness." *Theory and Society* 5(2):229–42.

Elias, Norbert. 1994. *The Civilizing Process.* Oxford: Blackwell.

Elliott, Sinikka, and Elyshia Aseltine. 2013. "Raising Teenagers in Hostile Environments: How Race, Class, and Gender Matter for Mothers' Protective Carework." *Journal of Family Issues* 34(6):719–44.

Emerson, Robert M., Rachel I. Fretz, and Linda L. Shaw. 1995. *Writing Ethnographic Fieldnotes.* Chicago: University of Chicago Press.

Emirbayer, Mustafa. 1997. "Manifesto for a Relational Sociology." *American Journal of Sociology* 103(2):281–317.

Erikson, Kai. 1976. *Everything in Its Path. Destruction of Community in the Buffalo Creek Flood.* New York: Simon & Schuster.

Fassin, Didier. 2013. *Enforcing Order: An Ethnography of Urban Policing.* Cambridge, UK: Polity.

Fassin, Didier. 2015. *At the Heart of the State: The Moral World of Institutions.* London: Pluto Press.

Ferreira Rubio, Delia. 2013. "Argentina: Two Cases." Pp. 22–41 in *Dangerous Liaisons: Organized Crime and Political Finance in Latin America and Beyond*, edited by K. Casas-Zamora. Washington, DC: Brookings Institution Press.

Flom, Hernán. 2018. "Who Protects Whom? Politicians, Police and the Regulation of Drug Trafficking in Argentina." Working Paper 426. Kellogg Institute for International Studies, Univeristy of Notre Dame. Retrieved June 1, 2018 (https://kellogg.nd.edu/who-protects-whom-politicians-police-and-regulation-drug-trafficking-argentina).

Flores Pérez, Carlos Antonio. 2014. "Political Protection and the Origins of the Gulf Cartel." *Crime, Law and Social Change* 61(5):517–39.

Font, Enrique. 2011. "El porqué del aumento de crímenes en Rosario." *La Capital*, September 28. Retrieved June 1, 2018 (https://www.lacapital.com.ar/policiales/el-queacute-del-aumento-criacutemenes-rosario-n385562.html).

Foucault, Michel. 1977. *Discipline and Punish: The Birth of the Prison.* New York: Pantheon Books.

Frederic, Sabina. 2013. "La Formación Policial en Cuetión: Impugnción, Valoración y Transmisión de los 'Saber Hacer' Policiales." Pp. 271–301 in *De Armas Llevar: Estudios Socioantropológicos sobre los Quehaceres de Policías y Fuerzas de Seguridad*, edited by S. Frederic, M. Galvani, J. G. Zucal, and B. Renoldi. La Plata: Universidad Nacional de La Plata, Facultad de Periodismo y Comunicación Social.

Frederic, Sabina, Mariana Galvani, José Garriga Zucal, and Brígida Renoldi, eds. 2013. *De Armas Llevar: Estudios Socioantropológicos sobre los Quehaceres de Policías y Fuerzas de Seguridad.* La Plata: Universidad Nacional de La Plata, Facultad de Periodismo y Comunicación Social.

Friman, H. Richard. 2009. "Drug Markets and the Selective Use of Violence." *Crime, Law and Social Change* 52(3):285–95.

Gambetta, Diego. 1993. *The Sicilian Mafia: The Business of Private Protection.* Cambridge, MA: Harvard University Press.

Garland, David. 1996. "The Limits of the Sovereign State: Strategies of Crime Control in Contemporary Society." *British Journal of Criminology* 36(4):445–71.

Garrido, Elena Azaola, and Miquel Ángel Ruiz Torres. 2011. "Poder y abusos de poder entre la Policía Judicial de la Ciudad de México." *Iberoamericana* 11(41):99–113.

Garriga Zucal, José. 2013. "Un Correctivo: Violencia y Respeto en el Mundo Policial." Pp. 147–72 in *De Armas Llevar: Estudios Socioantropológicos sobre los Quehaceres de Policías y Fuerzas de Seguridad*, edited by S. Frederic, M. Galvani, J. G. Zucal, and B. Renoldi. La Plata: Universidad Nacional de La Plata, Facultad de Periodismo y Comunicación Social.

Garriga Zucal, José. 2016. *El Verdadero Policía y sus Sinsabores: Esbozos para una Interpretación de la Violencia Policial.* La Plata: Universidad Nacional de La Plata, Facultad de Periodismo y Comunicación Social.

Gay, Robert. 2005. *Lucia: Testimonies of a Brazilian.* Philadelphia: Temple University Press.

Ginzburg, Carlo. 1989. *Clues, Myths, and the Historical Method.* Baltimore, MD: Johns Hopkins University Press.

Ginzburg, Carlo. 1992. *The Cheese and the Worms: The Cosmos of a Sixteenth-Century Miller.* Reprint edition. Baltimore, MD: Johns Hopkins University Press.

Glanc, Laura, and Pablo Glanc. 2013. "La Paradoja de de la Seguridad en la Ciudad de Buenos Aires: ¿Proteger a las 'Amenazas Urbanas' de los 'Garantes' de la 'Seguridad'?" Pp. 209–40 in *De Armas Llevar: Estudios Socioantropológicos sobre los Quehaceres de Policías y Fuerzas de Seguridad*, edited by S. Frederic, M. Galvani, J. G. Zucal, and B. Renoldi. La Plata: Universidad Nacional de La Plata, Facultad de Periodismo y Comunicación Social.

Goffman, Alice. 2009. "On the Run: Wanted Men in a Philadelphia Ghetto." *American Sociological Review* 74(3):339–57.

Goffman, Alice. 2014. *On the Run: Fugitive Life in an American City.* Chicago: University of Chicago Press.

Goldman, Francisco. 2007. *The Art of Political Murder. Who Killed the Bishop?* New York: Grove Press.

Goldstein, Daniel. 2012. *Outlawed. Between Security and Rights in a Bolivian City.* Durham, NC: Duke University Press.

Goldstein, Paul J. 1985. "The Drugs/Violence Nexus: A Tripartite Conceptual Framework." *Journal of Drug Issues* 15(4):493–506.

González, Cecilia. 2013. *Narcosur: La Sombra del Narcotráfico Mexicano en la Argentina*. Buenos Aires: Marea Editorial.

Goodman, Ryan. 2017. "Can We Please Stop Talking about 'Collusion'?" *New York Times*, November 2. Retrieved June 1, 2018 (https://www.nytimes.com/2017/11/02/opinion/collusion-meaning-trump-.html).

Granovetter, Mark. 2007. "The Social Construction of Corruption." Pp. 152–72 in *On Capitalism*, edited by V. Nee and R. Swedberg. Stanford, CA: Stanford University Press.

Gray, John. 2015. "Steven Pinker Is Wrong about Violence and War." *Guardian*, March 13. Retrieved June 1, 2018 (https://www.theguardian.com/books/2015/mar/13/john-gray-steven-pinker-wrong-violence-war-declining).

Gunst, Laurie. 1995. *Born Fi' Dead: A Journey through the Yardie Posse Underworld*. New York: Canongate Books.

Gupta, Akhil. 1995. "Blurred Boundaries: The Discourse of Corruption, the Culture of Politics, and the Imagined State." *American Ethnologist* 22(2):375–402.

Hagan, John, Joshua Kaiser, and Anna Hanson. 2016. "The Theory of Legal Cynicism and Sunni Insurgent Violence in Post-Invasion Iraq." *American Sociological Review* 81(2):316–46.

Hagedorn, John. 2015. *The Insane Chicago Way: The Daring Plan by Chicago Gangs to Create a Spanish Mafia*. Chicago: University of Chicago Press.

Hall, John A., and G. John Ikenberry. 1989. *The State*. London: Open University Press.

Inner-City Boys. Chicago: University of Chicago Press.

Harrington, Joseph E. and Andrzej Skrzypacz. 2011. "Private Monitoring and Communication in Cartels: Explaining Recent Collusive Practices." *American Economic Review* 101(6): 2425–49.

Hathazy, Paul. 2013. "(Re)Shaping the Neoliberal Leviathans: the Politics of Penality and Welfare in Argentina, Chile and Peru." *European Review of Latin American and Caribbean Studies* 95 (October):5–25.

Hathazy, Paul. 2016. "Remaking the Prisons of the Market Democracies: New Experts, Old Guards and Politics in the Carceral Fields of Argentina and Chile." *Crime, Law and Social Change* 65(3):163–93.

Hays, Sharon. 1996. *The Cultural Contradictions of Motherhood*. New Haven, CT: Yale University Press.

Hazen, Jennifer M., and Dennis Rodgers, eds. 2014. *Global Gangs: Street Violence across the World*. Minneapolis: University of Minnesota Press.

Heath, Anthony F., Lindsay Richards, and Nan Dirk de Graaf. 2016. "Explaining Corruption in the Developed World: The Potential of Sociological Approaches." *Annual Review of Sociology* 42(1):51–79.

Hinton, Mercedes S. 2006. *The State on the Streets: Police and Politics in Argentina and Brazil*. Boulder, CO: Lynne Rienner.

Hobson, John. 2006. "Mann, the State and War." Pp. 150–66 in *An Anatomy of Power: The Social Theory of Michael Mann*, edited by J. A. Hall and R. Schroeder. Cambridge, UK: Cambridge University Press.

Hochschild, Arlie, and Anne Machung. 1990. *The Second Shift*. New York: Avon Books.

Holland, Alisha C. 2017. *Forbearance as Redistribution: The Politics of Informal Welfare in Latin America*. Cambridge, UK: Cambridge University Press.

Human Rights Clinic. 2017. *Human Rights Abuses and State Complicity in Coahuila, Mexico*. Austin: University of Texas School of Law.

Imbusch, Peter, Michel Misse, and Fernando Carrión. 2011. "Violence Research in Latin America and the Caribbean: A Literature Review." *International Journal of Conflict and Violence* 5(1):87–154.

Jaffe, Rivke. 2013. "The Hybrid State: Crime and Citizenship in Urban Jamaica." *American Ethnologist* 40(4):734–48.

Jancsics, David. 2014. "Interdisciplinary Perspectives on Corruption." *Sociology Compass* 8(4):358–72.

Jarecki, Eugene. 2012. *The House I Live In*. Retrieved, January 30, 2019 (http://www.pbs.org/independentlens/films/house-i-live-in/).

Jessop, Bob. 2016. *The State: Past, Present, Future*. Malden, MA: Polity.

Johnston, Michael. 2014. *Corruption, Contention and Reform: The Power of Deep Democratization*. Cambridge, UK: Cambridge University Press.

Jones, Nikki. 2009. *Between Good and Ghetto: African American Girls and Inner-City Violence*. New Brunswick, NJ: Rutgers University Press.

Kakar, Sudhir. 1996. *The Colors of Violence: Cultural Identities, Religion, and Conflict*. Chicago: University of Chicago Press.

Kalven, Jaime. 2016. "House of Cards: How the Chicago Police Department Covered Up for a Gang of Criminal Cops (Part 3)." *Intercept*, October 6. Retrieved June 1, 2018. (https://theintercept.com/2016/10/06/

how-the-chicago-police-department-covered-up-for-a-gang-of-criminal-cops/).

Kandori, Michihiro, and Hitoshi Matsushima. 1998. "Private Observation, Communication and Collusion." *Econometrica* 66(3): 627–52.

Katz, Jack. 2001. "From How to Why: On Luminous Description and Causal Inference in Ethnography (Part I)." *Ethnography* 2(4):443–73.

Katz, Jack. 2002. "From How to Why: On Luminous Description and Causal Inference in Ethnography (Part 2)." *Ethnography* 3(1):63–90.

Keohane, Robert. 1986. "Reciprocity in International Relations." *International Organization* 40(1):1–27.

Kertzer, David I. 2008. *Amalia's Tale: A Poor Peasant, an Ambitious Attorney, and a Fight for Justice*. Boston: Houghton Mifflin Harcourt.

Kessler, Gabriel, and Matías Bruno. 2018. "Inseguridad y Vulnerabilidad al Delito." Pp. 329–56 in *La Argentina en el Siglo XXI*, edited by J. Piovani and A. Salvia. Buenos Aires: Siglo XXI.

King, Desmond, and Patrick Le Gales. 2012. "State." Pp. 107–19 in *The Wiley-Blackwell Companion to Political Sociology*, edited by E. Amenta, K. Nash, and A. Scott. Malden, MA: Wiley-Blackwell.

Kirk, David S., and Mauri Matsuda. 2011. "Legal Cynicism, Collective Efficacy, and the Ecology of Arrest." *Criminology* 49(2): 443–72.

Kirk, David S., and Andrew Papachristos. 2011. "Cultural Mechanisms and the Persistence of Neighborhood Violence." *American Journal of Sociology* 116(4):1190–233.

Kirk, David S., Andrew V. Papachristos, Jeffrey Fagan, and Tom R. Tyler. 2012. "The Paradox of Law Enforcement in Immigrant Communities: Does Tough Immigration Enforcement Undermine Public Safety?" *Annals of the American Academy of Political and Social Science* 641(1):79–98.

Koonings, Kees, and Dirk Kruijt, eds. 2007. *Fractured Cities: Social Exclusion, Urban Violence and Contested Spaces in Latin America*. London: Zed Books.

Koonings, Kees, and Dirk Kruijt, eds. 2015. *Violence and Resilience in Latin American Cities*. London: Zed Books.

Kotlowitz, Alex. 1991. *There Are No Children Here: The Story of Two Boys Growing Up in the Other America*. New York: Doubleday.

Kraska, Peter B., and Victor E. Kappeler. 1997. "Militarizing American Police: The Rise and Normalization of Paramilitary Units." *Social Problems* 44(1):1–18.

Larkins, Erika Mary Robb. 2015. *The Spectacular Favela: Violence in Modern Brazil*. Oakland: University of California Press.

Lasa, María de los Ángeles. 2015. "Narco Made in Argentina." *La Nación*, October 7. Retrieved June 1, 2018 (http://www.lanacion.com.ar/1834560-narco-made-in-argentina).

LeBlanc, Adrian Nicole. 2004. *Random Family: Love, Drugs, Trouble, and Coming of Age in the Bronx*. New York: Scribner.

Lessig, Lawrence. 2013. "'Institutional Corruption' Defined." *Journal of Law, Medicine & Ethics* 41(3):553–55.

Loyal, Steven, and Stephen Quilley. 2017. "The Particularity of the Universal: Critical Reflections on Bourdieu's Theory of Symbolic Power and the State." *Theory and Society* 46(5):429–62.

Maher, Lisa, and David Dixon. 2001. "The Cost of Crackdowns: Policing Cabramatta's Heroin Market." *Current Issues in Criminal Justice* 13(1):5–22.

Malešević, Siniša. 2017. *The Rise of Organised Brutality: A Historical Sociology of Violence*. New York: Cambridge University Press.

Manzetti, Luigi. 2009. *Neoliberalism, Accountability, and Reform Failures in Emerging Markets: Eastern Europe, Russia, Argentina, and Chile in Comparative Perspective*. University Park: Pennsylvania State University Press.

Marshall, Robert C., and Leslie M. Marx. 2014. *The Economics of Collusion: Cartels and Bidding Rings*. Cambridge, MA: The MIT Press.

Marwell, Nicole P. 2016. "Rethinking the State in Urban Outcasts." *Urban Studies* 53(6):1095–98.

Massey, Douglas S. 1990. "American Apartheid: Segregation and the Making of the Underclass." *American Journal of Sociology* 96(2):329–57.

McAdam, Doug, Sidney Tarrow, and Charles Tilly. 2001. *Dynamics of Contention*. New York: Cambridge University Press.

McAdam, Doug, Sidney Tarrow, and Charles Tilly. 2008. "Methods for Measuring Mechanisms of Contention." *Qualitative Sociology* 31(4):307.

McCart, Michael R., Daniel W. Smith, Benjamin E. Saunders, Dean G. Kilpatrick, Heidi S. Resnick, and Kenneth J. Ruggerio. 2007. "Do Urban Adolescents Become Desensitized to Community Violence? Data from a National Survey." *American Journal of Orthopsychiatry* 77(3):434–42.

Melotto, Mariano. 2013. "Aprender a Desear lo Posible: La Construcción de la Vocación y el Espíritu de Cuerpo en Escuelas de Formación Básica Policial." Pp. 241–70 in *De Armas Llevar: Estudios Socioantropológicos sobre los Quehaceres de Policías y Fuerzas de Seguridad*, edited by S. Frederic, M. Galvani, J. G. Zucal, and B. Renoldi. La Plata: Universidad Nacional de La Plata, Facultad de Periodismo y Comunicación Social.

Menjívar, Cecilia, and Shannon Drysdale Walsh. 2017. "The Architecture of Feminicide: The State, Inequalities, and Everyday Gender Violence in Honduras." *Latin American Research Review* 52(2):221–40.

Merton, Robert K., and Elinor Barber. 1976. *Sociological Ambivalence and Other Essays*. New York: Free Press.

Messi, Virginia. 2003. "Los narcos del conurbano se secuestran y matan entre ellos." *Clarín*, September 21. Retrieved June 1, 2018 (https://www.clarin.com/policiales/narcos-conurbano-secuestran-matan_0_r1VfGfexAFl.html).

Messi, Virginia. 2010. "San Martín: Radiografía de la guerra narco en un polo clave." *Clarín*, January 3. Retrieved June 1, 2018 (https://www.clarin.com/ediciones-anteriores/san-martin-radiografia-guerra-narco-polo-clave_0_BJ3goqwRTte.html).

Messi, Virginia. 2012. "En una cocina de droga, cae el capo narco de la Villa Korea." *Clarín*, November 3. Retrieved June 1, 2018 (https://www.clarin.com/policiales/cocina-droga-narco-villa-korea_0_Hks_1-AjDQg.html).

Mills, C. Wright. 1959. *The Sociological Imagination*. New York: Oxford University Press.

Miron, Jeffrey A. 2001. "Violence, Guns, and Drugs: A Cross-Country Analysis." *Journal of Law and Economics* 44(S2):615–33.

Mische, Ann. 2008. *Partisan Publics: Communication and Contention across Brazilian Youth Activist Networks*. Princeton, NJ: Princeton University Press.

Morenoff, Jeffrey D., Robert J. Sampson, and Stephen W. Raudenbush. 2001. "Neighborhood Inequality, Collective Efficacy, and the Spatial Dynamics of Urban Violence." *Criminology* 39(3):517–58.

Morgan, Kimberly J., and Ann Shola Orloff, eds. 2017. *The Many Hands of the State: Theorizing Political Authority and Social Control*. New York: Cambridge University Press.

Moser, Caroline, and Cathy McIlwaine. 2004. *Encounters with Violence in Latin America*. New York: Taylor and Francis.

Müller, Markus-Michael. 2010. "Community Policing in Latin America: Lessons from Mexico City." *European Review of Latin American and Caribbean Studies/Revista Europea de Estudios Latinoamericanos y Del Caribe* (88):21–37.

Müller, Markus-Michael. 2012a. "Addressing an Ambivalent Relationship: Policing and the Urban Poor in Mexico City." *Journal of Latin American Studies* 44(2):319–45.

Müller, Markus-Michael. 2012b. "The Rise of the Penal State in Latin America." *Contemporary Justice Review* 15(1):57–76.

Müller, Markus-Michael. 2016. *The Punitive City: Privatised Policing and Protection in Neoliberal Mexico*. Chicago: University of Chicago Press.

Natarajan, Mangai. 2006. "Understanding the Structure of a Large Heroin Distribution Network: A Quantitative Analysis of Qualitative Data." *Journal of Quantitative Criminology* 22(2):171–92.

Navarro, Fernando, ed. 2016. *Dársela en la Pera: Violencia y Adicciones en la Provincia de Buenos Aires*. Buenos Aires: Marea Editorial.

Naylor, R. Thomas. 2009. "Violence and Illegal Economic Activity: A Deconstruction." *Crime, Law and Social Change* 52(3):231–42.

Nelson, Brian. 2006. *The Making of the Modern State: A Theoretical Evolution*. New York: Palgrave Macmillan.

Nivette, Amy E., Manuel Eisner, Tina Malti, and Denis Ribeaud. 2015. "The Social and Developmental Antecedents of Legal Cynicism." *Journal of Research in Crime and Delinquency* 52(2):270–98.

O'Donnell, Guilermo. 1993. "On the State, Democratization and Some Conceptual Problems: A Latin American View with Glances at Some Postcommunist Countries." *World Development* 21(8):1355–69.

Oliveira, Alicia, and Sofía Tiscornia. 1997. "Estructura y prácticas de las policías en la Argentina: Las redes de ilegalidad." Paper presented at "Seminario Control Democrático de los Organismos de Seguridad Interior en la República Argentina," Centro de Estudios Legales y Sociales, Buenos Aires, April 7–8.

Osofsky, Joy D. 1999. "The Impact of Violence on Children." *Future of Children* 9(3):33–49.

Ossona, Jorge Luis. 2014. *Punteros, Malandras y Porongas: Ocupación de Tierras y Usos Políticos de La Pobreza*. Buenos Aires: Siglo XXI Editores.

Ossona, Jorge Luis. 2017. "Lo paradójico de la violencia es que la financia el propio estado." *Clarín*, December 24. Retrieved June 1, 2018 (https://www.clarin.com/politica/jorge-ossona-paradojico-violencia-financia-propio_0_HyX4dYTMf.html).

Ousey, Graham C., and Matthew R. Lee. 2002. "Examining the Conditional Nature of the Illicit Drug Market–Homicide Relationship: A Partial Test of the Theory of Contingent Causation." *Criminology* 40(1):73–102.

Pachirat, Timothy. 2011. *Every Twelve Seconds: Industrialized Slaughter and the Politics of Sight*. New Haven, CT: Yale University Press.

Pardoy, José Luis, and Alejandra S. Inzunza. 2014a. "Compran cárteles a sheriffes de EU." *El Universal*, October 7. Retrieved June 1, 2018 (http://archivo.eluniversal.com.mx/primera-plana/2014/impreso/los-8216sheriffes-8217-que-cayeron-en-las-redes-del-narco-47157.html).

Pardoy, Jose Luis, and Alejandra S. Inzunza. 2014b. "US Police Corrupted by Mexico's Cartels along Border." *InSight Crime: Investigation and Analysis of Organized Crime*, October 21. Retrieved June 1, 2018 (https://www.insightcrime.org/news/analysis/us-police-corrupted-by-mexican-cartels-along-border/).

Parker, Robert Nash, and Kathleen Auerhahn. 1998. "Alcohol, Drugs, and Violence." *Annual Review of Sociology* 24(1):291–311.

Penglase, R. Ben. 2014. *Living with Insecurity in a Brazilian Favela: Urban Violence and Daily Life*. New Brunswick, NJ: Rutgers University Press.

Peralta, Elena. 2003. "En el Riachuelo hay mucho más plomo que los niveles permitidos." *Clarín*, December 5. Retrieved June 1, 2018 (https://www.clarin.com/ediciones-anteriores/riachuelo-plomo-niveles-permitidos_0_ryfbUekgRFe.html).

Perlman, Janice. 2010. *Favela: Four Decades of Living on the Edge in Rio de Janeiro*. New York: Oxford University Press.

Perry, Alex. 2018. *The Good Mothers: The True Story of the Women Who Took on the World's Most Powerful Mafia*. New York: HarperCollins.

Pinker, Steven. 2012. *The Better Angels of Our Nature: Why Violence Has Declined*. New York: Penguin.

Ralph, Lawrence. 2014. *Renegade Dreams: Living through Injury in Gangland Chicago*. Chicago: University of Chicago Press.

Raspall, Tomás. 2012. "El Plan Unidad Cinturón Sur: Impactos de una Nueva Política de Seguridad en un Gran Cconjunto Urbano de la Ciudad de Buenos Aires." *Revista INVI* 27(74):123–46.

Reding, Nick. 2009. *Methland: The Death and Life of an American Small Town*. New York: Bloomsbury.

Reinarman, Craig, and Harry G. Levine, eds. 1997. *Crack in America: Demon Drugs and Social Justice*. Berkeley: University of California Press.

Resignato, Andrew J. 2000. "Violent Crime: A Function of Drug Use or Drug Enforcement." *Applied Economics* 32:681–88.

Reuter, Peter. 2009a. "Systemic Violence in Drug Markets." *Crime, Law and Social Change* 52(3):275–84.

Reuter, Peter. 2009b. "Violence and Illegal Economic Activity: A Deconstruction." *Crime, Law and Social Change* 52(3):275–84.

Rios, Victor M. 2010. *Punished: Policing the Lives of Black and Latino Boys*. New York: New York University Press.

Rivlin, Gary. 2010. *Broke, USA: From Pawnshops to Poverty, Inc.—How the Working Poor Became Big Business*. New York: HarperCollins.

Rodgers, Dennis. 2006. "The State as a Gang: Conceptualizing the Governmentality of Violence in Contemporary Nicaragua." *Critique of Anthropology* 26(3):315–30.

Rodgers, Dennis. 2017. "Of Pandillas, Pirucas, and Pablo Escobar in the Barrio." Pp. 65–84 in *Politics and History of Violence and Crime in Central America*, edited by S. Huhn and H. Warnecke-Berger. New York: Palgrave Macmillan.

Rodgers, Dennis, Jo Beall, and Ravi Kanbur, eds. 2012. *Latin American Urban Development into the Twenty First Century: Towards a Renewed Perspective on the City*. New York: Palgrave Macmillan.

Rodgers, Dennis, and Bruce O'Neill. 2012. "Infrastructural Violence: Introduction to the Special Issue." *Ethnography* 13(4):401–12.

Roldán, Mary. 2002. *Blood and Fire: La Violencía in Antioquía, Colombia, 1946–1953*. Durham, NC: Duke University Press.

Ronconi, Lucas, and Zarazaga, Rodrigo. 2017. "The Tragedy of Clientelism: Opting Children Out." IZA Discussion Paper No. 10973. Social Science Research Network. Retrieved June 1, 2018 (https://ssrn.com/abstract=3029845).

Roth, Philip. 2017. *Why Write? Collected Nonfiction 1960–2013*. New York: Library of America.

Rothstein, Bo, and Aiysha Varraich. 2017. *Making Sense of Corruption.* Cambridge, UK: Cambridge University Press.

Ruiz, Adolofo. 2013. "'El narco les paga a altos jefes como Sosa.'" *Página/12,* September 22. Retrieved June 1, 2018 (https://www.pagina12.com.ar/diario/elpais/1-229600-2013-09-22.html).

Sahlins, Marshall D. 1972. *Stone Age Economics.* Chicago: Aldine-Atherton.

Sahlins, Marshall D. 1977. "Poor Man, Rich Man, Big-Man, Chief: Political Types in Melanesia and Polynesia." Pp. 220–31 in *Friends, Followers, and Factions: A Reader in Political Clientelism,* edited by S. Schmidt, L. Guasti, C. Landé, and J. Scott. Berkeley: University of California Press.

Saín, Marcelo. 2004. *Política, Policía y Delito: La Red Bonaerense.* Buenos Aires: Capital Intelectual.

Saín, Marcelo. 2008. *El Leviatán Azul: Policía y Política en La Argentina.* Buenos Aires: Siglo XXI.

Saín, Marcelo. 2015. *La Regulación del Narcotráfico en la Provincia de Buenos Aires.* Buenos Aires: Universidad Metropolitana para la Educación y el Trabajo.

Saín, Marcelo. 2017. *Por qué Preferimos No Ver la Inseguridad (Aunque Digamos lo Contrario).* Buenos Aires: Siglo XXI.

Salahub, Jennifer Erin, Markus Gottsbacher, and John de Boer, eds. 2018. *Social Theories of Urban Violence in the Global South: Towards Safe and Inclusive Cities.* Abingdon, UK: Routledge.

Salzinger, Leslie, and Teresa Gowan. 2018. "Macro Analysis: Power in the Field." Pp. 61–94 in *Approaches to Ethnography: Analysis and Representation in Participant Observation,* edited by C. Jerolmack and S. R. Khan. New York: Oxford University Press.

Sampson, Robert J., and Dawn J. Bartusch. 1998. "Legal Cynicism and (Subcultural?) Tolerance of Deviance: The Neighborhood Context of Racial Differences." *Law & Society Review* 32(4): 777–804.

Sampson, Robert J., Stephen W. Raudenbush, and Felton Earls. 1997. "Neighborhoods and Violent Crime: A Multilevel Study of Collective Efficacy." *Science* 277(5328):918–24.

Sampson, Robert, and William Julius Wilson. 1995. "Toward a Theory of Race, Crime, and Urban Inequality." Pp. 37–54 in *Crime and Inequality,* edited by J. Hagan and R. Peterson. Stanford: Stanford University Press.

Santamaría, Gema, and David Carey. 2017. *Violence and Crime in Latin America: Representations and Politics.* Norman: University of Oklahoma Press.

Saralegui, Rafael. 2017. "El Juez Infiltrado." *Revista Anfibia.* Retrieved June 1, 2018 (http://www.revistaanfibia.com/cronica/el-juez-infiltrado).

Schneider, Jane. 2018. "Fifty Years of Mafia Corruption and Anti-Mafia Reform." *Current Anthropology* 59(S18):S16–27.

Schneider, Jane, and Peter T. Schneider. 2003. *Reversible Destiny: Mafia, Antimafia, and the Struggle for Palermo.* Berkeley: University of California Press.

Schneider, Jane, and Peter T. Schneider. 2008. "The Anthropology of Crime and Criminalization." *Annual Review of Anthropology* 37:351–73.

Schor, Juliet B. 2004. "From Obscurity to People Magazine." *Social Problems* 51(1):121–24.

Schreiner, Daniel, and Silvina Tamous. 2016. "Narcos en Rosario: Los monos, historia negra de un clan sangriento." *Infobae*, September 10. Retrieved June 1, 2018 (http://www.infobae.com/sociedad/policiales/2016/09/10/narcos-en-rosario-los-monos-historia-negra-de-un-clan-sangriento/).

Seri, Guillermina. 2012. *Seguridad: Crime, Police Power, and Democracy in Argentina.* New York: Continuum International.

Sharma, Aradhana, and Akhil Gupta. 2006. "Rethinking Theories of the State in an Era of Globalization." Pp. 1–42 in *The Anthropology of the State: A Reader,* edited by A. Sharma and A. Gupta. Malden, MA: Wiley-Blackwell.

Shay, Jonathan. 1995. *Achilles in Vietnam: Combat Trauma and the Undoing of Character.* New York: Simon & Schuster.

Shepard, Edward M., and Paul R. Blackley. 2005. "Drug Enforcement and Crime: Recent Evidence from New York State." *Social Science Quarterly* 86(2):323–42.

Slater, Tom. 2017. "Territorial Stigmatization: Symbolic Defamation and the Contemporary Metropolis." Pp. 111–25 in *The Sage Handbook of New Urban Studies,* edited by J. Hannigan and G. Richards. London: Sage.

Slater, Tom. Forthcoming. *Shaking Up the City.* Berkeley, CA: University of California Press.

Snow, David A., and Robert D. Benford. 1988. "Ideology, Frame Resonance, and Participant Mobilization." *International Social Movement Research* 1:197–217.

Snow, David A., and Robert D. Benford. 1992. "Master Frames and Cycles of Protest." Pp. 133–55 in *Frontiers in Social Movement Theory,* edited by A. D. Morris and C. McClurg Mueller. New Haven, CT: Yale University Press.

Snyder, Richard, and Angelica Durán-Martínez. 2009. "Does Illegality Breed Violence? Drug Trafficking and State-Sponsored Protection Rackets." *Crime, Law and Social Change* 52(3):253–73.

Sobering, Katherine. 2016. "Producing and Reducing Gender Inequality in a Worker-Recovered Cooperative." *Sociological Quarterly* 57(1):129–51.

Sobering, Katherine. 2018. "Workplace Equality in Argentine Worker-Recuperated Businesses." Dissertation, University of Texas at Austin.

Soss, Joe, Richard C. Fording, and Sanford F. Schram. 2011. *Disciplining the Poor: Neoliberal Paternalism and the Persistent Power of Race.* Chicago: University of Chicago Press.

Soss, Joe, and Vesla Weaver. 2017. "Police Are Our Government: Politics, Political Science, and the Policing of Race-Class Subjugated Communities." *Annual Review of Political Science* 20:565–91.

Sozzo, Máximo. 2014. "Delito Común, inseguridad y respuesta estatales: Inercia e innovación durante la década kirchnerista a nivel nacional en Argentina." *Cuestiones de Sociología* 10:1–15.

Stacey, Judith. 2004. "Marital Suitors Court Social Science Spin-Sters: The Unwittingly Conservative Effects of Public Sociology." *Social Problems* 51(1):131–45.

Staniland, Paul. 2012. "Organizing Insurgency: Networks, Resources, and Rebellion in South Asia." *International Security* 37(1):142–77.

Steinmetz, George. 2014. "On Bourdieu, Sur l'État: Field Theory and the State, Colonies, and Empires." *Sociologica* 3:1–13.

Stephenson, Svetlana. 2017. "It Takes Two to Tango: The State and Organized Crime in Russia." *Current Sociology* 65(3):411–26.

Stuart, Forrest. 2016. *Down, Out, and Under Arrest: Policing and Everyday Life in Skid Row*. Chicago: University of Chicago Press.

Sullivan, Esther. 2017. "Displaced in Place: Manufactured Housing, Mass Eviction, and the Paradox of State Intervention." *American Sociological Review* 82(2):243–69.

Tamous, Silvina. 2017. "Las jefas de la droga." *Revista Veintitres*. Retrieved June 1, 2018 (https://www.veintitres.com.ar/).

Taylor, Guy. 2008. "Paco: Drug War Blowback in Argentina." *NACLA*. Retrieved June 1, 2018 (http://nacla.org/news/paco-drug-war-blowback-argentina).

Thomas, William, and Dorothy S. Thomas. 1928. *The Child in America*. New York: Knopf.

Tilly, Charles. 1985. "War Making and State Making as Organized Crime." Pp. 334–52 in *Organized Crime: Critical Perspectives in Criminology*, edited by F. Varese. Vol. 1. London: Routledge.

Tilly, Charles. 1996. "Invisible Elbow." *Sociological Forum* 11(4):589–601.

Tilly, Charles. 2002. *Stories, Identities, and Political Change*. Lanham, MD: Rowman & Littlefield.

Tilly, Charles. 2005. *Trust and Rule*. New York: Cambridge University Press.

Transparency International. 2016. *A Transparency Agenda for Argentina*. Transparency International. Retrieved June 1, 2018 (https://www.transparency.org/news/feature/a_transparency_agenda_for_argentina).

UCA (Universidad Católica Argentina). 2016. *Barómetro del Narcotráfico y las Addiciones en la Argentina*. Buenos Aires: Universidad Católica Argentina.

Ugolini, Agustina. 2010. "Proximidades y Distanciamientos: Un Análisis Etnográfico de las Configuraciones Sociales de una Comisaría del Conurbano Bonaerense." Paper presented at VI Jornadas de Sociología de la UNLP, La Plata, Argentina, December 9–10. Retrieved June 1, 2018 (http://memoria.fahce.unlp.edu.ar/trab_eventos/ev.5472/ev.5472.pdf).

Ugolini, Agustina. 2013. "Reuniendo Cómplices: Sociabilidad Cotidiana y Lazos de Complicidad entre Policías." Pp. 379–407 in *De Armas Llevar. Estudios Socioantropológicos sobre los Quehaceres de Policías y Fuerzas de Seguridad*, edited by S. Frederic, M. Galvani, J. G. Zucal, and B. Renoldi. La Plata: Universidad Nacional de La Plata, Facultad de Periodismo y Comunicación Social.

Ugolini, Agustina. 2016. *Legítimos Policías: Etnografía de lo Ilegal entre Policías de la Provincia de Buenos Aires*. Buenos Aires: Editorial Antropofagia.

UNDP (United Nations Development Program). 2013. "Citizen Security with a Human Face: Evidence and Proposals for Latin America." *Regional Human Development Report, 2013–2014: Executive Report*. New York: UNDP. Retrieved June 1, 2018 (http://www.undp.org/content/dam/rblac/docs/Research%20and%20Publications/IDH/IDH-AL-ExecutiveSummary.pdf).

Ungar, Mark. 2011. *Policing Democracy: Overcoming Obstacles to Citizen Security in Latin America*. Baltimore, MD: Johns Hopkins University Press.

United Nations Office on Drugs and Crime (UNODC). 2016. *World Drug Report*. Vienna: United Nations.

Valdés Castellanos, Guillermo. 2013. *Historia del Narcotráfico en México*. Mexico City: Aguilar.

van Dun, Mirella. 2014a. "Exploring Narco-Sovereignty/Violence: Analyzing Illegal Networks, Crime, Violence, and Legitimation in a Peruvian Cocaine Enclave (2003–2007)." *Journal of Contemporary Ethnography* 43(4):395–418.

van Dun, Mirella. 2014b. "'It's Never a Sure Deal': Drug Trafficking, Violence, and Coping Strategies in a Peruvian Cocaine Enclave (2003–2007)." *Journal of Drug Issues* 44(2):180–96.

Varese, Federico. 2011. *Mafias on the Move: How Organized Crime Conquers New Territories*. Princeton, NJ: Princeton University Press.

Varese, Federico. 2014. "Protection and Extortion." Pp. 343–58 in *The Oxford Handbook of Organized Crime*, edited by L. Paoli. Oxford: Oxford University Press.

Vargas, Robert. 2016. *Wounded City. Violent Turf Wars in a Chicago Barrio*. New York: Oxford University Press.

Vaughan, Diane. 2004. "Public Sociologist by Accident." *Social Problems* 51(1):115–19.

Venkatesh, Sudhir. 2008. *Gang Leader for a Day: A Rogue Sociologist Takes to the Streets*. New York: Penguin.

Verdery, Katherine. 2018. *My Life as a Spy: Investigations in a Secret Police File*. Durham, NC: Duke University Press.

Wacquant, Loïc. 2007. "Territorial Stigmatization in the Age of Advanced Marginality." *Thesis Eleven* 91: 66–77.

Wacquant, Loïc. 2008. *Urban Outcasts: A Comparative Sociology of Advanced Marginality*. London: Polity.

Wacquant, Loïc. 2009. *Punishing the Poor: The Neoliberal Government of Social Insecurity.* Durham, NC: Duke University Press.

Wacquant, Loïc. 2010. "Urban Desolation and Symbolic Denigration in the Hyperghetto." *Social Psychology Quarterly* 20(3):1–5.

Wacquant, Loïc. 2015. "Revisiting Territories of Relegation: Class, Ethnicity and the State in the Making of Advanced Marginality." *Urban Studies Journal* 53(6):1077–88.

Wacquant, Loïc, Tom Slater, and Virgílio Pereira. 2014. "Territorial Stigmatization in Action." *Environment & Planning A* 46(6):1270–80.

Weber, Max. 1946. *From Max Weber: Essays in Sociology*, edited by H. H. Gerth and C. W. Mills. New York: Oxford University Press.

Weber, Max. 1978. *Economy and Society.* Berkeley: University of California Press.

Weiss, Linda. 2006. "Infrastructural Power, Economic Transformation, and Globalization." Pp. 167–86 in *An Anatomy of Power: The Social Theory of Michael Mann*, edited by J. A. Hall and R. Schroeder. Cambridge, UK: Cambridge University Press.

Werb, Daniel, Greg Rowell, Gordon Guyatt, Thomas Kerr, Julio Montaner, and Elizabeth Wood. 2011. "International Journal of Drug Policy Effect of Drug Law Enforcement on Drug Market Violence: A Systematic Review." *International Journal of Drug Policy* 22(2):87–94.

Wilding, Polly. 2010. "'New Violence': Silencing Women's Experiences in the Favelas of Brazil." *Journal of Latin American Studies* 42(4):719–47.

Wilkinson, Steven. 2004. *Votes and Violence.: Electoral Competition and Ethnic Riots in India.* Cambridge, UK: Cambridge University Press.

Williams, Phil. 2009. "Illicit Markets, Weak States and Violence: Iraq and Mexico." *Crime, Law and Social Change* 52(3):323–36.

Williams, Raymond. 1978. *Marxism and Literature.* New York: Oxford University Press.

Williams, Terry. 1992. *Crackhouse: Notes from the End of the Line.* Reading, MA: Addison-Wesley.

Wilson, William Julius. 1996. *When Work Disappears: The World of the New Urban Poor.* New York: Vintage.

Yashar, Deborah. 2012. "Institutions and Citizenship: Reflections on the Illicit." Pp. 432–58 in *Shifting Frontiers of Citizenship: The Latin American Experience*, edited by M. Sznajder, C. A. Forment, and L. Whitehead. Boston: Brill.

Zarazaga, S. J. Rodrigo. 2014. "Brokers beyond Clientelism: A New Perspective through the Argentine Case." *Latin American Politics and Society* 56(3):23–45.

Zelizer, Viviana A. 2012. "How I Became a Relational Economic Sociologist and What Does That Mean?" *Politics & Society* 40(2):145–74.

Zimring, Franklin, and Gordon Hawkins. 1997. *Crime Is Not the Problem: Lethal Violence in America.* New York: Oxford University Press.

Zubillaga, Verónica, Manuel Llorens, and John Souto. 2015. "Being the Mother of an Empistolado within the Everyday Armed Violence of a Caracas Barrio." Pp. 162–88 in *Violence at the Urban Margins*, edited by J. Auyero, P. Bourgois, and N. Scheper-Hughes. New York: Oxford University Press.

Index

The Ambivalent State: Police-Criminal Collusion at the Urban Margins. Javier Auyero, Oxford
University Press (2019). © Oxford University Press.
DOI: 10.1093/oso/9780190915537.001.0001